MAY ALL BE FED

DIET
FOR A
NEW
WORLD

JOHN ROBBINS

MAY ALL BE FED

DIET
FOR A
NEW
WORLD

Including Recipes
by Jia Patton and Friends

AVON BOOKS ◆ NEW YORK

Some of the material in chapters 3, 4, and 5 was adapted from *Diet for a New America* by John Robbins, with permission from Stillpoint Publishing, Walpole, New Hampshire. The excerpt from the 1991 *State of the World Report* on page 37 is reprinted with permission from Worldwatch Institute. The excerpts from Worldwatch Paper No. 103, *Taking Stock: Animal Farming and the Environment*, by Alan Durning and Holly Brough on pages 41, 42, 43, and 44 are reprinted with permission from Worldwatch Institute. The excerpt from *Present Moment, Wonderful Moment* by Thich Nhat Hanh on pages 27-28 is reprinted with permission from Parallax Press. The excerpts on pages 40 and 41 from *Beyond Beef: The Rise and Fall of the Cattle Culture* by Jeremy Rifkin are reprinted with permission of the author. "The Meat-Eater" by R.J. Matson, page 32. Reproduced with permission.

The authors would like to acknowledge those who contributed recipes for adaptation to *May All Be Fed*. Our sincere thanks to Joy A. Nandi, Kenneth Austin (Luma Restaurant, New York City), Butterflies, Terry Cooper (Honey Rose Baking Company, Encinitas, California), Sylvia Crary (Country Life Ministries, Portage, Wisconsin), Cary Diane DeLano, Judy DelaRosa (Restaurant Keffi, Santa Cruz, California), Marilyn Diamond, Wind Golds, Tracy Jones, Tami Patton, Virn Patton, Jennifer Raymond, Ocean Robbins, Joanne Sepaniak, Lelanya Sovinsky, Rose Thompson, and Maureen Vivano (Moosewood Restaurant, Ithaca, New York).

AVON BOOKS
A division of
The Hearst Corporation
1350 Avenue of the Americas
New York, New York 10019

Copyright © 1992 by John Robbins and Jia Patton
Cover floral design by Kathy Hendrickson
Back cover author photograph by Anthony Loew
Published by arrangement with the authors
Library of Congress Catalog Card Number: 92-12596
ISBN: 0-380-71901-0

Published in hardcover by William Morrow and Company, Inc.; for information address Permissions Department, William Morrow and Company, Inc., 1350 Avenue of the Americas, New York, New York 10019.

The William Morrow and Company edition contains the following Library of Congress Cataloging in Publication data:
Robbins, John.
  May all be fed: diet for a new world / John Robbins; recipes by Jia Patton and friends.
  p. cm.
  Includes index.
1. Food habits–United States. 2. Animal Food. 3. Cookery.
I. Patton, Jia. II. Title.
TX371.R623 1992   92-12596
613.2-dc20   CIP

First Avon Books Trade Printing: October 1993

AVON TRADEMARK REG. U.S. PAT. OFF. AND IN OTHER COUNTRIES, MARCA REGISTRADA, HECHO EN U.S.A.

Printed in the U.S.A.

ARC 10 9 8 7 6

*This book
is dedicated to you,
dear reader.*

*May it touch you
with love,
with peace,
and with healing.*

Acknowledgments

My deepest thanks and heartful appreciation to:

Deo and Ocean Robbins, whose love, laughter, and dedication made it possible for this book to be written.

Harriet Bell, Jody Rein, and everyone else at William Morrow who has done so much behind the scenes to bring this book to the public.

Patti Breitman, who, disguised as a literary agent, was really the godmother of this book.

Jia and Adam Patton, who worked so hard on the marvelous recipes.

Richard Curtis, who so beautifully crafted the graphs, charts, and tables.

Ann Mortifee, whose love moves mountains.

John McDougall, M.D., Michael Klaper, M.D., T. Colin Campbell, Ph.D., Neal Barnard, M.D., Jeremy Rifkin, Dean Ornish, M.D.,

Acknowledgments

Frances Moore Lappé, Harvey and Marilyn Diamond, and the many other colleagues and friends upon whose work I have gratefully built.

Patricia Carney, Earle Harris, Mary Quillin, Shams Kairys, Eleanor Wasson, Richard Glantz, Claire Townsend, Arnoldo Gil-Osorio, Gary and Emily Dunn, Ian and Terry Thierman, Kali Ray, Bud Hayes, Dennis Leuer, and the rest of the dedicated staff and volunteers at the EarthSave Foundation, for their ongoing commitment to the cause.

Hal and Linda Kramer, Jay and Lawrie Harris, Mel Skolnick and Elizabeth Brenhouse, Sandy and Bob Mintz, Jack and Shannon Van Zandt, the Phoenix family, Dan and Joy Millman, Morty Cohen, Olivia Newton-John and Matt Latanzi, Robert Lynch, Paul Wenner, Rick Ralston, Dean Fernandez, Toni Denning, Emo Phillips, Patricia and Oliver Markley, John Seed, Joanna Macy, Sally Randel, Donald Epstein and Jackie Knowles, and Judy and Joe Manzone—for the many kinds of wonderful support they have given over the years to me, to EarthSave, and to the creation of a sustainable and healthy world.

My thanks, too, to all the many people who have worked and continue to work so hard to bring sanity and compassion into our society. The number of names is so long that I cannot list you all, but you are in my heart, and this is your book as well as mine.

Contents

Contents

Introduction

I love good food. I love eating it, I love preparing it, and I love sharing it with others.

Only in a prosperous society could we ever forget that food is one of life's primary blessings. I am one who sometimes forgets and takes food for granted, but I'm grateful when I remember that food is precious.

A few years ago, I wrote a book called *Diet for a New America*. Since then I have received more than thirty thousand heartfelt letters from people thanking me and saying the book changed their lives. These letters provide unmistakable testimony to something medical science has been documenting for years. Countless people report that their minds have become sharper and clearer. Their capacity for pleasure and enjoyment has increased. They've lost weight; their cholesterol levels are way down; they don't need the blood pressure medication and diabetes pills they had been told they would have to take for the rest of their lives; their joints don't hurt anymore; their sexual functioning has returned; they don't have the headaches or constipation they did previously; they don't catch colds or flus anymore. They are learning to eat well, and their bodies are thanking them with pleasure and health.

Dear reader, I honor you for your desire to more fully understand the implications of your eating habits. I respect you for your urge to become more aware and capable of making life-affirming choices about what you put into your body. The decisions you make at a grocery store, at a restaurant, and in your own kitchen have an importance that is often overlooked: They help to determine the quality and nature of the life that will be yours thereafter. Every time you shop, every time you prepare food, and every time you sit down to eat, you have an opportunity to say "Yes!" to a healthier you.

The question is, how are you to take the fullest possible advantage of these many opportunities?

The book you are now holding can guide you toward your personal answer to this question. Its purpose is to enrich all your dining experiences with greater understanding, so they may be times of sustaining and nourishing pleasure.

I've noticed that you can learn something interesting about another person if you find out what constitutes the optimum kind of meal to him or her. To me, the best meals may be elaborate or they may be simple, they may be occasions of quiet solitude or of joyous festivity, but they are each in their own way holy. To me, the best meals speak of beauty, balance, and grace. They help you to relax, to enjoy yourself and others. They nurture your senses and your soul. They provide you with wholesome food, and bring health and happiness into your life.

May All Be Fed is an invitation to eating with gratitude for the blessed gift of life—and to understanding how our food choices affect our health and our world.

In a culture that is as commercialized and depersonalized as ours can be, bringing consciousness and thankfulness to our meals is no small achievement. It is, in fact, an act of liberation. To this end I find it important to ask whether the habits I have developed are freely chosen ones that authentically serve my health and happiness and genuinely express my respect for life, or whether they have been "chosen" for me by commercial or other self-interested forces with ulterior motives. To discover what we need and feel is not as easy as it sounds, because in contemporary society a great deal of effort is devoted to keeping us from doing so. Entire industries are focused on maintaining the illusion that we can be happy, well-fed, and "real" only if we consume their products.

Remarkably, these forces beset us not only through advertisements, marketing campaigns, and other obvious efforts to control our food choices for commercial purposes. Their agendas are also found frequently, and with dire consequences, in classrooms, in governmental agencies, and in hospitals.

May All Be Fed exposes the commercially motivated programming that has shaped and continues to shape much of the prevailing food consciousness in our society. This is the conditioning that, whether we know it or not, often determines the food choices we make. By recognizing the nature and power of these influences, we cease to be their pawns and can joyously take back our control and self-determination over how, what, and why we eat.

The price we unknowingly pay for remaining in the grip of this programming is staggeringly high. Today, a greater percentage of the human race is overweight than at any time in history. Meanwhile, a greater percentage of the human race suffers from malnutrition than at any other time in recorded history. These two developments stem from a common source. *May All Be Fed* exposes some of the forces at work in our world that cause the affluent to be burdened with unnecessary disease, and also cause poorer people to be deprived of the right to ample and wholesome food. It lifts the veils of deception that hide and perpetuate the darker side of our society's eating habits. And it reveals the steps we can take to free ourselves to safer, more enlightened, and secure lives.

There are few places where the spiritual, political, personal and ecological dimensions of our lives meet as fully as they do when we sit down to our breakfasts, lunches, and dinners. The first part of *May All Be Fed* shows in clear human terms the extraordinary importance of our becoming more responsible and more conscious in our food awareness and actions. You will see what is to be gained not only in terms of your individual health, but also for infants and children, for the world's less fortunate, for the very future of humanity, and for the essential ecological systems on which all Earthly life depends. In a few places—notably in Chapter 3—I felt that material from my previous book was of such crucial importance to the themes of *May All Be Fed* that I have, with the kind permission of the good people at Stillpoint Publishers, excerpted portions from *Diet for a New America*.

In the book's second part, you will find a wide range of superb and healthy recipes. Many of the recipes were first formulated by Jia Patton, then enhanced and perfected by the outstanding chefs and recipe experts chosen for the task by William Morrow, publisher. Some of the recipes are based on the most popular dishes from a number of the nation's best vegetarian restaurants. Others are based on the contributions of other excellent cooks. I asked this team to create the recipes (and the section on stocking a healthy pantry) in order to help make the time you spend preparing food easier and more productive, and your meals filled with more pleasure and health. In the most practical way, the recipes are here to help you unify your relationship to food with your deepest capacity to enjoy life.

Throughout the recipe section you will find sidebars—statistics, quotes, and facts—that provide a continual reminder of how interconnected we are with all forms of life on this planet, and how our attitudes and decisions concerning food have an impact upon ourselves, other people, and indeed upon the entire Earth community. You'll see why I have come to the startling conclusion that a reduction in meat consumption may well be the most potent single act we can take to halt the destruction of our environment and preserve our precious natural resources.

You have entered a path that leads to increased health and a greater capacity to experience the richness of life. When you prepare the recipes in this book for people who find this way of eating to be new, you will have cause for happiness, for you will be touching their lives with a vision of health and hope. Every time you make a choice that expresses respect for life, you bring a little more love into your body, into your family, into our society, and into a world that is calling out for this blessing.

May this book give strength and heart to your life.

May all be fed,
May all be healed,
May all be loved.

JOHN ROBBINS
Santa Cruz, California

"Lord, make me an instrument of thy peace.
Where there is hatred, let me sow love.
Where there is injury, pardon.
Where there is doubt, faith.
Where there is despair, hope.
Where there is sickness, joy.
Where there is darkness, light.

O Divine Master,
Grant that I may not so much seek to be consoled as to console.
Not so much to be understood as to understand.
Not so much to be loved as to love.
For it is in giving that we receive,
In pardoning that we are pardoned,
And in dying that we are born to eternal life."

—FRANCIS OF ASSISI

PART ONE

ONE

The Grace of Eating

"The person who eats beer and franks
with cheer and thanks
will probably be healthier
than the person who eats sprouts and bread
with doubts and dread."
Diet for a New America

"Any time we eat it's holy.
We should have ritual and ceremony,
not just gobbling down some food to keep alive."
M.F.K. Fisher

Eating used to be a time for family bonding. It used to be a time when people said grace, relaxed together, and appreciated each other's company. It used to be a time when the heart was fed.

It could be that way again.

I want it to be. I don't want to celebrate Thanksgiving only one day each November.

Bless this food.
Bless these people.
Bless this house.
Bless this world.

More times than I care to remember I have lost touch with feelings of gratefulness. My tendency is to give thanks only when things seem to be going well. When events aren't proceeding according to my personal preferences, I sometimes lose sight of my blessings.

This is a loss. It is also one of the reasons why people have traditionally said grace before meals. The saying of grace is, at least in its original intent, a way of connecting to our sense of gratitude and kinship with life. It is a means of caring for ourselves. It is a way to slow down, to relax, to let go of the busyness and worries of the day, and to be open to the food we're about to receive. It enables us to acknowledge and bond with the others with whom we are sharing the meal. It is a way to join with them, and all the people and elements that have made our meal possible, in a spirit of appreciation.

Taking time to say grace not only blesses the food, it blesses the people who take the time to say it.

It is not so much the words we say as the state of mind and heart we evoke that is important. It is a way to honor the deep human need to express our common unity in the mystery of life.

We give thanks for this food.
We give thanks for each other.
We give thanks for our lives.

I once thought that saying grace was just an empty ritual, merely another timeworn habit. But I am learning that things happen when we share expressions of blessing, things that make a deeply important difference to the quality of our lives. We are reminded. A connection is restored. We become better able to appreciate each other and the living Earth that sustains us all.

And, we become more receptive to our food. . . .

A Magical Gift

Eating is essentially an act of communion with the living forces of nature. Sadly, because of the habitual attitudes that many of us have learned to carry toward food, we often take it for granted. We forget that food is a magical gift. We forget that food is precious.

Let us bless the source of life
That brings forth bread from the Earth.
Let our lives be a blessing
To the Earth that sustains us,
And to all the creatures that,
Like us,
Call this planet home.

Some spiritual traditions propose that the development of our spiritual selves requires a certain kind of nourishment from our food, a nourishment that is only available to us when we eat with an attitude of reverence.[1] Our capacity to experience the finer dimensions of consciousness depends upon our spiritual natures being adequately nourished, and this, according to these traditions, depends in part upon the state of mind in which we eat.

When it can be so much more enriching to eat in a relaxed mood, why is it that we often eat so fast and unconsciously? How is it that for many of us this experience, which is among the most basic connections that we have with our bodies, has become so marked by confusion and dissatisfaction?

The "Clean-Your-Plate Club"

Many of us were conditioned early in our lives to experience eating as something other than an act of self-care and self-respect. Many of us were not stroked with love while being breast-fed, but were bottle-fed according to an externally imposed schedule, without a sense of respect for the needs, wisdom, and natural rhythms of our bodies. Many of us were forced to eat food we did not want.

Later, many of us learned that "cleaning our plates" as quickly as

possible earned the approval of our mothers, who saw our zeal as re-
assurance that we were healthy and that the food they had prepared for
us was good. I remember, as a little boy, hearing adults exhort me to
finish my meal with the command "*Down the hatch!*"

We have all been inundated by advertisements that trivialize eating,
that reduce eating to a form of amusement or entertainment, to something
shallow and commercial. Accordingly, we often eat hurriedly, and tend
to swallow without fully chewing and savoring our meals. In fact, for
many people in our society, eating consists of a mechanical routine of
shoveling food in and swallowing it down in a process uninterrupted by
feelings of pleasure, joy, or gratitude.

When I was growing up in Los Angeles, I often watched a popular
television show hosted by Engineer Bill. The children who were guests
on the show regularly took part in a milk-drinking contest, and those of
us watching at home were strongly encouraged to play along. The contest
worked like this: Engineer Bill would push a button and shout "*Green
Light,*" whereupon we would pour our milk down our throats just as fast
as we possibly could, until he pushed another button and shouted "*Red
Light,*" whereupon we were to stop. Then came the go-ahead "*Green
Light,*" again, and so on until we had finished our milk. The child who
drank the fastest and finished first won.

I also remember the Popeye cartoons. When the hero was in a jam
and needed energy, he would literally pour an entire can of spinach
down his throat, swallowing the contents in one gulp.

What messages were being conveyed to us through these and other
similar television shows? That swallowing without chewing, and eating
in a hurry, are commendable? The irony is that these were shows that
actually were trying to point us in healthy directions. The people who
developed and produced them believed that by encouraging young people
to drink their milk and eat their spinach they were supporting our well-
being.

There are countless television shows and movies in which dramatic
events take place during a meal. In the movies and on television we see
business lunches, we see people discuss matters that are very emotional,
we see them argue and become upset at meals. But how often do we see
people who are simply sitting quietly, contentedly absorbed in the relaxed
pleasure of taking nourishment?

One fast-food-chain television commercial shows a group of skate-
boarding teenagers who appear to be hysterical with joy, consuming
hamburgers as they skateboard through a restaurant. In another ad, a
snack food company presents us with a scene of youngsters gleefully

gobbling potato chips while on rides at an amusement park. In yet another example, basketball player Michael Jordan is shown leaping high into the air, grabbing a bottle of Coke, and guzzling the stuff down while in midair. These messages not only commercialize and trivialize the act of eating, they also convey the idea that eating or drinking at top speed is fun. Nowhere to be seen in these advertisements is the bloating and indigestion—and possibly even the bleeding ulcers, the heart attacks, the dangerously high blood pressure, the obesity, and the cancers—that may develop from such an attitude toward food.

Of all the cultures in the world, ours may well be the one in which people eat the fastest. We are the people who have the hardest time slowing down enough to fully appreciate the relaxed art of dining. As Dr. Bernie Siegel put it:

Relaxation and meditation are perhaps especially difficult for Americans. Our constant mental diet of advertising, noise, violence, and media stimulation makes it very difficult to endure even a few minutes of inactivity and quiet.[2]

Eating in a hurried or unconscious way, as so many of us have learned to do, is like receiving a love letter from the Earth but never taking the time to carefully read it.

Saying Grace

Many of us know how hectic and frazzled our lives can become, and we don't need to be reminded that this constant commotion is not the healthiest way to live. Living in this world, how can we come to eat with a more tranquil and self-caring attitude?

There are many ways to establish peace and appreciation as the primary tones of one's meal. A common method is simply to take a few moments to observe silence, perhaps holding the hands of the others at your table if that is comfortable. You can recite together a favorite poem or prayer that expresses the kind of feeling you want to invoke. One person can read a short piece that he or she finds particularly meaningful. Or a number of people can share in a short reading, each taking a few lines or a stanza.

There are as many ways to say grace as there are hearts that have known the joy of gratitude.

One method is for each person simply to take a turn naming something for which he or she is grateful:

First child: *"I'm grateful for our kitty-cat Muffins, and for my little sister to play with."*
Second child: *"I feel thankful for this food, and for the sunshine."*
Adult: *"I feel grateful that we are all together, and for the love I feel for each of you."*

Some families like to sing together. Others like to allow time for spontaneous expressions that anyone at the table, regardless of age, might want to make. There are an infinite number of ways to express the prayers of our hearts, to dedicate our meals, to feel our appreciation for the source of our food and our drink.

If you are eating alone, you can take a moment to hold your bowl or plate, smelling the aromas and enjoying the peace of your solitude.

What's important is to find a way to bless your meals that feels comfortable to you. Restoring the intimacy of our relationships with one another and with the entire Earth community is a natural human urge. The act of blessing our food and giving thanks for our lives is as ancient as humanity. It is a profoundly spiritual act, and reminds us that we are not alone in our prayers.

Throughout history, men, women, and children in all cultures and lands have gathered together at mealtimes to align themselves with the greater forces of the universe. In forests and mountains, in humble abodes and great mansions, beneath star-filled skies and beside hearths, people have always given voice to this instinct. In taking the time to create a nourishing relationship with the great mystery, we enter the timeless world of myth, fable, proverb, and story. In offering to the rest of creation the gift of our heartfelt appreciation, we become more fully expressed, more receptive to our food, and more fully human.

Beautiful God,
Beautiful Earth.
Show us how to help.
Make us strong so that we can bring more love into the world.
Make us strong so that we can bring more peace into the world.
Thank you for this food.
Beautiful God,
Beautiful Earth.

Pleasure Is Healthy

Given the amount of time most of us spend talking and thinking about food, and all the energy that goes into preparing it, transporting it, and obtaining it, it is remarkable that we don't take more time to truly enjoy it.

This is sad. For when we eat too fast, or under conditions that are not conducive to relaxation, we often end up feeling unsatisfied. If we haven't had a fair share of pleasure and enjoyment in our meal, some part of us feels deprived and undernourished.

As a product of this culture, I had always assumed that the pleasure I took in tasting my food while it was in my mouth was basically divorced from what happened to my food once it reached my stomach. There, I assumed, was where digestion took place. The truth, however, is that digestion begins in the mouth, and our saliva is almost as crucial a digestive catalyst as the gastric enzymes our stomachs secrete. In the communication within the human body, the mouth tells the stomach what's coming and helps it to prepare. How easily we forget that the tastes and other mouth experiences of eating are indispensable parts of the process by which we are nourished, by which Nature communicates with us and sustains us.

I am learning that it helps to breathe deeply every so often during a meal. If we pause from time to time and take a deep breath, we become more relaxed and in touch with our body rhythms. Just as a flame is fanned by a breeze that provides it with more oxygen, so too does the digestive fire burn more cleanly and completely when we pause in our eating in order to take a deep breath.

For the power of God's angels enters into you with the living food which the Lord gives you from his royal table....Breathe long and deeply at all your meals, that the angel of air may bless your repasts. (The Essene Gospel of Peace)

To Chew...Or Not to Chew

It is no secret that our bodies secrete different chemicals depending on our moods and emotional states. But I'm learning how deeply the way we digest and assimilate our food is affected by what we are thinking and feeling as we eat.

Eating slowly has been shown to aid digestion. As Drs. Jeffrey Migdow and James Loehr explain:

The glands in your mouth produce two kinds of saliva. When the diner is relaxed and ready to eat, the parotid glands produce saliva that contains digestive enzymes and is watery; it easily digests food being chewed. Under stress, however, the sublingual glands exude a thick saliva that is devoid of digestive enzymes.[3]

Studies by Dr. Tomozaburo Ogata of the School of Medicine at the University of Tokyo reveal that chewing stimulates the parotid glands, located on each side of the jaw behind the ears, to release parotin hormones. This in turn encourages the thymus to create T-cells, the guardians of our immune system. It appears from this and other research that eating peacefully can contribute to a strengthened immune system.[4]

We are beginning to understand the wisdom in the old saying:

Nature will castigate those who don't masticate.

A friend of mine, Lino Stanchich, is a teacher of health practices who is certain of the benefits of thorough chewing.[5] The impetus for his work came from his father, Antonio Stanchich, who was a prisoner during World War II in a German concentration camp. The conditions there, as I am sure you are aware, were horrible beyond comprehension. People were grossly underfed, and many died of starvation each day. It was two years after Antonio's capture that the camp was finally liberated. By that time, of the thirty-two men who had been sent to the camp with Antonio, only two others remained alive. The three survivors, Antonio and two of his friends, had shared a method by which they had managed to endure. The secret? They religiously chewed their meager rations hundreds of times.

After the war, Lino, an Italian citizen, found himself trapped in Yugoslavia. When he tried to escape, he was sentenced to two years of hard labor in a Yugoslavian prison. The rations there were also abysmally scant. But Lino remembered his father's advice to chew and chew what food there was, and as a result survived the ordeal. Now Lino loves to share with others the benefits he has learned from taking the time to slow down and savor food, chewing it fully.

"Good to Meet You, Mr. Food"

Another friend of mine, Geneen Roth, has done wonderful work in unearthing the emotional roots of overeating. She says that deciding if you're hungry is like deciding if you're in love; if you don't know for sure, you're probably not.

I think she's right. Eating *is* like lovemaking. It is best when it is not rushed, when it is approached with respect and with passion, with reverent appreciation for our hungers and our desires, and their fulfillment.

Bringing consciousness to our eating helps us to connect with ourselves, to be aware of what is going on in our bodies, our feelings, our minds, and in the world. Thich Nhat Hanh, the Buddhist monk who was nominated for the Nobel Peace Prize by Dr. Martin Luther King, Jr., speaks of the importance of doing everyday things as mindfully as possible. He delights in making daily activities into meditational arts. When it comes to eating,

When the food is on the table and everyone is seated, we practice breathing: "Breathing in, I calm my body—breathing out, I smile," three times. We can recover ourselves completely after three breaths like this.

Then, we look at each person as we breathe in and out in order to be in touch with ourselves and everyone at the table. We don't need two hours in order to see another person. If we are really settled within ourselves, we only need to look for one or two seconds, and that is enough to see our friend. I think that if a family has five members, only about five or ten seconds is needed to practice this "looking and seeing."

After breathing, we smile. Sitting at the table with other people, we have a chance to offer an authentic smile of friendship and understanding. It is very easy, but not many people do it. We look at each person and smile at him or her. Breathing and smiling together are very important practices. If the people in a family cannot smile at each other, the situation is a very dangerous one.

After breathing and smiling, we look down at the food in a way

*that allows the food to become real. This food reveals our connection
with the Earth. Each bite contains the life of the sun and the Earth.
The extent to which our food reveals itself depends on us. We can see
and taste the whole universe in a piece of bread! Contemplating our
food for a few seconds before eating, and eating in mindfulness, can
bring us much happiness.*

*Having the opportunity to sit with our family and friends and
enjoy wonderful food is something precious, something not everyone
has. Many people in the world are hungry. When I hold a bowl of
rice or a piece of bread, I know that I am fortunate, and I feel
compassion for all those who have no food to eat and are without
friends or family. This is a very deep practice. We do not need to go
to a temple or a church in order to practice this. We can practice it
right at our dinner table. Mindful eating can cultivate seeds of
compassion and understanding that will strengthen us to do
something to help hungry and lonely people be nourished."* [6]

Including the World's Hungry

Thich Nhat Hanh speaks of taking a moment, as we are about to be
served, to look at our empty plates and to recall that there are many
people on this Earth whose plates are also empty—but unlike ours, their
plates will not soon be filled with nourishing food.

I want to find ways to help those who are without the necessities of
life. I want to find ways to live more simply so that I can use my time
and energy to help bring more social justice and economic and environmental sanity into the world.

I do not always consciously say or do anything special to include the
world's hungry at my table. Sometimes it is enough to simply offer thanks
for the food and the blessings of life. The world's hungry do not need a
special invitation. They are already there, in our hearts.

May all be fed,
May all be healed,
May all be loved.

Each of us is personally affected by the tragedy of human hunger, by
the fact that forty thousand children starve to death every day. Some of
us may not know the exact numbers, but we are all aware that there is

enormous suffering in the world caused by hunger and starvation. Perhaps at those times when we rush to "shovel down" our food, it is because we believe at some level of our psyches that if we do not grab ours while there is some to grab, then there may not be any left for us. Sadly, when we react in this way to the fear of hunger, we weaken not only our health, but also our peace and personal power, and thus decrease our ability to respond creatively and effectively to whatever challenges confront us, including the fact of hunger.

The existence of so much human hunger in the world is a reality we cannot deny. It is a reality that challenges us deeply: It asks us to become more fully human. The response that each of us makes to the world's hunger is central to the process of our unfolding and growth, essential to the process by which we learn to become more authentic, responsible, and whole human beings. When we try to push the world's hungry away from our minds, we go psychically numb. When we remember those who are without food, something is awakened within us. Our own deeper hungers come to the surface—our hungers to live fully, to bring our lives into alignment with our compassion, to make our lives expressions of our spirits.

There are many forms of hunger. There is the hunger for food, and there is the hunger for love, for purpose, for truth. There is the hunger for health, for happiness. There is the hunger for companionship, for inner peace, for the sense that we belong. There is the hunger for laughter, and there is the hunger for God.

The hunger that lives in the human heart is part of the kinship that threads us all together. We are interdependent beings with a profound need both to give and to receive from each other. For what one of us is lacking, another has in abundance, whether that be a bowl of rice, a skill, a wisdom, a capacity for joy, a knowledge, or a courageous heart. Our urges and our gifts, our longings and our offerings, are all needed and are all indispensable.

If we are touched by the images of men, women, and children that we have seen starving for food, it is because they are a reflection of our own need. They are a reminder not only of that part of us that is hungry, but also of that part of us that needs to give in order to be whole.[7]

Each of us responds to the fact of world hunger in ways as individual as our fingerprints. For a long time I didn't want to face the reality of human hunger, because I didn't want to feel as powerless as I thought it would make me feel. I wanted to feel in charge and in control. I didn't want to feel vulnerable. I was sure that the sight of human beings without food would make me pathetically aware of my inability to help in any significant way.

But something called me to look. Something inside me began to rise, helping to open my eyes and heart to this fundamental and often painful reality.

I found that facing the fact of human hunger activated forces within me that needed expression. It saddened me, frightened me, and sometimes made me outraged. But when I acknowledged this sometimes horrifying reality, something was called forth in me that needed to flow outward to life, that wanted to touch and explore and meet the world, that wanted to respond to this pain. I had feelings about this, human responses, and I needed to give them voice. I couldn't sit on the sidelines, passively watching others starve and die.

What has happened as a result has taken me on a journey. It has meant making a sincere attempt to understand the implications of my life choices. It has meant becoming more socially conscious, more aware of the impact that my lifestyle and activities have on the fate of those who suffer. It has led me to ask whether the beliefs and habits I have about food truly serve life's purpose. It has caused me to question many of the prevailing assumptions of our culture.

Most important of all, it has reminded me that food is precious.

Take my hand, now, and we will see where this journey might lead us.

TWO

A Bite Felt
'Round the World

"To a man with an empty stomach, food is God."
Mahatma Gandhi

"To be a vegetarian is to disagree—
to disagree with the course of things today.
Starvation, world hunger, cruelty, waste, wars—
we must make a statement against these things.
Vegetarianism is my statement.
And I think it's a strong one."
Isaac Bashevis Singer

There is an old story about a man who lived a long and worthy life. When he died, the Lord said to him, "Come, I will show you hell."

He was taken to a room where a group of people sat around a huge pot of stew. Each held a spoon that reached the pot, but had a handle so long it couldn't be used to reach his or her mouth. Everyone was famished and desperate; the suffering was terrible.

After a while, the Lord said, "Come, now I will show you heaven."

They came to another room. To the man's surprise, it seemed identical to the first room—a group of people sat around a huge pot of stew, and each held the same long-handled spoon. But here everyone was nourished and happy, and the room was full of joy and laughter.

THE MEAT-EATER

"I don't understand," said the man. "Everything seems to be the same, yet they are so happy here, and they were so miserable in the other place. What in heaven's name is going on?"

The Lord smiled. "Ah, but don't you see? Here they have learned to feed one another."[1]

A Food Factory in Reverse

Less than half the harvested agricultural acreage in the United States is used to grow food for people. The majority of it is used instead to grow livestock feed.

There was a time when I would have said that this makes no difference. I would have said that the livestock feed ends up as the meat that people eat, so the land used for livestock feed is still feeding people.

But I have learned something that has changed this perspective.

It takes sixteen pounds of grain to produce a pound of feedlot beef.[2] It takes only one pound of grain to produce a pound of bread.

It is hard to grasp how immensely wasteful the feed conversion ratio for beef is. By cycling our grain through livestock and into beef, we end up with only 6 percent as much food available to feed human beings as we would have if we ate the grain directly.

To understand the return on the investment we make by feeding our grain to livestock, imagine the following scenario: You take $1000 to the bank and deposit it in your account. Later, you return to the bank to withdraw the money. You would probably expect to collect the original $1000 that you deposited, plus a little interest, wouldn't you?

Well, in this case things work out a little differently. The bank teller hands you only $60. That's it. That is all you get. Not only do you get no interest, you have lost $940 of your original $1000.

This is equivalent to the loss of available food when we cycle our grain through cattle. We get back only one pound of beef for every sixteen pounds of grain we invest.

Love is feeding everybody. (Dennis Weaver)

To feed one meat eater for a year requires three-and-a-quarter acres of land. To feed one vegetarian for a year requires one half acre of land.

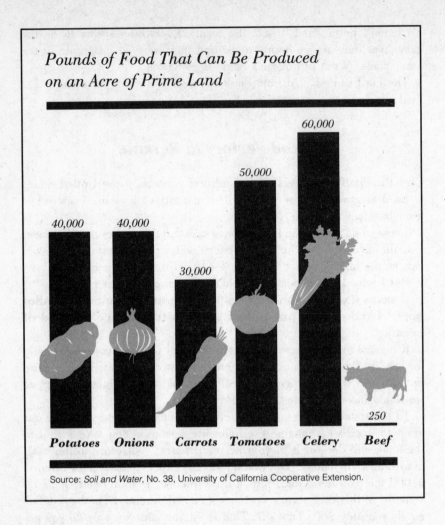

*Pounds of Food That Can Be Produced
on an Acre of Prime Land*

40,000	40,000	30,000	50,000	60,000	250
Potatoes	Onions	Carrots	Tomatoes	Celery	Beef

Source: *Soil and Water*, No. 38, University of California Cooperative Extension.

In other words, a given amount of land can feed more than six times as many people eating a vegetarian diet than those eating a meat-based diet.[3]

University of California Cooperative Extension agricultural experts analyzed the yield per acre of various food crops. An acre of prime land, according to their findings, annually yields forty thousand pounds of potatoes, or forty thousand pounds of onions, or thirty thousand pounds of carrots, or fifty thousand pounds of tomatoes, or sixty thousand pounds of celery. But if that acre of land is used to produce beef, the yield is a paltry two hundred and fifty pounds.[4]

Forty thousand children starve to death on this planet every day.
(Institute for Food and Development Policy)

How Not to Feed One Another

The livestock population of the United States today daily consumes enough grain and soybeans to feed more than five times the entire human population of our country.[5] We feed these animals more than 80 percent of the corn we grow, and more than 95 percent of the oats.[6]

I had assumed that the great quantities of grain exported by the United States went to feed hungry people. But I was wrong. Two thirds of all the grain exported to other countries from the United States goes to feed livestock rather than to feed people. Only a tiny minority of the people in most of these countries can afford meat. In fact, many people go to bed hungry every night, and mothers must often watch helplessly as their children starve.

Malnutrition is the principal cause of infant and child mortality in developing nations. In some of these countries, malnutrition is so widespread that newborn babies have only a 50:50 chance of reaching the age of four. In Guatemala, much of the land and other resources for food production is given over to producing meat, while 75 percent of the children under five years of age are undernourished. The meat produced doesn't go to those in need. It goes to those who can afford it. Every year Guatemala exports forty million pounds of meat to the United States.[7]

In Costa Rica, beef production quadrupled between 1960 and 1980. But most Costa Rican beef is exported to the United States. As more and more Costa Rican land is turned over to meat production, the population has less and less to eat. Today, even with much of the country's original tropical rain-forest sacrificed to beef production, the average family in Costa Rica eats less meat than the average American housecat.

I had never really grasped how exorbitantly wasteful a meat-based diet is until I learned that **if Americans reduced their meat consumption by 10 percent, enough grain would be saved to feed sixty million people.**[8] That is close to the total number of people who die of hunger-related disease each year!

Of course, this doesn't mean world hunger would be solved simply if Americans ate 10 percent less meat. There are difficult economic, social, and political realities that must be faced.

35

But this startling statistic does dramatize the severe waste of resources involved in meat production.

In a world where a child dies of hunger-caused disease every two seconds, only an ignorant society can continue to view meat as a status symbol.

The Great Debate

In the years since my book *Diet for a New America* became a best-seller, I've had many occasions to discuss these matters with representatives from the Beef Council, the National Cattlemen's Association, the National Livestock and Meat Board, and other meat industry organizations. Usually these debates follow a fairly predictable pattern; we disagree on just about everything, and not a lot gets resolved. But on one occasion, the experience was different. A debate was to be broadcast on national radio, and the meat industry was taking it seriously. They sent as their spokesman an extremely well spoken man with several Ph.D.s, whom I will call Dr. Mark Seligson. (I have changed his name, and for the sake of clarity, made a few other minor changes in the conversation that follows.)

The show began with the usual polite introductions, but I could tell this was not going to be a picnic at the beach. Dr. Seligson was clearly a formidable adversary, a man who knew his intellectual strength and used it. It didn't take long. Within seconds of beginning, the power of this man's mind was being used in all its force to vindicate the industry he served.

When the topic turned to world hunger, he moved forward in his seat, eager for combat. I knew this was going to be interesting.

He began by saying that the corn and soybeans fed to animals are not suitable for human consumption. I replied that this is true; but it's also true that the land used to grow these crops could just as easily be used to grow varieties for people.

"Well," he said, looking not in the slightest disturbed, "I'll admit that far greater quantities of grain would be available for human consumption with a more plant-based diet. But that would have no real effect on world hunger." He paused for effect, then continued, "After all, we have immense quantities of grain already in storage."

I felt a sadness come over me. Not because I had lost a point in the contest. I knew in fact that what I would say next would turn the tide of the argument in a different direction than he imagined. No, I was sad because for a moment I wished that what he was saying and implying was true. If only we had so much grain stored that world food security was assured! It is true, as I proceeded to explain, that up until quite recently we did have mountains of grain in storage, because for years world per capita grain production was climbing. What many people don't realize, however, is that we reached, and then passed, the apex of this curve, and for a number of years now, throughout the world, per capita grain production has been declining precipitously. We do have surplus grain in storage, but much less than most people think. To document my point, I quoted from Worldwatch Institute's prestigious 1991 *State of the World* report:

World carryover stocks, perhaps the best short-term measure of food security, totaled a record 461 million tons of grain in 1987, enough to feed the world for 102 days. But in each of the next three years world grain consumption exceeded production, leading to a 173-million-ton drop in stocks.... By 1990, carryover stocks had dropped to 290 million tons, enough for just 62 days.[9]

I then mentioned that in 1991, world grain production dropped by nearly 5 percent, a decline of 86 million tons. Even if the U.S. were to put back into production all the 28 million acres idled under commodity supply-management programs, world per capita grain production would still be dropping dramatically.

This information seemed to catch my worthy opponent off guard; he obviously respected Worldwatch's credibility and did not dispute the figures.

"Why, that would mean," he said, his eyes blinking rapidly, "that if this trend continued unabated, world grain stocks would be totally depleted in just five years. Even if this trend is somehow halted, we are already in a precarious position."

I nodded, and for the moment at least it seemed that we were no longer opponents, but two people joined in a search for understanding.

I mentioned that more than one hundred nations depend increasingly on U.S. grain exports. If the United States were to experience another harvest anything like the one we had in 1988, in which a drought lowered grain production below domestic consumption, the consequences to the world's hungry would be extremely severe.

Suddenly, Dr. Seligson's previous demeanor was back in place. He announced forcefully: "The drought of 1988 was exceptional, and we aren't likely to see anything like it again."

"It may be reassuring to believe that," I responded, "but such comfort is unfortunately hardly warranted. Climatologists and environmentalists are warning us ever more stridently of the growing likelihood of another drought as greenhouse gases accumulate in the atmosphere, altering the climate and creating the very conditions that can cause droughts. They point out that the seven hottest years in recorded history have all been since 1980. Four times in the past twelve years the U.S. grain harvest has been seriously damaged by unusually hot summers."

What would be the consequences of another U.S. harvest like 1988, I asked. Dr. Seligson was quiet, contemplating the question. Referring again to the Worldwatch report, I explained that such an event would immediately force millions more of the world's poor to the brink of starvation. As Third World governments tried desperately to import enough high-priced grain to avoid widespread starvation, there would be little or no foreign exchange available for debt payments. Major international banks would be faced with massive defaults and income loss. As the implications of food scarcity spread beyond the Third World, interest rates would climb, further threatening the viability of the world's financial institutions.

I could feel my adversary listening intently. Speaking slowly, I acknowledged that this is a frightening scenario. However, there are alternatives to the direction we are presently taking, I told him, alternatives that would place us on safer ground. **If Americans were to reduce our meat consumption by only 10 percent, it would free land and resources to grow over twelve million tons of grain annually for human consumption, more than enough to adequately feed every one of the forty to sixty million human beings who will starve to death on the planet this year.**[10]

To complete my turn, I quoted Albert Schweitzer:

I would daily throw out crumbs for the sparrows in the neighborhood. I noticed that one sparrow was injured, so that it had difficulty getting about. But I was interested to discover that the other sparrows, apparently by mutual agreement, would leave the crumbs which lay nearest their crippled comrade, so that he could get his share, undisturbed.

At this juncture, I thought I had spoken rather well, so I settled back and allowed Dr. Seligson finally to have his turn. In truth, I don't think I could have continued to monopolize the microphone much longer. He was impatient to say his piece.

He spoke at length, and although I disagreed with much of what he said, I found listening to his eloquent use of his rhetorical skills to be a fascinating experience. His primary point, to which he returned several times, and each time with greater emphasis, was that world hunger is not a consequence of meat consumption. It is, he announced triumphantly, "a question of the enormous explosion in population. Every year there are ninety-three million more homo sapiens upon this planet. That is why we have starving people."

A satisfied smile crossed Dr. Seligson's face. Evidently he felt that his point was conclusive.

"Well said," I acknowledged. "But don't you think that the growing population is even more reason to have an agriculture that feeds people, not livestock? With more and more people, isn't the need becoming greater every year to use our land efficiently?"

Dr. Seligson looked deflated. "I hadn't thought of it quite that way," he said, his voice now subdued.

"And what if we couple rising population numbers with deteriorating life-support systems?" I continued. "We are losing twenty-four billion tons of topsoil worldwide every year. Our croplands, forests, and grasslands are degrading; our biologically productive land area is shrinking. Acid rain, ozone layer depletion, air pollution, the extinction of species, water loss, soil erosion, and many other environmental degradations are steadily diminishing our food-producing capability. In almost every country in the world more and more forests are being cut down to clear land to grow cattle feed or to graze cattle. Prairies, grasslands, and rangelands are being destroyed by the overgrazing of livestock. And cropland soils are eroding under the stress of producing the vastly greater quantities of grain needed for a meat-based diet than for a plant-based one. Isn't it time we began to see meat as the extravagance it is?"

The room was feeling tense. I finished by saying that it is easy for us to talk about hunger, well-fed as we are. I quoted Ring Lardner:

I've known what it is to be hungry, but I always went right to a restaurant.

A Shift of Monumental Proportions

As the debate continued that day, it became obvious that as educated as Dr. Seligson was, he had paid very little attention to the fundamental shift that has taken place in world agriculture in this century. In times past, people toiled in the fields to grow grain for people to eat. But today, ever more land is used to grow feed for livestock or to graze cattle.

This shift has gone relatively unnoticed, even though it may be the most important change in the history of world agriculture. One of the most brilliant social commentators of our time, Jeremy Rifkin, author of a dozen extremely influential books and President of the Foundation on Economic Trends, writes:

Cattle and other livestock are devouring much of the grain produced on the planet. It need be emphasized that this is a new phenomenon, unlike anything ever experienced before.[11]

The results are not pretty:

*Contrary to popular belief, the poor are getting poorer each year. . . . Increased poverty has meant increased malnutrition. On the African continent, nearly one in every four human beings is malnourished. In Latin America, nearly one out of every seven people goes to bed hungry each night. In Asia and the Pacific, 28 percent of the people border on starvation, experiencing the gnawing pain of a perpetual hunger. In the Near East, one in ten people is underfed. Chronic hunger now affects upwards of 1.3 billion people, according to the World Health Organization—a statistic all the more striking in a world where one third of all the grain produced is being fed to cattle and other livestock. **Never before in human history has such a large percentage of our species—nearly 25 percent—been malnourished.***[12]

There is another corresponding reality that is also unique to our times. Never before has as great a percentage of the human race been over-

weight. While an unprecedented number of human beings are malnourished, the world's beef-eating populations have become so
overweight that we have seen in this century the emergence of a social
behavior never seen before in human history—a phenomenon to which
we have given the ironic name "dieting." The rise of grain-fed beef has
brought in its wake two realities that are reverse images of each other:
While more and more of the world's children are going hungry, 80 percent
of the nine-year-old girls in California have already been on their first
diet. Rifkin writes:

*While millions of American teenagers anguish over excess pounds,
spending time, money, and emotional energy on slimming down,
children in other lands are wasting away, their physical growth
irreversibly stunted, their bodies racked with parasitic and
opportunistic diseases, their brain growth diminished by lack of
nutrients in their meager diets.*[13]

Rifkin concludes:

*The transition of world agriculture from food grain to feed grains
represents an . . . evil whose consequences may be far greater and
longer lasting than any past examples of violence inflicted by men
against their fellow human beings.*[14]

The End of Food Self-Sufficiency
in the Third World

Most of the nations that now import grain from the United States were
once self-sufficient in grain. The main reason they aren't any longer is
the rise in meat production and consumption.

Worldwatch Institute recently released a remarkable report entitled
Taking Stock: Animal Farming and the Environment, which lists nation
after nation where food deprivation has followed the switch from a grain-
based diet to a meat-based one.

In Taiwan, for example, per capita consumption of meat and eggs
increased 600 percent from 1950 to 1990. With this change, vastly
increased amounts of grain have gone to livestock, raising the annual
per capita grain use in the country from 375 pounds to 858 pounds.[15]

Despite steadily growing harvests, Taiwan could only keep up with the demand for feed by turning to imports from abroad. In 1950, Taiwan was a grain exporter; in 1990, the nation imported, mostly for feed, 74 percent of the grain it used.[16]

In mainland China, the report continues, the situation is similar. Increased meat consumption has meant less grain available to feed people:

Since 1978 ... meat consumption has more than doubled, to twenty-four kilograms. ... Though the country's farmers have been able to grow sufficient feed grain for the swelling meat industry so far, few observers expect them to keep pace for much longer. The share of Chinese grain fed to livestock rose from 7 percent in 1960 to 20 percent in 1990.[17]

Shortages and hunger today seriously threaten the peoples of the former Soviet Union. In almost every report that we get on hunger in the area, the emphasis is on the lack of meat. We hear interviews with Russian citizens who complain that there is no sausage on the shelves, and with Russian butchers who tell of difficulties getting cows to market. They seem to be unaware that "getting meat back on the shelves" is not the best solution for a country needing to feed its people in a hurry. They seem not to realize that there are better and more productive ways to solve the problem of hunger than to step up beef production. In fact, rising meat consumption has severely aggravated the country's problems. In 1991, Worldwatch noted:

Since 1950, meat consumption has tripled and feed consumption quadrupled. Use of grain for feed surpassed direct human consumption in 1964 and has been rising ever since. Soviet livestock now eat three times as much grain as Soviet citizens. Grain imports have soared, going from near zero in 1970 to twenty-four million tons in 1990, and the USSR is now the world's second largest grain importer.[18]

Twenty-five years ago, livestock consumed only 6 percent of Mexico's grain. Today, the figure is over 50 percent. This is the same trend we see throughout the Third World.

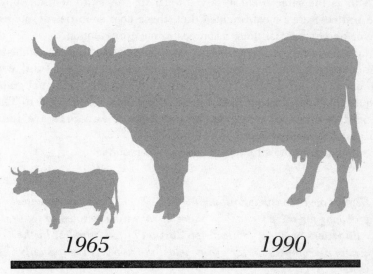

1965   1990

Source: *The Mexican Food Crisis* by David Barkin and Bill DeWalt; and *Taking Stock: Animal Farming and the Environment* by Worldwatch Institute

We see the same trend in the Middle East and North Africa—increases in grain-fed livestock require more imported feed. The richest Middle Eastern countries maintain high levels of meat consumption only by depending heavily on imported feed and meat. In the poorer countries, the demand for meat is causing deepening hardship.[19]

Twenty years ago, Egypt was self-sufficient in grain. Then, livestock ate only 10 percent of the nation's grain. Today, livestock consumes 36 percent of Egypt's grain. As a result, Egypt must now import eight million tons of grain every year.[20]

Twenty-five years ago, Syria was a barley exporter. But in the intervening years, livestock has consumed increasing amounts of the country's grain. Now, despite a phenomenal 1000 percent increase in the land area devoted to producing barley, Syria must import the cereal.[21]

Only thirty years ago, sorghum was almost unknown in Mexico. But by 1980, it covered literally twice the acreage of wheat.[22] What caused sorghum's incredible takeover of Mexican agricultural land? Sorghum isn't grown for humans. It is fed to livestock. Twenty-five years ago, livestock consumed only 6 percent of Mexico's grain. Today, the figure is over 50 percent.[23]

This is the same trend we see throughout the Third World. Copying the United State's meat-oriented diet, these poor countries devote ever-larger percentages of their resources to meat production.

In country after country the pattern is repeated. Livestock industries are consuming feed to such an extent that now almost all Third World nations must import grain. You might think that this additional grain is required to feed growing human populations. **But 75 percent of Third World imports of corn, barley, sorghum, and oats are fed to animals, not to people.**[24]

Summarizing the situation, Worldwatch reports:

Higher meat consumption among the affluent frequently creates problems for the poor, as the share of farmland devoted to feed cultivation expands, reducing production of food staples. In the economic competition for grain fields, the upper classes usually win.[25]

In country after country, the demand for meat among the rich is squeezing out staple production for the poor.

There Goes Latin America

As more and more land is used to grow livestock feed and to graze livestock, economics forces even more people off their land. Deprived of the land they need to grow food to feed their families, they descend into the ever-tightening grip of poverty and hunger.

Since 1960, the number of landless people in Central America has multiplied fourfold.[26] International lending agencies such as the World Bank and the Inter-American Development Bank have responded with billions of dollars in loans. But because these loans have often been to the livestock industry, they have not challenged the use of resources to benefit the wealthy at the expense of the poor.

While a typical acre of land in Latin America can easily produce over twelve hundred pounds of grain per year, that same land used to graze cattle barely yields fifty pounds of meat.[27] Yet American aid has propped up Latin America's livestock industry. As economist Bruce Rich said:

No other single commodity in developing countries has ever received such extraordinary outside support.

We might hope that this heightened beef production would be of at least some use to the impoverished masses in these poor countries. But over half of Latin America's beef production is exported, and the rest is too expensive for any but the wealthy to purchase.[28] From 1960 to 1980, beef exports from El Salvador increased over sixfold.[29] Meanwhile, increasing numbers of small farmers lost their livelihood and were pushed off their land. Today, 72 percent of all Salvadoran infants are underfed.[30]

In Brazil, major portions of the Amazon tropical rain forests have been destroyed so that wealthy multinational corporations can produce beef for the wealthy. Corporations including Volkswagen, Nestlé, Mitsubishi, Liquigas, King Ranch, and Swift-Eckrich have bulldozed and burned literally hundreds of millions of acres, replacing the world's oldest and richest ecosystems, home to two million or more species of plant and animal life, with a single crop—pasture grass for cattle.[31] And again, the beef produced has not gone to feed hungry Brazilians; it has been primarily exported to Western Europe, the Middle East, and North America.[32] In 1987 the United States imported three hundred million pounds of meat from countries in Central and South America.[33] It's impossible to ignore the fact that the same land that fed all those cattle could have fed many people.

With the help of international lending institutions, Brazil has mounted an enormous effort to increase agricultural production, but this has been primarily meat-oriented production and for export. Twenty-five years ago, soybeans were planted almost nowhere in Brazil. Today, this crop is the nation's number one export—but almost all of it goes to feed Japanese and European livestock.[34] Twenty-five years ago, one third of the Brazilian population suffered from malnutrition. Today, the figure has risen to two thirds.[35]

Throughout the Third World, the production of meat is devastating the natural ecosystems, monopolizing the best local land, undermining the local food supply, and undercutting the efforts of the people to become food self-reliant. There are today millions of human beings in less-developed countries who are living and dying in despair, going hungry while their land, labor, and resources are being exploited so a tiny minority of people can eat meat.

Cultures that are rich with countless years of human tradition are being extinguished. To native peoples, land is life. But many indigenous peoples are watching their ancestral homelands being destroyed to produce meat. In the hope of survival, they often migrate hundreds or even thousands of miles to urban slums, where all that awaits them is a life of grinding poverty. Some families, especially children, take to scavenging refuse dumps on the margins of cities, hoping to find edible leftovers discarded by the affluent. In some cases, parents who cannot feed their children sell them to wealthier families as servants, or abandon them altogether.

May All Be Fed

Reversing the spread of hunger will take an enormous effort. It will mean challenging the assumptions of a meat-based culture. It will mean questioning social systems that are stacked in favor of the rich and against the poor, and developing social models in which the rich and the poor work together for a common good, rather than perceive each other as enemies. It will mean challenging the tightly concentrated distribution of economic control that denies access to land and purchasing power for so many people. It will mean reversing the trend toward the ever-greater concentration of wealth in ever fewer hands. It will mean building our lives upon the certainty that all humanity is connected.

If humanity finally sheds the onerous and degrading specter of starvation, it will be because we have decided not to treat food and the resources needed to produce it just like any other commodity, but have come to see food as a basic and universal human right. It will be because we have found ways to ensure security for **all** people, to stabilize our numbers, and to heal the planet's deeply injured life-support systems. It will be because we have ceased to support regimes that resist the changes needed to end hunger, and have realized that only when none of us fears hunger can any of us truly find peace.

The day that hunger is eradicated from the Earth there will be the greatest spiritual explosion the world has ever known. Humanity cannot imagine the joy that will burst into the world on the day of that great revolution. (Federico García Lorca)

Reversing the spread of hunger will mean learning to create a world based on cooperation and on the affirmation of the human spirit. It will mean all of us remembering to include in our hearts, as we eat, the reality that elsewhere on this planet there are people without food. It will mean examining all of our public policies and personal lifestyles in the light of our desire to touch as many people as possible with a message of hope for a better world.

THREE

To Grow Up Big and Strong

*"Loyalty to a petrified opinion
never yet broke a chain
or freed a human soul."*
Mark Twain

I am sitting in elementary school. The teacher has brought out a colored chart and is telling us kids how important it is to eat meat, drink our milk, and get lots of protein. I am listening to her and looking at the chart, which makes it all seem so simple. I believe my teacher, because I sense that she believes what she is saying. She is sincere. She is a grown-up. Besides, the chart is decorated and fun to look at. It must be true.

Protein, I hear—that's what's important. Protein. And you can only get good quality protein from meats, eggs, and dairy products. That is why they make up two of the four basic food groups on the chart.

I am impressed. At lunch, I spend the last ten cents of my weekly allowance for a second carton of milk.

Now I am an adult and, looking back, I know my teacher had all she could handle to keep control of the classroom and teach a few basic skills. When teaching aids were given to her that helped get the class's attention, and helped ease her burden, she was grateful. She surely had little time to wonder about the political dynamics that led to the development of those aids. How was she to know that the pretty chart was actually the outcome of extensive political lobbying by the meat and dairy industries?[1] How could she know that many millions of dollars had been poured into the campaigns that produced those charts? My teacher believed what she taught us, and never for a moment suspected she was being used to relay a commercial message.

Our innocent and captive little minds soaked it all up like sponges. And most of us have been willing, regular, and unquestioning consumers of large amounts of meat and dairy products ever since. Even those few of us who have chosen not to may still be haunted by the voices of our teachers and the lessons of those charts. If we listen, we may hear a voice in the back of our minds whispering, *"Maybe you aren't getting enough protein. . . ."*

Step Right Up, Step Right Up

We have come to believe we need lots of protein. But is this belief justified?

Objective authorities say no. The World Health Organization, the Food and Nutrition Board of the National Academy of Sciences, and the National Research Council say that at the very maximum we need only 8 percent of our total daily calories from protein.[2] They arrive at this 8 percent figure, incidentally, by adding in a "safety" factor of an extra 30 percent.

Building in an extra 30 percent margin may seem like a good idea. But one passionate nutritional expert, Dr. David Reuben, spoke for many informed scientists when he was asked just who it is that needs the extra 30 percent allowance of protein. He answered:

The people who sell meat, fish, cheese, eggs, chicken, and all the other high prestige and expensive sources of protein. Raising the amount of protein you eat by 30 percent raises their income by 30 percent. It also increases the amount of protein in the sewers and septic tanks of your neighborhood 30 percent as you merrily urinate away everything that you can't use that very day. It also deprives the starving children of the world of the protein that would save their

*lives. Incidentally, it makes you pay 30 percent of your already
bloated food bill for protein that you will never use. If you are an
average American family, it will cost you about $40 a month to
unnecessarily pump up your protein intake. That puts another $36
billion a year into the pockets of the protein producers.*[3]

There is no question that meat, dairy products, and eggs are high in
protein. But the average American consumes 90 to 120 grams of protein
per day—while the ideal protein intake for a human being is 20 to 40
grams per day.[4] Most Americans today are worried about "getting enough
protein," but, in fact, are eating far more than necessary, and far more
than is healthy.

Getting Enough Protein

**Human mother's milk provides 5 percent of its calories as pro-
tein.** Nature seems to be telling us that little babies, whose bodies are
growing the fastest they will ever grow in their lives, and whose protein
needs are maximum, are best served when 5 percent of their food calories
come as protein.

How hard is it to get 5 percent of your calories from protein? Not
hard at all, as you can see from the chart on page 385, which shows
the percentage of calories from protein, fat, and carbohydrate in various
foods.

If we ate nothing but wheat (16 percent protein), or oatmeal (15
percent), or even pumpkin (12 percent), we would easily be getting more
than enough protein. In fact, if we ate nothing but the common potato
(11 percent protein) we would still be getting enough protein. There
have been circumstances when people have been forced to satisfy their
entire nutritional needs with potatoes and water alone. Individuals who
have lived for lengthy periods of time under those conditions showed no
signs whatsoever of protein deficiency.[5] This fact does not mean potatoes
are a particularly high source of protein. They are not. But what it does
show is the contrast between how low our protein needs really are, and
how exaggerated are the beliefs most of us have come to accept about
them.

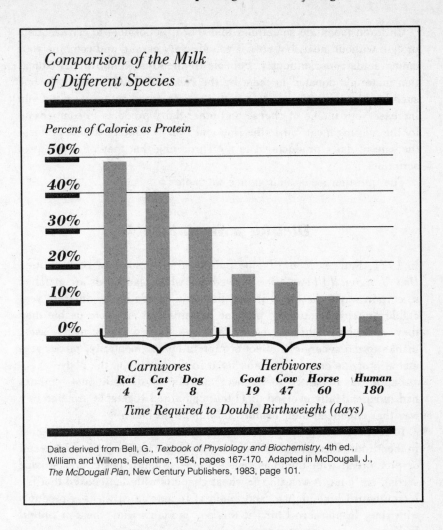

Comparison of the Milk of Different Species

Percent of Calories as Protein

Carnivores

Rat	Cat	Dog
4	7	8

Herbivores

Goat	Cow	Horse	Human
19	47	60	180

Time Required to Double Birthweight (days)

Data derived from Bell, G., *Texbook of Physiology and Biochemistry*, 4th ed., William and Wilkens, Belentine, 1954, pages 167-170. Adapted in McDougall, J., *The McDougall Plan*, New Century Publishers, 1983, page 101.

Learning to Shout "Hooray!" for Meat and Milk

I am back in elementary school again. The teacher is telling us that animal protein is superior to vegetable protein. It's the only "complete" protein. That sounds good. I have learned to root for the "good guys" on television shows, and now I learn that "good" protein comes only from animal products. Inside I shout "Hooray!" for meat and milk. At lunch, I wish my mother had put more bologna on my sandwich, so I could be stronger and better at football.

Children today are sometimes told that it is possible to get adequate protein without meat, but only if you are very careful and combine your amino acids conscientiously. Schools frequently use nutritional education materials donated to them by the National Dairy Council. In one such booklet, children are told that it is safe not to eat meat only if you increase your intake of cheese and other dairy products to compensate for the missing meat. Since the National Dairy Council exists to promote the sale of dairy products, it is not surprising that they offer this prescription.

The question is, is their stance warranted?

Diet for a Small Planet

In 1971, Frances Moore Lappé published an influential book entitled *Diet for a Small Planet*.[6] She showed that when plant foods are matched in certain ways, the result is that the amino acids in the different vegetable proteins combine to produce proteins that are more usable than they would be by themselves. In fact, she showed that in many cases, thanks to the synergistic effect of protein complementarity, mixed vegetable proteins come to outrank meat in their value to the body.

Lappé was delighted to discover that almost all traditional societies had independently evolved diets that combined vegetable proteins in a way that enhanced their combined amino acid patterns.

In Latin America, it was corn tortillas with beans, or rice with beans. In the Middle East, it was bulgur wheat with garbanzo beans (chickpeas), or pita bread with hummus (made from garbanzo beans and sesame seeds). In India, it was rice or wheat chapatis with dal (cooked lentils). In southern China, Japan, and much of Indonesia, it was soy products with rice. In northern China it was soy products with wheat or millet. In Korea it was soy foods with barley.

Lappé's enthusiasm for protein combining was contagious. Her book was beautifully written, and it was full of charts and tables that gave the details of how complementary vegetable proteins increased each other's nutritional value. Furthermore, Lappé tapped a deep and powerful spring in the human psyche when she showed the terrible waste of a meat-centered diet, and how it is part of a pattern of consumption that deprives millions of people the essentials of life. Her book sold more than three million copies.

Many people whose "nutritional education" had hitherto been overseen by the National Dairy Council and the Beef Council now saw, for the first time, scientific evidence that they did not have to eat meat in order to get enough protein. Numerous individuals were freed from thinking that only animal products could meet their dietary needs.

Lappé wrote *Diet for a Small Planet* specifically to show how wasteful a meat-centered diet is and to show that animal proteins aren't necessary for a balanced diet. Meanwhile, though, she was learning more and revising her thinking about the need to combine vegetable proteins. Lappé became convinced that her emphasis in *Diet for a Small Planet* on protein complementarity had been misplaced. So she revised her book, and in 1982 reissued an almost completely new tenth anniversary edition.[7] Now she said:

*In 1971 I stressed protein complementarity because I assumed that the only way to get enough protein . . . was to create a protein as usable by the body as animal protein. In combating the myth that meat is the only way to get high-quality protein, I reinforced another myth. I gave the impression that in order to get enough protein without meat, considerable care was needed in choosing foods. Actually, it is much easier than I thought. . . . **With a healthy, varied diet, concern about protein complementarity is not necessary.**[8]*

It is very rare when public figures are humble enough to publicly correct themselves, especially when the position they are abandoning is one that has made them famous. I deeply admire this kind of integrity and honesty.

In the original edition of *Diet for a Small Planet*, over 200 of the 280 pages deal specifically with the ins and outs of protein combining. In the 1981 edition, however, only about 60 of the 455 pages deal with this matter, mostly as an explanation of how the author's point of view has changed.

In the new *Diet for a Small Planet*, the woman who brought the concept of complementing vegetable proteins to the world goes out of her way to show that it isn't necessary. She writes:

If people are getting enough calories, they are virtually certain of getting enough protein.[9]

53

Enough Is Enough

What are we to make of this turnaround? Could it be that the whole concern about getting enough protein is actually just a relic from a less-enlightened past, with nothing to support it except the propaganda of the meat, dairy, and egg industries?

This, remarkably, seems to be the case. It is not only Frances Moore Lappé whose mind has changed as new evidence has come in from protein research. The editors of the most rigorous scientific journals now are likewise convinced.[10] An editorial in the medical journal *Lancet* reports:

> *Formerly, vegetable proteins were classified as second-class, and regarded as inferior to first-class proteins of animal origin, but this distinction has now been generally discarded.*[11]

A clinical study reported in the *Journal of the American Dietetic Association* compared the intake of the essential amino acids in the diets of meat eaters, lacto-ovo vegetarians (those consuming dairy products and eggs), and pure vegetarians (no eggs or dairy products). This study was uncompromising—it set the protein requirements for each amino acid at a height that would easily cover the needs of even growing children and pregnant women. The researchers found, however, that not only did all three diets provide sufficient protein, **they were all well above sufficient:**

> *Each group exceeded twice its requirement for every essential amino acid and surpassed this amount by large amounts for most of them.*[12]

Many consider Nathan Pritikin among the foremost experts on nutrition and health in modern times. Thousands of people came to his Longevity Centers. Some came in wheelchairs or were preparing for coronary bypass operations. Many went jogging home a month later. Most improved tremendously. The heart of Pritikin's program was diet. He said:

*Vegetarians always ask about getting enough protein. But I don't
know any nutrition expert [who] can plan a diet of natural foods
resulting in a protein deficiency, so long as you're not deficient in
calories. You need only 5 or 6 percent of total calories in protein . . .
and it is practically impossible to get below 9 percent in ordinary
diets.*[13]

It seems Nature intends us to have enough protein. By simply following
the instinct of hunger and eating enough natural food of whatever kind,
it is almost impossible to be deficient in this vital nutrient.

I admit that I have sometimes had a hard time accepting this truth.
When I first became a vegetarian, I often worried about the adequacy
of my protein intake. But dispassionate appraisal of the evidence has
forced me to conclude that the "problem" of where vegetarians will get
their protein, even those who completely forego dairy products and eggs,
has no basis in reality.[14]

In fact, researchers who set out to design diets deficient in protein
often have a devil of a time. It is possible, but it is far from easy, and
the "solution" usually involves large quantities of junk food. A member
of a team of Harvard researchers commented:

*It is difficult to obtain a mixed vegetable diet which will produce an
appreciable loss of body protein without resorting to high levels of
sugar, jams, jellies, and other essentially protein-free foods.*[15]

Growing Up Big and Strong

I am back in the classroom again. My teacher is telling us kids that if
we want to be big and strong we had better eat lots of protein, and that
when we work hard and play hard we need even more protein. I'm
thinking of my Superman comic books, and remembering the pictures
of Charles Atlas on the back, with his huge muscles and rippling vitality.
Squinting my eyes a little, I resolve to bite the bullet and ignore my
intense dislike for meatloaf. Some things are more important than whether
they taste good or not.

Most of us, naturally, still believe what our teachers taught us. But
one man who doesn't quite go along with all this is a man who might
be capable of kicking sand in even Charles Atlas's face. I am speaking

of Arnold Schwarzenegger, the virtual symbol of male muscular development. In his book on bodybuilding, he writes:

Kids nowadays ... tend to go overboard [on] protein—something I believe to be totally unnecessary ...[I state in] my formula for basic good eating: Eat about one gram of protein for every two pounds of body weight.[16]

To meet Arnold Schwarzenegger's protein quota, you'd do fine without meat, dairy products, or eggs. If you ate only broccoli, people might wonder if you had lost your marbles, but you'd get more than three times Schwarzenegger's suggested requirement of protein.

When it comes to protein and physical work, it turns out that once again my teacher, bless her heart, didn't quite hit the nail on the head.[17] True, we need protein to replace enzymes, rebuild blood cells, grow hair, produce antibodies, and to fulfill certain other specific tasks. But there is virtually no greater demand for any of these functions caused by hard physical work. If we are working or playing hard, it is not more protein we need, but rather more carbohydrates to burn, because it is carbohydrates that provide our fuel.

Study after study has found that protein combustion is no higher during heavy exercise than under resting conditions. This fact helps explain why Dave Scott could win the grueling Ironman triathalon six times on a vegetarian diet. And why Sixto Lenares, who holds the world record for the twenty-four-hour triathalon, can swim 4.8 miles, cycle 185 miles, and run 52.4 miles in a single day without any meat, dairy products, or eggs in his diet.

The popular idea that we need extra protein if we are working hard turns out to be simply another part of the whole mythology of protein, the conditioning foisted upon us by those who profit from our meat habit. Such thoughts have been planted in our minds since we were little children, and they have, for many of us, become so much a part of our psychic landscape that we simply "know" they are true. We take them for granted, as given facts, much as people once took for granted that the world was flat.

As a result, even though modern nutritional science tells us clearly that our protein needs are met without any fuss, many of us are still haunted by the fear that if we do not eat enough protein, we may end up looking like one of the people on a CARE poster.

Though we know that most anything in excess can be harmful, be it aspirin or alcohol, sex or sunshine, we rarely apply this understanding to our protein consumption. We have for the most part been so afraid of not getting enough protein that we have ignored the growing body of scientific research that points to **the serious health consequences of ingesting too much.**

Osteoporosis and the Protein Connection

If my grade school teacher is still alive, she is probably in her sixties. If she is like most other women of that age in the United States, her "old bones" are probably not quite what they used to be. She may be a little stooped over with age; and she may well have lost height from the days when she towered over a classroom of youngsters who looked up to her.

Actually, if she is like most women that age in the United States, her "old bones" are far indeed from what they once were. They have lost significant amounts of minerals, especially calcium, and as a result are fragile and weak. It is not at all uncommon for the mineral losses in the bones of postmenopausal women to cause them chronic back pain, while making them susceptible to frequent fractures. Often these women find themselves increasingly stooped over, for their weakened vertebrae just cannot support the body load.

I remember my teacher fondly, and wouldn't wish this fate on her for all the world. But in one quarter of sixty-five-year-old women in the United States, bone mineral losses (called "bone resorption") are so severe the condition is given the clinical name "osteoporosis."[18] For a person technically to qualify for this diagnosis she must have lost 50 to 75 percent of the original bone material from her skeleton. **One out of every four sixty-five-year-old women in our culture has lost over half her bone density.[19] Today, more women die from the effects of osteoporosis than from cancer of the breast and cervix combined.**

I used to believe that bones lost calcium only if there was not enough calcium in the individual's diet. The dairy industry is the foremost proponent of this point of view, and the solution its spokesmen propose, not all that shockingly, is for us all to drink more milk and eat more dairy products. In fact, the dairy industry has spent a great deal of money promoting this "solution," and because dairy products are high in calcium, it does at first glance seem logical. But current nutritional research clearly indicates a major flaw in this perspective.[20] **Osteoporosis is a condition caused by a number of factors, the most important of which is excess dietary protein.**[21]

Many research teams, working independently, have studied the effect of low- and high-protein diets on calcium balance and have reported their findings in the scientific literature.[22] Invariably, their studies have shown two things: (1) Low-protein diets create a positive calcium balance, meaning bones are not losing calcium; and (2) High-protein diets create a negative calcium balance, meaning osteoporosis is developing.

One long-term study found that even with as little as 75 grams of daily protein (less than three quarters of what the average meat-eating American consumes), more calcium is lost in the urine than is absorbed by the body from the diet—a negative calcium balance.[23] In every study the same correspondence was found: the more protein taken in, the more calcium the body loses. This is true even if the dietary calcium intake is as high as 1400 milligrams per day, far higher than the current American standard.

Regardless of how much calcium we take in, the more protein in the diet, the more calcium we lose. The result is that high-protein diets in general, and meat-based diets in particular, lead to a gradual but inexorable decrease in bone density and the development of osteoporosis.[24]

Summarizing the medical research on osteoporosis, one of the nation's leading medical authorities on dietary associations with disease, Dr. John McDougall, says:

I would like to emphasize that the calcium-losing effect of protein on the human body is not an area of controversy in scientific circles. The many studies performed during the past fifty-five years consistently show that the most important dietary change that we can make if we want to create a positive calcium balance that will keep our bones solid is to decrease the amount of proteins we eat each day. The important change is not to increase the amount of calcium we take in.[25]

Osteoporosis
Around the World

Throughout the world, the incidence of osteoporosis correlates directly with protein intake. In any given population, the greater the intake of protein, the more common and more severe the incidence of osteoporosis.[26] In fact, world health statistics show that osteoporosis is most common in exactly those countries where animal products are consumed in the largest quantities—the United States, Finland, Sweden, Israel, and the United Kingdom.[27]

After studying the medical research on osteoporosis, Nathan Pritikin commented:

African Bantu women take in only 350 milligrams of calcium per day. They bear nine children during their lifetime and breast-feed them for two years. They never have calcium deficiency, seldom break a bone, rarely lose a tooth. Their children grow up nice and strong. How can they do that on 350 milligrams of calcium a day when the [current] recommendation is 1200 milligrams? It's very simple. They're on a low-protein diet that doesn't kick the calcium out of the body.... In our country, those who can afford it are eating 20 percent of their calories in protein, which guarantees negative mineral balance, not only of calcium, but of magnesium, zinc, and iron. It is all directly related to the amount of protein you eat.[28]

The Bantus consume much less calcium than Americans. Yet, even their oldest women are essentially free of osteoporosis,[29] while the condition is epidemic among older American women. Representatives of the dairy industry have argued that the Bantus' far higher bone densities on much lower calcium intakes may be due to genetic factors. But genetic relatives of the Bantus who live in the United States and eat the standard American diet have been found to have levels of osteoporosis that equal those of their white neighbors.[30] Thus, the only sensible conclusion, in light of the research, is that the Bantus' far lower protein consumption has kept their bones healthier.[31]

At the other end of the scale from Bantus are native Eskimos. If osteoporosis were a calcium-deficiency disease it would be unheard of among these people. With a diet that includes such delicacies as fish bones, they have the highest dietary calcium intake of any people on Earth—more than 2000 milligrams a day.[32] On the other hand, if osteoporosis were caused by excess protein in the diet, they would suffer greatly from the disease, because their diet is centered on fish, walrus, and whale, and it is the very highest in the world in protein—250 to 400 grams a day.[33] As it happens, unfortunately, the native Eskimo people have one of the highest rates of osteoporosis in the world.[34]

The dairy industry likes to present dairy products as an answer to osteoporosis:

For strong bones—drink milk and eat cheese! (National Dairy Council)

But studies comparing the bone densities of people with different diets show a pattern completely opposed to what the dairy industry would teach us to expect. Those countries in which the population consumes large amounts of dairy products and calcium have much higher rates of osteoporosis than countries where the populations consume little or no dairy products and little calcium.[35]

In 1989, the *British Medical Journal* published a comprehensive review of the scientific literature on calcium intake and osteoporosis. The authors were far from impressed with the idea that increased calcium intake can offset bone loss. They called the idea *"clearly misleading and not supported by experimental observation."*[36]

Animal Protein: The Primary Factor in Osteoporosis

Even conservative medical investigators no longer deny the connection between excess protein and osteoporosis. In a report published in *Lancet*, Drs. Aaron Wachman and Daniel Bernstein commented on work sponsored by the U.S. Department of Health and Harvard University. They called the connection between meat-based diets and the increasing incidence of osteoporosis an *"inescapable"* conclusion.[37]

Today, the meat and dairy industries still defend their products by claiming that animal protein does not cause calcium loss. Yet more than one hundred studies and research papers published in peer-reviewed

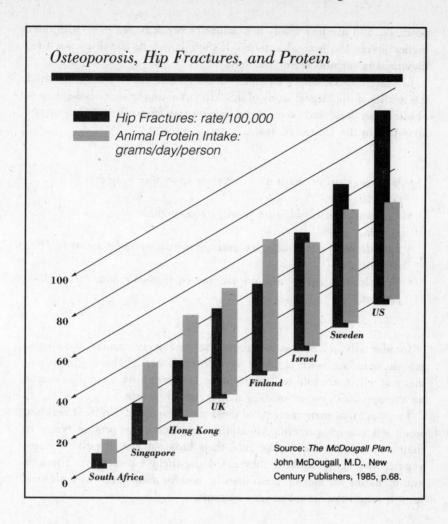

Osteoporosis, Hip Fractures, and Protein

Hip Fractures: rate/100,000

Animal Protein Intake:
grams/day/person

US

Sweden

Israel

Finland

UK

Hong Kong

Singapore

South Africa

100

80

60

40

20

0

Source: *The McDougall Plan,*
John McDougall, M.D., New
Century Publishers, 1985, p.68.

scientific journals have found a direct and consistent association between animal protein consumption and calcium loss in the urine. Three published studies that did not find this connection, all conducted by the same researcher, were all financially supported by the meat and dairy industries.[38] And impartial investigators who have examined these studies have raised serious questions about the methodology.[39]

As this tug-of-war goes on, many elderly meat-eating women feel helpless as they watch their skeletons crumble. In contrast, older women who have eaten vegetarian diets for many years know a very different experience of aging. They tend to remain active, can maintain erect postures, and are less likely to fracture or break bones even with their higher levels of physical activity. If their bones do break or fracture, they heal faster and more completely.[40]

In March 1983, the *American Journal of Clinical Nutrition* reported the results of the largest study of this kind ever undertaken. Researchers at Michigan State and other major universities found that, by the age of sixty-five in the United States:

- *Male vegetarians have an average measureable bone loss of 3 percent;*
- *Male meat eaters have an average measureable bone loss of 7 percent;*
- *Female vegetarians have an average measureable bone loss of 18 percent; and*
- *Female meat eaters have an average measureable bone loss of 35 percent.*[41]

Incidentally, a USDA survey found that among vegetarians, the biggest protein overdose is in children aged three to eight. These youngsters, many of whom are told to "drink three glasses of milk a day," consume an average 209 percent of their actual protein needs.[42]

I suspect that many parents of these children are afraid their children won't get enough protein. Attempting to placate the protein tyrant in their own minds, they make sure their kids eat lots of milk, cheese, yogurt, and eggs, thinking they are doing them a good turn. The kids end up eating far more protein than is good for them, even with all their growth requirements taken into account.

Protein Overdose

Remarkably, even some of the studies funded by the dairy industry, presumably for the purpose of showing the benefits of milk for women susceptible to osteoporosis, have, in fact, ended up showing something quite different. In one Dairy Council–sponsored study, it was found that women who drank an extra three eight-ounce glasses of low-fat milk every day for a year showed no significant increase in calcium balance. Even with all the extra milk-derived calcium, they were still in negative calcium balance. The scientists who conducted the test said that the reason the women continued to have a negative calcium balance and continued to develop osteoporosis was, in fact:

...the average 30 percent increase in protein intake during milk supplementation.[43]

The researchers stated that the additional protein load from the milk tended to wash calcium and other minerals out of the subjects' bodies, thus keeping them in negative calcium balance.

The evidence is massive and consistent. As milk consumption increases, there is a corresponding rise in calcium intake. But there is an equally corresponding increase in the amount of calcium lost in the urine.[44] In 1984, the *British Medical Journal* published a report indicating that calcium intake is, in fact, completely irrelevant to bone loss. The researchers enlisted post-menopausal women, who were divided into three groups: (1) those whose diets contained less than 550 milligrams of calcium; (2) those who consumed between 550 milligrams and 1100 milligrams of calcium; and (3) those whose diets provided more than 1100 milligrams of calcium.

At the end of two years, there was no difference in bone demineralization among the three groups. In fact, the women who consumed less than 550 milligrams of calcium daily showed bone loss similar to those who took in as much as 2000 milligrams a day.[45]

Many other studies show the same thing. At the Mayo Clinic, Dr. B. Lawrence Riggs measured bone densities and calcium intake in women for more than four years. Reporting his findings in the August 1, 1986 issue of *Science*, he noted:

[There is a] large body of evidence indicating no relationship between calcium intake and bone density.... **We found no correlation at all between calcium intake and bone loss, not even a trend.**

After a thorough review of the scientific literature, John McDougall, M.D., concluded:

In most published studies about calcium, the correlation between dietary calcium intake and bone density has been weak or nonexistent.[46]

Quite frankly, the more I have studied the medical literature, the harder it has gotten for me to listen to the dairy industry's promotion of *"milk for strong bones."* In spite of its high calcium content, milk, because of its high protein content, appears actually to contribute to the accelerating development of osteoporosis. The occurrence of this condition has reached truly epidemic proportions in the United States, and the promotion of dairy products as an "answer" to the suffering of millions seems to me to be not only self-serving, but even criminal.

There are, of course, other factors in addition to animal protein consumption that contribute to osteoporosis. Postmenopausal women are at highest risk. Small-boned, light-skinned Caucasian women are susceptible, as are women who bear no children and those who have had their ovaries removed. Lack of weight-bearing exercise is a significant factor, as is the consumption of soft drinks, junk food, and excess salt. Smoking increases risk, as do certain anticonvulsant medications. Yet, even though the list of factors that can contribute to osteoporosis is long, excess protein consumption towers above them all as the chief causative influence we can control.

A Word About Menopause, Estrogen, and Osteoporosis

Menopause is a natural process in which a woman's ovaries gradually decrease their production of estrogen and her menstrual periods come to an end. Menopause usually occurs between the ages of forty-eight and fifty-two in women consuming the standard American high-fat, high-animal-protein diet. (In women consuming a low-fat vegetarian diet, it occurs a few years earlier.)

Estrogen replacement therapy (ERT) is effective in preventing osteoporosis in postmenopausal women (and in women who have had hysterectomies). There are other advantages to ERT also. But at what cost?

Synthetic estrogen was first isolated in the 1920s, but its use did not become widespread until the 1960s, when it was hailed by Robert Wilson in his popular book *Feminine Forever*. By 1975, more than half the postmenopausal women in the United States were being prescribed estrogen.[47] The fad began to wane, however, in the late 1970s, when reports began to show that women on estrogen therapy were far more likely to develop ovarian and uterine cancer.

The risk becomes greater the longer a woman takes estrogen. According to one study, with one to five years of treatment, the risk of uterine cancer increases 560 percent.[48] With seven or more years of treatment, the risk increases 1400 percent![49]

Recently, estrogen replacement therapy has been on the upswing, with studies showing that adding progesterone on top of estrogen for at least ten days each month lessens the increase in uterine cancer risk. However, the addition of progesterone to estrogen treatment has serious drawbacks. It increases the rate of heart disease by decreasing high-density lipoprotein (HDL) levels, and it substantially increases the risk of breast cancer.[50]

In 1989, the *New England Journal of Medicine* reported that when estrogen is given in combination with progesterone for more than six years, the rate of breast cancer is increased by 440 percent![51]

There are other problems with estrogen replacement therapy. Rates of gallbladder disease, pulmonary embolism, diabetes, and hypertension all increase.[52] Women tend to be unhappy with the weight gains it often brings, and with the indefinite continuation of their menstrual periods. Estrogen replacement therapy is of little value in easing the mood swings, depression, and other emotional difficulties sometimes associated with menopause.[53]

Furthermore, to be effective against osteoporosis, estrogen therapy must be maintained indefinitely. If estrogen treatments are discontinued, any bone density retained because of the treatments is quickly lost.[54]

The good news is that for the vast majority of women, estrogen replacement therapy is altogether unnecessary in the prevention of osteoporosis—if they follow a diet that is low in animal protein and get plenty of exercise.

There's More

As a product of this culture, I must acknowledge that I, too, learned to think of protein as an unquestioned good. Bringing my thinking and actions up to date has not always been easy. Yet an impartial review of the scientific literature leaves me no choice but to conclude that not only osteoporosis, but many other diseases as well, are directly linked to animal protein consumption. The more animal protein specific populations consume, the higher their rates of kidney stones and other kidney diseases, heart disease, stroke, diabetes, and many forms of cancer.[55] The mechanisms that link animal protein to cancer rates are not yet fully understood, but the evidence is mounting rapidly. Dr. Myron Winick, director of Columbia University's Institute of Human Nutrition, says the data indicates:

a relationship between high-protein diets and cancer of the colon.[56]

The meat and dairy industries like to question the credentials of anyone who suggests their products might not promote optimum health. But it would be hard to dispute the standing of T. Colin Campbell, a professor in the Division of Nutritional Sciences at Cornell University and former senior science advisor to the American Institute for Cancer Research. He says there is:

a strong correlation between dietary protein intake and cancer of the breast, prostate, pancreas, and colon.[57]

Dr. Campbell is the director of the China-Oxford-Cornell Study, the largest and most comprehensive investigation of the connections between diet and disease in world medical history. In the May 8, 1990 *New York Times*, health editor Jane Brody hailed it as *"the grand prix of all epidemiological studies."*

Dr. Campbell was a meat eater for many years, but gave meat up because, as he put it, *"the mounting evidence could no longer be ignored."*

The culprit in many of the most prevalent and deadly diseases of our time, according to this prodigious study, is none other than the very thing many of us have been taught to hold virtually sacred—animal protein. Data from the China-Oxford-Cornell Study reveal that people who derive 70 percent of their protein from animal products (as Americans typically do) have major health difficulties compared to people who derive just 5 percent of their protein from animal sources. **They have seventeen times the death rate from heart disease, and**

women are five times more likely to die of breast cancer.[58] Summarizing the implications of this extraordinary data, Campbell leaves little doubt as to his opinion of the protein consumption patterns of our society:

Excessive animal protein is at the core of many chronic diseases.

Now What?

I am back in my grade school classroom. The teacher is telling us about the importance of eating lots of meat and drinking lots of milk, because we need lots of protein. She is pointing to the colorfully decorated chart that makes it all seem so simple. Her voice rings with authority, because she believes every word she is saying and that what she is telling us is for our own good.

I am listening, but not completely. I'm thinking about my pet kitten, about how furry and cuddly and playful he is, and about a neighbor's dog who recently had puppies.

My teacher's voice passes over me and slides away. My attention drifts, and I glance at the wall and happen to notice another chart, one with a photograph of a hungry family. It is plea for help.

That day at lunch I decide to save my milk money and give it to people who do not have enough to eat.

FOUR

Who Decides What You Eat?

*"Yes, sometimes unusual things happen
after a switch to a vegetarian diet.
I've seen a number of cases in which the
poor people broke out in violent attacks of good
health, followed by bouts of physical
exercise and sweet thoughts."*
Anonymous

*"The person who is afraid to alter his living habits,
and especially his eating and drinking habits,
because he is afraid that other persons may
regard him as queer, eccentric, or fanatic
forgets that the ownership of his body,
the responsibility for its well-being,
belongs to him, not them."*
Dr. Paul Brunton

I t is now the 1990s. It has been four decades since I sat in my grade
school classroom.

In front of me is a coloring book found today in public schools.
Purporting to teach children how to eat well, it has been supplied to
school systems by the dairy industry. I don't know how many states use

this particular coloring book, but I know that it is representative of many of the "nutritional education" materials used throughout the United States.

I open the coloring book and see the outline drawing of a man's face. "Color Dad," I am told.

That sounds fair enough. But look what happens next. How we are to color in Dad's face is not left entirely up to our imaginations. There are rules to follow:

1. If Dad drank milk today, we are to draw a "happy face." If he did not, then we are to draw a "sad face."
2. If he had ice cream today, we are to color his hair brown; if he did not, we are to color his hair blue.
3. If he had butter, we are to color his eyes blue. If he didn't have any butter, we are to color his eyes red.
4. If he had cheese, we are to color his face pink. If he didn't have any cheese, we are to color his face green.

It is unlikely that you had this particular coloring book when you were in grammar school, because this one is a recent publication. But it is quite probable that if you went to public school in the United States, you were given similar materials.

When that happened, you probably got out your crayons and began busily coloring away. There is one thing, though, that I am willing to bet you didn't do.

You didn't raise your hand and say, "Excuse me, teacher, but I have some questions. What are the health consequences of eating a lot of milk, butter, ice cream, and cheese? Aren't these all high in butterfat? And isn't butterfat a highly saturated fat? And don't dairy fats carry pesticide residues at very high levels of concentration? Oh, and there is one thing more, teacher: Who is it that profits from our believing that if we don't eat ice cream, butter, milk, and cheese we end up looking terrible, with red eyes, a green face, and blue hair?"

Hucksters in the Classroom

Knowing how malleable and impressionable youngsters are, I have often wondered about the forces that influence our children's thoughts and feelings about different foods. When we are young, we are by nature innocent and impressionable. We look instinctively to our parents and other adults for support, guidance, and example. Trusting, we soak up what we are told.

Unfortunately, there are people who see the innocence of children not as a call to be caring and supportive, but as an opportunity to promote the sale of their products.

The National Dairy Council is one of the leading suppliers of the materials used to teach nutritional education in America's school systems.[1] In some of our minds, the National Dairy Council may be a trustworthy organization concerned for human health. Even its name seems to suggest a group of elders whose purpose is wholesome and pure. When they told us to drink three glasses of milk a day, we dutifully obeyed. Little did we realize that this is an organization dedicated to getting the American public to buy as much milk, cheese, butter, yogurt, and ice cream as possible.

Because milk products are priced by federal law according to a structure that provides the dairymen more profit on higher-fat products, the dairy industry pushes those dairy products with the highest percentage of fat. It is not deterred by the fact that these are precisely the products that make the greatest contribution to heart disease, cancer, diabetes, and many other deadly diseases.

Kindergarten children have received National Dairy Council materials such as *Little Ideas*, a set of food pictures ostensibly designed to help preschoolers identify foods. The set starts with butter, and then continues with sixteen other milk products, most of which are high in saturated fat. The implicit message is that high-fat dairy products are the primary foods in the human diet.

First graders have gotten a curriculum package ironically called *Food: Your Choice*. This is a large box filled with colorful materials, including bright posters about making milk shakes and pancakes. The recipes happily call for cream and butter.

You may not think that ice cream, a product that derives up to 90 percent of its calories from fat and sugar, is the healthiest sort of food, but the Dairy Council is not hampered by such concerns. Their materials tell children:

Ice cream is a healthful food made from milk and cream along with other good foods.

The "*healthful milk group*" merrily recommended by the Council features another item that you may not have recognized as the type of food children should be encouraged to eat—chocolate pudding.

Claiming to be an unbiased source of nutritional information, the Dairy Council next tells children that to be healthy they should:

Drink milk at every meal and have . . . cheese, ice cream, baked custard, [and a] bowl of cream of tomato soup with butter.

Disguised as nutritional education, the advertising of dairy products continues throughout our children's school years. High school students receive such helpful Dairy Council publications as *A Boy and His Physique* and *A Girl and Her Figure*. What do you imagine overweight teenagers receive as their first diet suggestion from the Dairy Council?

[Drink] whole milk most of the time, skim milk part of the time, if you need to lose weight.

With a completely straight face, the "lower calorie" section of these booklets given to teenagers in our schools calls for ice cream.

But wait, that's not the worst. These publications are ostensibly designed to help youngsters lose weight and become healthy, but the "low calorie" sections suggest balls of cream cheese, softened with cream, and rolled in peanuts! This item derives nearly 90 percent of its calories from fat!

Given recommendations like these, it is hard to avoid the perception that the Dairy Council is primarily concerned with getting youngsters hooked on high-fat dairy products, and that providing sound nutritional education to children is merely a pretext.

Could part of the reason so many of us struggle with unhealthy food habits be that when we were young, vulnerable, and impressionable, we were "educated" by materials such as these?

Playing Games with Children's Minds

The National Dairy Council is not the only commercial interest that intentionally seeks to shape our beliefs about food to its own advantage and uses the public schools to accomplish this purpose.

A few years ago McDonald's ran a sixteen-page color insert in the *Chicago Tribune* that extolled the virtues of what it called a *"properly balanced diet."* It was an interesting version of "balance," in that it amounted to Big Macs, fries, and shakes. If this publication had been produced only as an advertisement, it would have been sad enough. But the insert was then distributed to the schools throughout the Chicago region, with the help of the Chicago Board of Education. The public relations company that developed the concept, the Aaron Cushman Agency, called it *"a combination textbook and advertisement."*

McDonald's has also presented youngsters with a colorful booklet proclaiming the nutritional benefits of its menu. Called *Good Food, Good Nutrition, and McDonald's,* the booklet concludes that a meal consisting of a cheeseburger, fries, a chocolate milk shake, and McDonaldland cookies is just what the doctor ordered. After all, they point out, such a meal is only 33.5 percent fat. Never mind that people who eat 33.5 percent fat have heart disease and cancer rates ten times higher than people who are considerably more moderate. And never mind that most of the fat in a McDonald's meal is highly saturated beef and dairy fat, which multiplies the danger many times over again.

By the way, there's a little trick that McDonald's uses in order to get the fat level of their meals to appear even that low. The cheeseburger, you see, is 41 percent fat. The fries are 47 percent fat. How do they get the percentage for the whole meal down from there? By adding sugar. The percentage of fat in the cookies and shake is significantly lower for the simple reason that these concoctions get most of their calories from sugar.

The Oscar Mayer company, a large producer of hot dogs, sausages, and cold cuts, also provides schools with nutrition tips. In one attractive booklet that is supplied free of charge to schools, the claim is made that sausage products are not fatty. To prove the point, the company provides an impressive graphic, comparing the fat content of hot dogs to other food products. Lo and behold, hot dogs do indeed come out looking the least fatty of them all.[2]

The comparison looks quite convincing if you don't happen to know how high in fat are the foods that have been chosen to be compared to hot dogs—margarine, mayonnaise, salad dressing, and cream cheese.

Similarly, the company has found a way to make their meats appear absolutely fabulous to schoolchildren in cholesterol comparisons. They simply compare them to eggs, which happen to be the highest of all foods in the human diet in cholesterol. In another instance, they proudly announce to schoolchildren that their wieners are filled with nutritional value. To prove it, they make a comparison to another food item, and sure enough, wieners come out clearly on top. Children might not realize that the product against which hot dogs look so good in comparison probably wasn't chosen to provide the stiffest possible competition. Wieners, it turns out, have less sugar and more nutrients than "*a 12-ounce can of Coke.*"[3]

Life in the Fat Lane

As our understanding of the relationship between diet and human health has been clarified, the meat and dairy industries have found themselves in an increasingly distressing position. Their products, which tend to be very high in saturated fat and cholesterol and provide no fiber, have been found to be responsible for an almost inconceivable amount of human suffering.

Time and time again, medical research has demonstrated the profound health advantages of a low-fat, high-fiber plant-based diet. And time and time again the meat and dairy industries have remained undaunted in their efforts to control our eating habits.

These industries have not always been able to avoid stumbling over the truth, but they have always managed to pick themselves up and carry on their efforts to hook us on their products as if nothing had happened. And it is not only children who are the target of their efforts.

The Beef Council has the dubious distinction of being the only two-time winner of the Harlan Page Hubbard Memorial Award for the year's most deceptive and misleading advertising.[4] This award is given annually by a coalition of consumer and public interest groups to expose the most dangerous lies and exaggerations of modern advertising. The "*Beef gives strength*" and similar beef campaigns have earned this distinction for their consistent attempts to deceive the public. The servings of steak shown in the ads are only three ounces, when the average beefsteak serving is six ounces. By concealing the fact that the serving shown in the ad is only half the size most people eat, the industry manages to convey the impression that servings of beef are much lower in fat than they actually are. In announcing the award, Bonnie Liebman of the Center for Science in the Public Interest also pointed out that the technicians who did the laboratory analysis for the Beef Council used scalpels to remove every possible bit of fat from the meat samples.[5] Thus the fat and calorie levels reported were not only for a serving size much smaller than consumers assumed it to be, but also for a serving which had been trimmed of fat to a degree no homemaker could possibly match.

The Beef Council found itself embarrassed again in the late 1980s when it hired actor James Garner to be the spokesman for a campaign claiming that beef is *"real food for real people."* Fortunately, Garner lived close to a "real hospital," because soon after the campaign began to air on national television, Garner's poor health required him to undergo quintuple bypass heart surgery.

In 1991, Frank Perdue, the East Coast chicken producer, began running a series of radio, television, and newspaper ads proudly announcing that his chickens would now carry nutrition labels to tell consumers *"things like how low in saturated fat a Perdue chicken is."* The catch is that while the USDA says a typical serving of chicken is about **five ounces,** Perdue lists the fat in **one ounce** of roasted chicken.[6]

Meanwhile, the California Milk Producers got into the act by presenting a series of ads in which hired celebrities proclaimed that *"everybody needs milk."* The Federal Trade Commission, however, didn't agree. It took legal steps toward prosecuting the milk producers and their advertising agency, calling the advertising *"false, misleading, and deceptive."*[7]

To this day, the meat and dairy industries continue to seek to convince us that their products are healthy. Steadfast in their purpose, they do not seem to be fazed by trifles like the truth, our health, or the health of our children.

Playing Politics with Our Food

The last few decades of scientific inquiry into the relationship between diet and disease have seen great advances in understanding. We now know, beyond any reasonable doubt, that diets high in fat, saturated fat, and cholesterol promote heart disease and cancer. We now know how to prevent many of the diseases that plague our society.

Yet the eating habits of most Americans have not adjusted to reflect this new understanding. Part of the reason is that our attitudes and feelings about various foods have been so heavily influenced by commercial interests. Another part of the reason is that many governmental agencies, under the sway of the "fat lobby," still propagate beliefs that have been disproven.

For more than thirty-five years schoolchildren throughout the United States were taught according to the precepts of the "basic four food groups." Generations of Americans have had the belief drummed into them that a balanced diet consists of having, every day, at least two servings from the meat group and at least two servings from the dairy group.

As a result, the belief in the necessity of meat and dairy products for our health has grown in our society to occupy the status of given truth.

Today the ideas behind the basic four food groups still provide the foundation of most diet planning in schools, in hospitals, in the military, in prisons, in government institutions, in public service cafeterias, and in households across the country. Unfortunately, these ideas have remarkably little to do with current information on creating good health in human beings.

Marion Nestle, who was managing editor of the Surgeon General's landmark report on Nutrition and Health in 1988, and now chairs New York University's Department of Nutrition, is not overly impressed with the food groups created by the USDA. She says:

The standard four food groups are based on American agricultural lobbies. Why do we have a milk group? Because we have a National Dairy Council. Why do we have a meat group? Because we have an extremely powerful meat lobby.

Had the creation of a plan for a balanced and health supporting diet been placed under the jurisdiction of the Department of Health and Human Services, or the Surgeon General, we would have seen very different results. But the food groups were in fact developed by the Department of Agriculture, and remain to this day under its auspices. This is a tragedy, because the Department of Agriculture is not primarily concerned with human health. Its principal mission, for which it was originally created, and for which it continues to be funded, is to promote the sale of agricultural products. This has led to something very different from guiding the eating habits of the country in a healthy direction. It has meant finding and maintaining markets for the meat and dairy industries.

Linda Schwartzstein, Associate Professor of Law at George Mason University, writes:

Congress has specifically given the USDA the mission of increasing demand for beef, pork, eggs, and dairy products. Under Congress' direction, the USDA collects money from all of the producers in these *industries, which it turns over to the Cattlemen's Beef Promotion and Research Board, the National Pork Board, the Egg Board, and the National Dairy Promotion and Research Board. These boards are appointed by the Secretary of Agriculture from members of the industry. The boards operate under the auspices of the USDA as government-sponsored trade associations. Their purpose is to protect the interests of their respective industries and to find effective means, such as advertisements, to increase the market for their products. As an example, in 1990 the National Dairy Promotion and Research Board spent $20.8 million to promote cheese, $15.8 million to promote fluid milk, $13.9 million to promote butter, $5.8 million to promote dairy calcium to female professionals, and $4.8 million to promote ice cream. It also arranged a coupon program in conjunction with the American Dairy Association, the International Ice Cream Association, and a cookie manufacturer to promote cookies and ice cream. Overall, $63.7 million was spent on advertising by this one promotion and research board alone. In contrast, the Food and Nutrition Service spent $8.7 million on its human nutrition information service. It does not take much skepticism to ask whether the agency that promotes cookies and ice cream can at the same time be given the responsibility for providing nutrition education and research to the American people.*

I have struggled against accepting the evidence that the USDA serves the meat and dairy industries more than it does public health. I have not wanted to believe this to be so, because I have wanted to believe that governmental agencies would at least be trying to look after the public interest. But the facts in this case, I am sorry to say, speak otherwise.

Giving Our Children Heart Disease and Calling It Nutrition

Perhaps the most blatant example of the Department of Agriculture's subservience to the meat and dairy industries at the expense of public health is the school lunch program. Each year, the USDA buys three to four billion dollars' worth of surplus foods, which it donates to the nation's schools. These donated items make up 20 to 30 percent of the food served in school lunches. This may sound as if the USDA were helping our children to eat well, but look again. The school lunch programs are being used by the Department of Agriculture to guarantee a market for the meat and dairy industries. By 1991, the evidence implicating high-fat, high-cholesterol animal products in the creation of heart disease, cancer, adult-onset diabetes, and obesity had become as massive and incontrovertible as the evidence linking smoking to lung cancer. Yet in 1991, 90 percent of the USDA surplus foods consisted of eggs, high-fat cheeses, butter, ground pork, ground beef, and whole milk.[8] If the USDA had intentionally gone out to obtain foods that would destroy the health of our children, they could hardly have done better. Furthermore, while the USDA donates hundreds of millions of dollars worth of high-fat cheeses, schools must pay for low-fat cheese.[9]

The results are catastrophic for the health of our children. A 1990 study in the *Journal of School Health* found that the average school lunch gets 39 percent of its calories from fat.[10] This, while the Surgeon General was saying that anything over 30 percent is dangerous, and health experts who were not as bound by political considerations were urgently calling for a reduction to 20 percent or less.

As a result of the USDA's programs, the average school lunch contains 1244 milligrams of sodium. Three meals a day at that rate would assault these young human bodies with 3732 milligrams of sodium—while the Food and Nutrition Board of the National Academy of Sciences recommends a daily sodium intake of 600 to 1800 milligrams for children aged seven to ten.

No wonder as many as one in eight school-age children in the United States have blood pressure levels that are unhealthfully high.[11] No wonder our children have the most clogged arteries of any children in the world, and their rate of atherosclerosis is increasing. No wonder the American Heart Association reports that in a recent seventeen-year period obesity in children aged six to eleven jumped a startling 54 percent, while obesity in children aged twelve to seventeen leaped 39 percent.[12]

School lunches are a nutritional nightmare. Meanwhile, the Department of Agriculture is providing three to four billion dollars a year worth of guaranteed business to the meat and dairy industries.

Who Decides What You Eat?

On April 15, 1991, the USDA announced that the basic four food group charts were at long last going to be modified. The change was not a major one: The four food groups themselves were not going to be significantly altered, nor were the number of servings recommended from each group.

What *was* going to be changed was the way the four food groups were depicted. The new version was to be a pyramid instead of a wheel, with the meat and dairy groups set at the narrow top of the pyramid. The new presentation would acknowledge both that animal products are higher on the food chain and that these foods ought to occupy a less important place in the human diet than fruits, vegetables, and grains.

While recognizing that this change amounted only to a small step, the nation's health community applauded the change, for it was at least in the right direction.

The meat and dairy industries, however, did not join in the applause. Instead, they pounced on the recently appointed Secretary of Agriculture, Edward Madigan, a former Congressman from the Illinois farm belt. After board members of the National Cattlemen's Association met with Madigan, their executive vice president, J. Burton Eller, Jr., was asked what had transpired. His reply left little doubt as to the purpose of the meeting: *"We complained loudly!"*[13]

Loudly enough, evidently. Almost immediately, Agriculture Secretary Madigan announced he was indefinitely delaying the new chart. He said it needed more study. He said it might be hard for some groups of youngsters to understand. He didn't mention that in fact the pyramid had already undergone extensive consumer tests and had been reviewed for the past two years by some thirty government and university experts.

In fact, the new food group model had already passed three years' worth of focus group tests and had been approved by a joint committee from the Departments of Agriculture and of Health and Human Services.[14]

The meat and dairy industries pleaded innocent. Alisa Harrison, director of information for the National Cattlemen's Association, said that the group had simply offered its comments to Madigan, *"as any U.S. citizen is encouraged to do."*[15]

A year later, after spending nearly $1 million of taxpayers' money to prove what earlier research had already shown, the USDA adopted the Food Guide Pyramid.

The sadness is that this still represents only a small step forward. Our children would still be taught as truth erroneous beliefs, beliefs that have been so relentlessly repeated that they continue to influence even those of us who know them to be awry. They will still be told to eat two to three servings from the meat group and two to three servings from the milk group every day.

A Different Picture

For the past forty years, nutritionists and cardiologists have increasingly urged Americans to adopt a healthier, more plant-based diet in order to avoid heart attacks, strokes, cancers, diabetes, and many of the other plagues of our time.[16] Literally thousands of articles published in the last few decades in the *New England Journal of Medicine*, the *American Journal of Clinical Nutrition*, the *Journal of the American Medical Association*, the *British Medical Journal*, *Lancet*, and other publications of similar stature have demonstrated that the less animal fat you take into your body, the healthier you will be. During the last few decades, the list of organizations telling us that cutting back the amount of fat, meat, and other animal products in our diets will make us a healthier people has grown to include almost every organization in the world concerned with human health. The U.S. Surgeon General, the Senate Select Committee on Nutrition and Human Needs, the National Research Council, the National Cancer Institute, the American Heart Association, the National Academy of Sciences' Food and Nutrition Board, the World Health Organization, the United Nations' Food and Agriculture Program, and hundreds of other similar organizations worldwide are all telling us the same thing: If you want to live a healthy life, eat more vegetables, eat more fruits, and eat more whole grains. Cut down on fat, especially saturated fat, and cut down on cholesterol.

In a nutshell, eat more plant foods and cut down on animal products.

The Evidence Mounts

Every week another report comes out implicating animal fat as a cause of human disease. The December 1990 edition of the *New England Journal of Medicine* reported the results of the largest study of diet and colon cancer ever conducted. After analyzing data from the health and diet histories of over eighty-eight thousand women, the report concluded that the more red meat and animal fat people eat, the more likely they are to develop cancer of the colon. The meat industry had already been put on the defensive, with scores of public health groups in effect telling

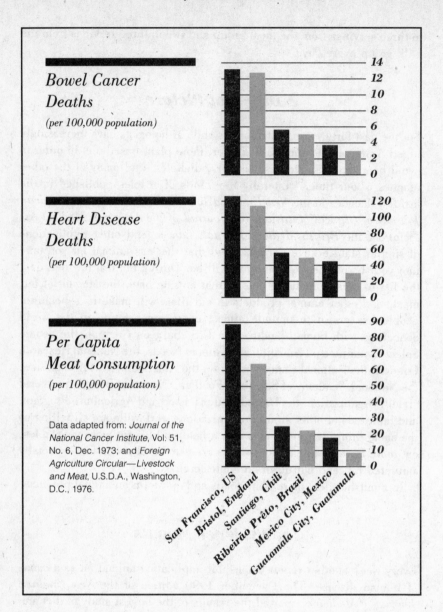

Bowel Cancer Deaths
(per 100,000 population)

Heart Disease Deaths
(per 100,000 population)

Per Capita Meat Consumption
(per 100,000 population)

Data adapted from: *Journal of the National Cancer Institute*, Vol. 51, No. 6, Dec. 1973; and *Foreign Agriculture Circular—Livestock and Meat*, U.S.D.A., Washington, D.C., 1976.

San Francisco, US
Bristol, England
Santiago, Chili
Ribeirão Prêto, Brazil
Mexico City, Mexico
Guatamala City, Guatamala

Americans to eat less meat. But now Dr. Walter Willet, the researcher at the Brigham and Women's Hospital in Boston who directed the study, concluded:

If you step back and look at the data, the optimum amount of red meat you eat should be zero.[17]

Reeling, the meat industry has looked to the conservative American Dietetic Association to support the old-guard philosophy and call for a reinstatement of meat's role as a healthy food. But the ADA was not of much help. Instead, the ADA came out with a position paper saying that people who do not consume meat are at lower risk not only for colon cancer, but also for heart disease, obesity, adult-onset diabetes, high blood pressure, osteoporosis, kidney stones, gallstones, diverticulosis, breast cancer, and lung cancer.[18]

The ADA position paper disappointed representatives of the meat industry, but it was justified by scores of international studies. The more fat that is consumed by the population of a particular country, the greater is the incidence of breast cancer in that country.[19] Cancers of the prostate, kidneys, testicles, uterus, lung, colon, and breast and lymphomas are all more common in populations that consume diets high in fat.[20]

So is high blood pressure. There are cultures in the world where high blood pressure is almost unheard of, even in older people.[21] What these societies have in common, and what our society does not have, is a diet that is low in sodium, fats and animal products and high in fiber.[22] When people in our society do adopt this type of diet, however, they find that their blood pressure levels almost immediately become lower and more healthy.[23]

High blood pressure, of course, is a serious problem because it leads to heart attacks and strokes. These tragedies occur because the blood vessels are diseased, a condition known as atherosclerosis. The consumption of meat and high-fat dairy products is known to be a leading cause of high blood pressure, atherosclerosis, heart attacks, and strokes.[24]

You may already know that blocked coronary arteries cause heart attacks, and blocked arteries leading to the brain cause strokes. But less publicized is the fact that blocked arteries leading to other parts of the body cause other problems, including lack of sexual response. In July 1985, *Lancet* published a major study of impotence in men. The

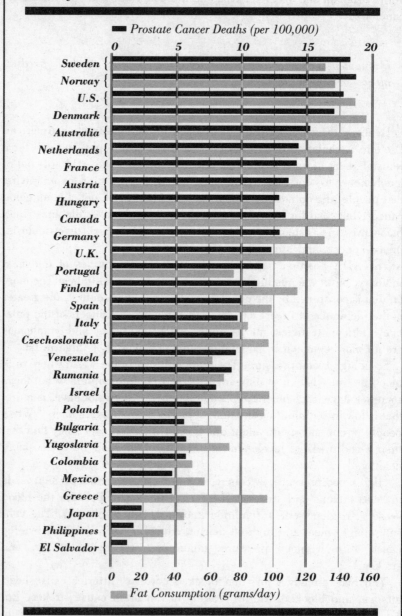

The More Fat Consumed, the Greater the Risk of Prostate Cancer Deaths

Prostate Cancer Deaths (per 100,000)

Fat Consumption (grams/day)

Data derived from: Reddy, B.S., et al. "Nutrition and Its Relationship to Cancer," *Advances in Cancer Research*.

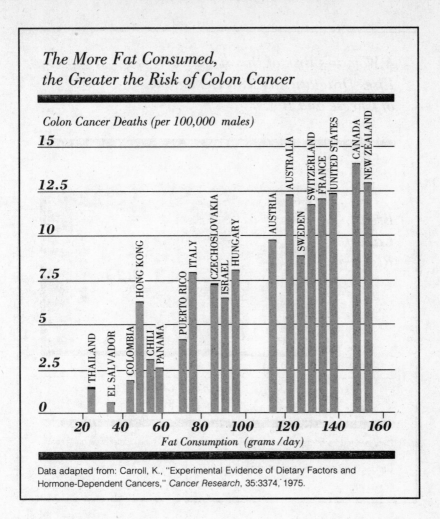

The More Fat Consumed, the Greater the Risk of Colon Cancer

Colon Cancer Deaths (per 100,000 males)

Fat Consumption (grams/day)

Data adapted from: Carroll, K., "Experimental Evidence of Dietary Factors and Hormone-Dependent Cancers," *Cancer Research*, 35:3374, 1975.

study concluded that impotence is directly associated with blocked arteries and atherosclerosis.[25] Low-fat, high-fiber plant-based diets have been shown to dramatically decrease arteriosclerotic deposits, freeing the circulation of blood throughout the cardiovascular system and allowing a full supply of blood to reach all the body's organs.[26]

Numerous studies have shown that diabetics also benefit, often dramatically, from low-fat, high-fiber plant-based diets.[27] So effective are these kinds of diets at bringing the blood sugar levels of most diabetics into balance that as many as 75 percent of adult-onset diabetics who require insulin can stop all medication soon after adopting them.[28] Al-

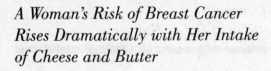

*A Woman's Risk of Breast Cancer
Rises Dramatically with Her Intake
of Cheese and Butter*

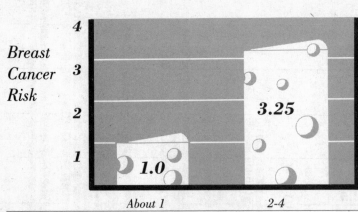

Breast
Cancer
Risk

3.25

1.0

About 1   2-4

Butter and Cheese
Times per Week

Data derived from Paper presented by Takeshi Hirayama at the Conference on Breast
Cancer and Diet, U.S.–Japan Cooperative Cancer Research Program, Fred Hutchison
Cancer Center, Seattle, Wa., March 14–15, 1977.

most 100 percent of those requiring diabetic pills can be freed of all
daily medication.[29]

In the last decade, the evidence that a high-fiber, low-fat plant-based
diet is of paramount importance in the prevention and treatment of a
broad spectrum of diseases has become incontrovertible. The *British
Medical Journal* reported that the fewer animal products people eat, the
lower their incidence of gallstones.[30] The *British Journal of Urology*
reported a direct correlation between the amount of animal protein people
consume and their likelihood of forming kidney stones.[31] The *Journal
of Asthma* reported that over 90 percent of asthmatics who followed a

diet without any meats or dairy products could reduce or entirely discontinue their medications.[32] *Lancet* reported that animal protein and animal fat aggravated arthritis symptoms, while 100 percent of the patients on a strict vegetarian diet noticed significant improvements.[33]

What Every Bite of Meat Costs

The world's longest ongoing investigation into heart disease and diet, the Framingham Heart Study, was begun in 1949. This enormous endeavor has proceeded under the able direction of William Castelli, M.D.

After many years of this work, Dr. Castelli was asked if he could say which food choices are the best. His response was to the point:

Vegetarians have the best diet. They have the lowest rates of coronary disease of any group in the country.... Some people scoff at vegetarians, but they have a fraction of our heart attack rate and they have only 40 percent of our cancer rate. They outlive us. On the average they outlive other men by about six years now.[34]

The six-year figure Castelli gives for the longer life expectancy for people who avoid meat is conservative compared to the numbers arrived at by other reputable researchers.[35]

It is interesting to speculate how much the eating of meat might shorten our life span. If we accept the conservative figure of six years for the length of time that the average vegetarian outlives the average meat eater, it turns out that for every minute people eat meat, they lose more than twelve minutes of their life spans.[36] Smokers, by way of comparison, lose approximately eight minutes off their life spans for each minute they smoke.

To me, length of life is actually a minor part of the story—the real issue is quality of life. For a person who is not burdened by clogged and hardened arteries, whose kidneys and skeleton are not under siege from excess protein, and whose cells are not driven to cancerous multiplication by too much fat, the experience of life is thoroughly different from the experience of someone whose diet is based on animal products. The real advantage is not merely a matter of life extension numbers, but can be found in a body that remains strong and supple and a mind that remains clear and flexible as the years go by. A valid test to a good eating plan is the one that not only lengthens our lives, but allows us the great blessing of good health throughout our years.

The Largest Study in History

In 1990, the global scientific community eagerly awaited the results of the largest and most important diet and health study ever undertaken.[37]

Conducted by an international team of scientists, the China-Oxford-Cornell Project on Nutrition, Health, and the Environment (also known as the China Health Project) was begun in 1983. When the first reports from the study were finally released, health organizations worldwide applauded the research enthusiastically, and over fifty papers on the study were published in scientific journals.

Representatives of the meat industry, however, did not find many reasons to celebrate. In fact, they were downright appalled.

The reason was that the mammoth study indicated that:

> ... *whether industrialized societies* ... *can cure themselves of their meat addictions may ultimately be a greater factor in world health than all the doctors, health insurance policies, and drugs put together.*[38]

The dairy industry also had reason to flinch, for the study confirmed not only that consumption of dairy products is completely unnecessary to prevent osteoporosis, but also that because dairy products are high in fat and protein, they contribute to cancer, heart disease, obesity, and many other diseases.[39]

The meat and dairy industries surely were not going to take a blow like this lying down. The trouble was, the study was being universally heralded. The best they could muster was to complain that the director of the study was a vegetarian, hoping this would cast doubt upon the study's findings.

The director of the study, T. Colin Campbell, actually has preeminent scientific stature. Formerly the senior science advisor to the American Institute for Cancer Research, he is currently Jacob Gould Schurman Professor of Nutritional Biochemistry at Cornell University. As to the charge that his dietary preferences affect his scientific conclusions, Campbell replied:

I was raised on a dairy farm and ate plenty of meat and eggs until about twenty years ago. I started doing nutritional research, and a decade or so after that my family made some major dietary changes. . . . I'm just paying attention to what the data are telling me: The scientific evidence came first.[40]

Campbell is one of many researchers who have dramatically reduced their intake of animal products because of the strength of the dietary evidence that has accumulated in the past twenty years. Not so long ago, the average American mother would have been more concerned for the health of her son or daughter if she learned that he or she had become a vegetarian than if she learned that her youngster had taken up smoking. But now the most credible medical journals are announcing that old ideas about meat eating being necessary and natural to human beings have been seriously in error. As the editor-in-chief of the prestigious *American Journal of Cardiology*, William C. Roberts, M.D., put it in a 1991 editorial:

Although we think we are one, and we act as if we are one, human beings are not natural carnivores. . . . When we kill animals to eat them, they end up killing us because their flesh . . . was never intended for human beings, who are naturally herbivores.

Reversing Heart Disease

While the China Health Project was a major blow to the meat and dairy industries' claim to be producing healthy products, it is not the only recent study that has given these reeling industries sleepless nights. The July 20, 1990 edition of the British medical journal *Lancet* reported a study that was deemed so important that *U.S. News and World Report* made it a cover story, while both *Time* and *Newsweek* featured it on their covers and called it *"revolutionary."*

The response of the meat and dairy industries, however, was markedly less enthusiastic. They called it *"irrelevant."*

Headed by Dr. Dean Ornish of the University of California at San Francisco School of Medicine, the study involved forty-eight people suffering from serious heart disease.[41] Twenty of the patients followed the American Heart Association dietary recommendations, which included reducing their fat intake to 30 percent of their calories and reducing their cholesterol intake to 300 milligrams daily. The program included moderate exercise and no smoking. But the twenty-eight other patients adopted a holistic approach and went much further. They reduced fat consumption to 10 percent and their daily cholesterol intake virtually to nil. They adopted a strict vegetarian diet, controlled stress through stretching and relaxation techniques, exercised, cut out all tobacco and caffeine, and met regularly for emotional support.

At the beginning of the study, both groups were tested, using angiography (dye-enhanced X rays of the interior of the arteries) and positron emission tomography (PET) scans. After a year on the program, both groups were tested again, and the results could hardly have been more dramatic. Most of the members of the group following the Heart Association recommendations, considered the standard medical treatment, were worse off than when they started. Their arterial blockages had worsened, and they were at increased risk for heart attacks. This was not surprising to the researchers, as the conventional treatment programs are not expected to cure or even arrest heart disease, only to slow down its progress.

What was astounding were the results for the group on the strict vegetarian diet. For 82 percent of these patients, not only did arterial clogging not get worse—it actually reversed!

For every indicator of health outcome, the contrast between the two groups was revealing. Incidences of chest pain (angina) **increased by 165 percent** in the group following the standard medical program. But in the vegetarian group, angina **was reduced by a phenomenal 91 percent.**

The consequences for the lives of these patients were impressive. When Werner Hebenstreit, seventy-five, began the program he could hardly walk without chest pain. "Now I can hike for six hours in the Grand Tetons at 8000 feet," he announced. Another patient, Don Vaupel, fifty, had been obese. He lost 82 pounds. At age fifty-three, Dwayne Butler drank too much and weighed 280 pounds. He had a history of getting into fistfights and his marriage was falling apart. He was ripe for a heart attack, with coronary artery blockages reaching 90 percent. A year on the program that included a strict vegetarian diet brought his blood cholesterol down from 340 to 149, he lost 85 pounds, his blood pressure dropped from 150/90 to 124/72, and his arterial blockages were significantly reversed; he is now proudly walking six miles a day. To top things off, he and his wife fell in love again.

When I asked Dr. Ornish whether the diet and program that got such outstanding results for his patients would be of value to people who were not as sick as those he had included in the study, he replied:

> *It's easier to prevent illness than to reverse it. The real point is that these simple changes increase the joy of living. You don't have to be sick to notice the improvements when you change your diet and lifestyle. People lose weight, they feel lighter, happier, freer, more full of joy. These simple changes can be very powerful. The implications of all this go way beyond treating and preventing heart disease.*[42]

Courage

I appreciate people who are willing to question the eating habits that our culture takes for granted. I respect people who have the courage to learn new ways of cooking and eating that contribute to their health and the health of our world.

Today, the Surgeon General and many established health organizations recommend reducing the fat component of your diet to 30 percent, and reducing your daily cholesterol intake to about 300 milligrams (from an average of about 500 milligrams).

Many scientists have expressed puzzlement that these recommendations are so conservative, when the medical literature clearly indicates that the optimum fat and cholesterol intake levels are much lower than those called for in the official guidelines. These recommendations will lower your risk of a heart attack from 50 percent to 35 percent, which is good. But why stop there when you can lower your risk to virtually nothing? Why settle for a diet that isn't as bad as what passes for "normal" in our society, but that still creates disease and suffering?

The China Health Project and Dr. Ornish's program are only a few in the vast body of studies reporting a consistent finding: Cancer, diabetes, stroke, hypertension, and heart disease risks are much lower with fat levels down closer to 10 or 15 percent, and with cholesterol either eliminated from the diet or drastically reduced.

T. Colin Campbell was involved in the original setting of the official guidelines. He was asked why, in view of the massive evidence indicating they are too conservative, they had not been set lower. He replied that it had been:

*. . . a practical matter. If we had given a figure lower than 30
percent, the public just wouldn't have taken us seriously. . . . If you
reduce fat to 20 percent, basically you have to drop animal foods
altogether. Even if you use low-fat milk or lean meats, you reduce
fat to only about 30 percent. . . . We would essentially have to tell
people they should convert to vegetarianism.*

In other words, an essentially vegetarian diet is clearly recognized to
be healthier than one following the official guidelines. There is no real
dispute about that. The only reason official recommendations fall short
of this is the belief that the average American would not be willing to
change that much.

But what kind of physician is it who knows what a patient must do
to become fully well, yet does not give the patient this information
because the doctor makes a judgement that the patient would not follow
the advice? Shouldn't the patient be given the information, and the right
to decide for himself or herself?

In October 1991, Dr. Campbell had the opportunity to address an
esteemed collection of physicians and researchers at the First National
Conference on the Elimination of Coronary Artery Disease, jointly sponsored by the Cleveland Clinic Foundation and the Caldwell B. Esselstyn
Foundation. The list of attendees read like a who's who in cardiology,
internal medicine, pediatrics, epidemiology, preventive medicine, ger-
ontology, and medical education. During the final hours of the conference, Dr. Campbell received a heartfelt ovation when he eloquently
stated that the time has come for the profession to begin to recommend
the healthiest dietary guidelines, rather than a political compromise:

*Why must we be reticent about recommending a diet which we know
is safe and healthy? We, as scientists, can no longer take the
attitude that the public cannot benefit from information they are not
ready for. We must have the integrity to tell them the truth and let
them decide what to do with it. We cannot force them to follow the
guidelines we recommend, but we can give them these guidelines
and let them decide. . . . **We must tell them that a diet of roots,
stems, seeds, flowers, fruits, and leaves is the healthiest diet,
and the only diet we can promote, endorse, and
recommend.**[43]*

90

I applaud Dr. Campbell for his courage. I don't want the average American's resistance to change to determine the level of health my diet provides me. I want to follow guidelines that lead to optimum health, not ones that reflect what most people are willing to follow. Many people seem to think they are healthy if they can walk to their car and work the remote control for their television. I want to be far healthier and more vital than that. I want to be as full of life and joy and energy as possible.

When we realize how askew are the eating habits of our culture, we are offered an opportunity to take a stand for ourselves and our children. It took courage for Dr. Campbell to call for a new level of integrity in medicine. It takes courage for each of us to make choices that are truly our own, to accept the challenge of being the unique human beings that we are.

I have stopped apologizing to others when my food preferences seem inconvenient to them. What I have realized is that it is vastly more than an inconvenience that millions of people are dying needlessly from diseases caused by meat and dairy consumption, and that millions of other people are going hungry while grain is fed to livestock to produce the very substances causing so much illness and suffering.

A Ray of Hope

There are many hopeful signs that a new and far healthier diet is beginning to emerge. In April 1991, virtually every major newspaper and newsmagazine in the country reported a major press conference held in Washington, D.C., by a remarkable collection of doctors and nutritionists. The purpose of the press conference? To announce the establishment of an entirely new four food groups plan.

Sponsored by the Physicians Committee for Responsible Medicine (PCRM), the new four food group system was designed to incorporate the enormous advances in understanding about diet and health that have been gained in recent years.

The meat industry immediately called its own press conference and tried to dismiss PCRM as being without scientific standing. But as Neal Barnard, M.D., the president of PCRM, officially unveiled the new four food groups, at his side were some of the physicians and scientists who have played leading roles in the advance of medical understanding that has taken place in these last few decades.

One of these men was Denis Burkitt, M.D., a man who has won world acclaim for two astonishing feats of medical detection. The first uncovered the causes and pioneered the cure for a form of cancer in children, now known as Burkitt's lymphoma. The second established the link between many of the killer diseases of the Western world, including cancer, and the lack of fiber in our diet.[44] Burkitt has earned and received as many accolades, honors, and recognition from the scientific community as any other physician alive today. Looking at the role our diets can play in preventing suffering and disease, he has called for sanity:

If people are falling over the edge of a cliff and sustaining injuries, the problem could be dealt with by stationing ambulances at the bottom, or erecting a fence at the top. Unfortunately, we put far too much effort into the positioning of ambulances and far too little into the simple approach of erecting fences.[45]

Also standing with Dr. Barnard were T. Colin Campbell, Ph.D., and Oliver Alabaster, M.D., Director of the Institute for Disease Prevention at The George Washington University.

Barnard spoke not only for the informed scientific community, but also for the hopes and dreams of every mother that her children should be given a healthy body and a healthy life:

Research is now clear and sufficient that the basic dietary guidelines taught to us as schoolchildren are wrong. Based on the knowledge we have today, we cannot go on recommending a diet based on the old four food groups. . . . Evidence has shown that most people who eat according to the old four food groups die earlier and have a greater risk of serious illness than many of those who eat differently.[46]

The new four food groups proposed by the Physicians Committee for Responsible Medicine consist of:

1. Whole grains (5 or more servings a day);
2. Legumes (2 to 3 servings a day);
3. Vegetables (3 or more servings a day); and
4. Fruits (3 or more servings a day).

The most striking thing about the new four food groups is that meats and dairy products, which constituted two of the old basic four, have lost their status. These products are not forbidden by the new guidelines, but they are considered merely optional, because medical studies clearly show they are not needed for human health, and in fact often contribute to disease. The new four groups reflect the massive amount of research telling us that the higher the consumption of meat and dairy products in any nation, the more its people suffer from illness. People whose dietary patterns are based upon grains, legumes, vegetables, and fruits inevitably have markedly better health. People basing their diets on these new four food groups are likely to be leaner, fitter, and healthier by every statistical measure than the followers of the old four food groups.

The proponents of the new grouping have made it clear they are not proposing to ban meats and dairy products from the menus and tables of America. Their call is not to eliminate animal products, but to cut back and shift them to a more secondary role. Their proposal is to bring our eating guidelines up to date. As Barnard said:

We're not saying that you can never have another scoop of Häagen-Dazs. But the basis of a healthful diet is not meat, fish, or cheese.

Your Own Department of Nutrition

The new four food groups are not fanatical or rigid. But neither are they a political construct, enslaved by meat and dairy industry pressures. Instead, they are what generations of innocent schoolchildren have all along trusted the basic four to be: a guide to healthy eating.

Michael Klaper, M.D., is a physician who has devoted his life to helping people become well through eating properly. He is one of many medical doctors who has seen in his own practice the staggering price the old basic four food groups have inflicted upon America in human suffering, health care costs, and lost productivity. If the nutrition planners in 1956 (when the old four food groups were just formulated) had had a crystal ball, he says, and could have gazed upon the eating habits that developed from the old basic four food groups—and if they could have peered into modern hospitals and seen the overflowing coronary care units, cancer wards, and surgical suites where diseased colons are removed and clogged arteries are bypassed—surely they would have taken us in a different direction.

But they did not have a crystal ball in 1956. And so we have witnessed the unfolding of an extraordinarily sad saga—great numbers of people in the richest nation in the history of the Earth eating themselves into diseases that could easily have been prevented through wiser food choices.

Dr. Klaper's remarks are typical of many in the health sciences who grasp the magnitude of what is at stake:

> *I am convinced that a proper diet is essential for maintaining or regaining one's physical well-being. . . . Every person is in charge of their own "Department of Nutrition," and, given the right guidelines, can make the best choices for themselves. One can benefit from the experience of the "Great American Dietary Catastrophe," and avoid the mistakes made by others. Even if you have been following a "junk food diet" for many years, it is never too late to begin to halt, or actually reverse, body damage that has been inflicted through unbalanced nutrition.*[47]

When asked what food choices he felt would be most healthful, he answered simply:

> *There is strong medical evidence that complete freedom from eating animal flesh or cow's milk products is a gateway to optimal nutritional health.*[48]

Living Health

There is a sadness that is only rarely spoken of in our culture. Programmed to eat improperly, and to live at a distance from the real needs of our physical selves, many of us have become gradually more distant from our natural state of health. We don't talk much about how it feels to be alienated from our bodies. We become resigned, and take it for granted that we will deteriorate physically as the years go by. Our bodies become something we are ashamed of, something we don't want to have attention drawn to, something we have to cart around. Our bodies cease to be a source of feeling, power, and pleasure.

The wonder is that in front of us now there lies the possibility of a new way of eating and a new way of living. We have the chance to free ourselves from the programming that has directed us toward disaster and to discover instead the pleasure of genuine natural health. We have the opportunity to learn how deeply satisfying it can be to live and function in a body that responds cleanly and clearly to life's challenges. We have the chance to see through the forces that have controlled our food choices for commercial gain and to discover how delightful it can be to have a body that is lean, fit, and responsive.

The joy is that we can take back our bodies, reclaim our health, and restore ourselves to balance. We can take power over what and how we eat. We can rejuvenate and recharge ourselves, bringing healing to the wounds we carry inside us, and bringing to fuller life the wonderful person that each of us can be.

I congratulate you for every move you make to take responsibility for your own health and well-being. I applaud you for being one of the special people who is willing to take a stand for yourself.

FIVE

What About Chicken, Fish, Milk, and Eggs?

"We were taken into a fast-food café where the order was fed into a computer. Our hamburgers, made from the flesh of chemically impregnated cattle, had been broiled over counterfeit charcoal, placed between slices of artificially flavored cardboard, and served to us by recycled juvenile delinquents."

Jean-Michel Chapereau

There are questions that often arise for people who are making positive changes, taking responsibility for their health, and challenging the "basic four food groups" orthodoxy. I am frequently asked what I think of eliminating red meat and substituting chicken and fish, cutting the skin off poultry and cooking it without fat, eating primarily low- or nonfat dairy products, and restricting egg-yolk intake to two or three a week. I wish I could be more enthusiastic about that approach, but a dispassionate appraisal of the data leads me to the conclusion that such a strategy is the equivalent of cutting smoking down to one pack a day.

Here's why....

WHAT ABOUT CHICKEN?

It is fairly common today for people to eat chicken rather than beef, thinking they are doing their bodies a good turn. It is true that if you eat only the white meat of the chicken, without the skin, and use nonfat cooking methods, you can significantly reduce the amount of fat in your meal. But the result is still very high in cholesterol and still markedly raises your blood cholesterol level and heart disease risk.[1]

Meat and poultry producers can legally make claims and implications about their products that are forbidden about other foods. Why? Because the FDA, which is mandated to watch over all other foods, has no jurisdiction over these products! You might wonder who does regulate meat and poultry products. In a classic example of dysfunctional bureaucracy, this responsibility is given to the very department that is mandated to *promote* their sale—the USDA!

The results are great if you're trying to deceive the public about the fat levels in meat and poultry.

Take, for example, a package of ConAgra's Kid Cuisine fried chicken dinner. The label merrily proclaims it is *"88 percent fat free."* This sounds wonderful, but the truth is the dinner is loaded with fat. Anytime a product presents "percent fat free" claims, you have cause to be wary, for there is a nifty little ploy to trick people into thinking a greasy product like fried chicken is actually low in fat.

There are several ways the fat content of food can be measured. The method generally recognized as the most accurate and reliable is to measure the percentage of total calories in a given food provided as fat.[2] A second method, useful in certain specific cases, is to measure the grams of fat in a serving of a given food. By those methods, meats, eggs, chicken, and almost all dairy products are seen for what they are—high-fat foods. The industries that profit from our consumption of these products, however, have realized that widespread understanding of this fact would erode their profits. In a case study example of the art of lying with statistics, they have come up with a method of measuring fat that disguises the high-fat levels of their products: They measure the percentage of fat by weight. When expressed as a percentage of a food's weight, the fat content of these foods sounds deceptively low.

For example, let's say you have a chunk of butter. This is a substance that is 100 percent fat. One hundred percent of the calories in the chunk of butter are fat. But let's say you dissolve it in a glass of hot water.

Now you've got a glassful of something that by the more impartial "percentage of calories as fat" method of conveying fat content is still 100 percent fat. This is as it should be, because the item has the same amount of fat as it did before you added the water and would clog up your arteries just the same.

But now witness the art of deception. What happens if you measure the amount of fat in the butter/water mixture by the "percentage of fat by weight method?" Even though 100 percent of the calories in the mixture still consist of fat, it may now be claimed to be "90 percent fat free."[3]

The FDA is trying to bring some sanity to food labeling regulations. But because the FDA has no authority over items containing meat or poultry, bogus "percent fat free" claims are still often found on these products.

There is another way that meat and poultry products can deceptively be made to appear to be healthier than they are. The FDA requires that package labels and health claims be based on realistic-size servings. But since this regulation doesn't apply to meat and poultry, producers are allowed to base their claims on serving sizes that are ridiculously low. For the innocent shopper, the result is bizarre. A can of USDA-regulated chicken soup will falsely seem to have less fat than a can of FDA-regulated vegetable soup.[4]

The standard that defines "low fat" is also much looser for meat and poultry products than for other foods. It has been pointed out many times that consumers would be best served if the USDA and the FDA adopted the same definition of "low fat." The meat and poultry industries, however, have adamantly opposed the idea. Their reason is simple. If meat and poultry products were held to the same standard as other foods, complained Gary Wilson of the National Cattlemen's Association, *"you [wouldn't] have any meat items being able to meet the criteria."*[5]

In March 1992, the USDA officially postponed for another year the deadline for new meat and poultry labels. When asked why, Secretary of Agriculture Madigan explained that the delay would save meat and poultry producers $210 million. He didn't mention the heart attacks, strokes, and cancers that people will suffer as a result of the move. Nor the $690 million the delay will cost American taxpayers.

The Truth
About Today's Chicken

Virtually all public health organizations have voiced major concerns about the safety of today's poultry products. The poultry industry disputes these allegations, claiming that today's chicken is safer than ever. In protest, its spokesmen point out that today less than one-half of 1 percent of all chickens are condemned for detectable disease, while twenty-five years ago, the figure was 10 percent. This drop shows, they say, that today's consumers can put their trust in poultry.

But can they? Six times during the last fifteen years, the USDA has weakened the poultry inspection system. Critics say the fact that comparatively few birds are condemned today testifies less to the safety of the product than to the sorry state of the inspection system.

What's the truth? On May 26, 1991, the *Atlanta Journal-Constitution* published the results of interviews with eighty-four federal poultry inspectors from thirty-seven processing plants in the five states that produce over half of all American chicken. The survey included about 5 percent of all the USDA inspectors monitoring poultry quality in the area.

If the poultry inspectors are to be believed, the chickens available for sale nationwide represent a health disaster. **In fact, sixty of the eighty-four poultry inspectors interviewed said that based on what they observe they no longer eat chicken.**

The comments of one chicken inspector were typical:

> *Would you like to go to a pasture with a chicken, cut him up, then drop him into a fresh manure pile, and eat him? That's what the product is like coming from chicken plants today.*

Inspectors are supposedly the consumer's defense against unsafe chicken. But according to these inspectors, every week millions of chickens leaking yellow pus, stained by green feces, contaminated by harmful bacteria, and marred by lung and heart infections and cancerous tumors are sold to consumers.

Inspectors try to do their jobs and provide protection to the consumer against unhealthy products, but they must stare eight hours a day at a speeding current of raw pink chicken carcasses. In 1957, when mandatory inspection of poultry began, inspectors looked at sixteen birds per minute. Today, the number has risen to thirty-five.

It is hardly possible under these circumstances to recognize any but the most obviously spoiled or blatantly diseased meat. The bacteria that cause serious problems in chicken are microscopic.

What happens if the inspectors do see a problem? Forty-eight of the eighty-four inspectors interviewed by the *Journal-Constitution* said they are routinely cursed, rebuked, and harassed by company officials or by their own government supervisors if they dare halt speeding production lines to scrutinize questionable meat.

A seven-year inspector explained:

> *It used to be that if [a bird] had a severe contamination, you condemned the sucker. But nowadays my own supervising inspector says, "There can be no more bad birds on your tally. You've had too many.*

These inspectors are frustrated because they want to do the job the public expects them to perform, but they cannot. Said William Freeman, an inspector at an Ellijay, Georgia, poultry plant, and a veteran of twenty-five years on the job:

> *The oath I took to be an inspector said if I ever saw anything wrong I was supposed to report it. But today I can't report anything. Today, if you blow the whistle, you're in trouble with the inspection service. I feel the oath I took is violated every day I work.*

This isn't the sort of comment that makes me feel confident in the inspection service. It makes me wonder just how contaminated are the chickens Americans consume. The *Atlanta Journal-Constitution* took poultry samples to USDA-approved commercial testing laboratories to find out, but they were rebuffed. The labs refused to test the samples for salmonella or for the related disease campylobacter. Why? Because, as Brian Shelton, the lab manager for Pathogen Control Associates explained:

> *I would expect an extremely high percentage of the chickens would test positive. Our poultry industry clients wouldn't like that.*

In other words, the labs were more concerned with protecting the public image of the poultry producers than with protecting public health.

The labs are probably right, though, that "*an extremely high percentage of the chickens would test positive.*" Dr. Norman Stern, a USDA microbiologist in Athens, Georgia, and an authority on campylobacter, found 98 percent of the precooked ready-to-eat store-bought chickens he tested in Georgia to be contaminated. Are these pathogens serious? The *New York Times* reported:

Campylobacteriosis causes typical food-poisoning symptoms: fever, chills, diarrhea, abdominal pain. Sometimes there may be more serious and permanent consequences, like arthritis. Occasionally, someone dies.[6]

An online inspector at a chicken-processing plant in Georgia voiced the inner feelings of most of today's inspectors:

I'm ashamed to even let people know I am a USDA inspector. There are thousands of diseased and unwholesome birds going right on down the lines.

An Assembly-Line Chicken in Every Pot

One of the reasons today's chickens are so unwholesome is the conditions in which the birds are raised. In *Diet for a New America*, I described in detail what I discovered when I visited modern factory farms and how this experience changed my life forever.[7] I will never be able to forget the birds crammed so tightly into warehouses they could hardly move, filthy with their own excrement, showing every evidence of having been driven insane by the stress of such a completely unnatural situation. So bad were the conditions, so inhumane the treatment of the birds, that I devoted the first part of that book to exposing the sordid truth.

I was warned by many people not to do that. I was told the matter was so unpleasant that people wouldn't want to read about it, and that it would cost me readers. But the degree of cruelty was so severe and so unrelenting, and today's chickens are as a result so sick, miserable, and filthy, that I felt people deserved to know.

Down through history animals have been killed for meat. And down through history there have been humanitarians who felt sufficiently disturbed by this that they chose to base their diet on plants rather than contribute to the killing. People like Plato, Leonardo da Vinci, Mahatma Gandhi, Henry David Thoreau, George Bernard Shaw, and many other spiritual giants became ethical vegetarians in order to take a stand on behalf of life.

Today, there is another issue to consider for those of us who wish our lives to be expressions of compassion. I am not talking now about the fact that the animals are killed. I am not even talking about the fact that the manner in which they are killed is inhumane. I am talking about the fact that we don't have barnyard chickens anymore, we have factory chickens. Virtually every chicken carcass sold in our markets and served in our restaurants is the outcome of a life that knew only deprivation and pain. The factory farm system is so systematically cruel that I have to wonder whether the chickens sold in our land today do not carry in their flesh some of the suffering they were forced to endure. If we feed ourselves on animals whose existence has been one long nightmare of pain, what will be the outcome in our lives?

I spoke earlier in this book about the importance of eating with respect for the living Earth community that provides our food. Is it possible to eat meat today with a genuine attitude of respect and love for the animal? Personally, I cannot see how. I cannot both love the animal and condone the conditions in today's factory farms and slaughterhouses. To eat meat, I would have to push out of my mind and heart the reality of the horrible conditions these animals are forced to endure. I would have to deny not just the agony of their deaths, but the torture and misery of their lives. I would have to believe I had never seen the eyes of these animals pleading to me, not heard their frantic and urgent cries. I would have to close my heart to them, and this is neither respect nor love.

WHAT ABOUT FISH?

People who eat fish instead of beef or chicken do have lower heart disease rates. A case in point is that of traditional Eskimos, who consume no beef or chicken but eat extremely high amounts of fish, and whose heart attack rates are quite low.[8] This is because many kinds of fish contain a polyunsaturated fat called eicosapentaneoic acid (EPA), which thins the blood and reduces the potential for the blood clots that often precipitate heart attacks.[9]

The influence of EPA and the other Omega–3 fatty acids found in fish is nevertheless a mixed blessing. While these substances in the diet do reduce heart attack incidence by thinning the blood, at the same time they raise the rate of hemorragic strokes and the incidence of impotence. Additionally, many studies have shown fish oils to interfere with the function of the human immune system's natural killer cells.[10]

There is another unfortunate side to the story. As I mentioned earlier, the high protein levels in fish cause Eskimos to have one of the highest osteoporosis rates in the world.[11]

The good news is that people who significantly reduce their consumption of all kinds of meats, fish, dairy products, and eggs show even lower heart disease rates than the Eskimos—and have extremely low rates of osteoporosis as well.

Both the federal government and the seafood industry have come under extensive fire in recent years from consumer advocacy groups for not doing enough to ensure a safe and wholesome seafood supply. In early 1992, the FDA conducted the first complete inspection of American seafood processing facilities. The FDA review was comprehensive, covering 3852 processing plants and encompassing manufacturers, growers, packers, and shippers. The results, however, were far from reassuring for anyone wanting to consume fish. As many as 20 percent of the samples analyzed showed clear signs of microbiological contamination, decomposition, and filth. The rate of violation found in fish exceeds that found in any other food commodity regulated by the FDA. A 1992 study in *Consumer Reports* magazine found widespread contamination and mislabeling of seafood in retail fish shops and supermarkets in New York and Chicago. Of the random samples purchased in the two cities, 29 percent were spoiled and 44 percent were contaminated with fecal bacteria.

Another factor to consider is the polluted environment from which today's fish may be taken. The sad reality is that our fresh and sea waters today are often heavily contaminated with pesticides and other toxic chemical residues. As a result, it is difficult to find fish from unpolluted waters.

These poisons don't affect just the creature that ingests them first. They accumulate in the animal's tissues, and then, as one organism is eaten by another, they build up in ever-increasing concentrations at each higher rung on the food chain.

Fish are at the top of an extremely long food chain. Therefore, a fish will house in its flesh the poisons accumulated by all the thousands of smaller fish it has eaten. And each of these smaller fish will have collected in its flesh all the toxins carried by thousands of still smaller fish. By this exponential progression, fish often become carriers of dangerously high concentrations of pesticides, insecticides, and other poisonous substances. For example, DDT was banned for most uses in the United States in 1972, and yet a frightening 1983 FDA survey found the presence of this human carcinogen in almost 90 percent of the domestic fish tested.[12] Fish caught downstream from paper mills are so dangerous that the EPA estimates that just one four-ounce serving of fish from these waters will often cause liver damage.[13]

If you are considering eating a particular kind of fish, you need to be aware of the level of pollution in the waters from which it has been taken. It helps, also, to know which fish tend to be the most dangerously contaminated.

1. Shellfish are frequently carriers of toxic levels of lead, cadmium, arsenic, and other heavy metals.[14]
2. Raw shellfish are particularly notorious for carrying dangerous microbes and toxins. As sushi, sashimi, and other raw fish dishes have become more popular in recent years, infections from parasitic worms have increased.[15]
3. Large predatory fish such as halibut, tuna, swordfish, shark, and marlin are often laden with methyl mercury, an extremely poisonous substance that attacks human nerve cells.[16]
4. Trout, carp, catfish, bass, bluefish, and mackerel tend to be very high in polychlorinated biphenyls (PCBs).[17]
5. The Center for Science in the Public Interest suggests that cod, haddock, pollock, and salmon are likely to be the safer fish choices.[18] They warn, however, that even with the least-contaminated fish, careful selection, proper handling, and thorough cooking are necessary to prevent serious problems.

Respect for Life

If you are considering eating fish, there is yet another factor to take into account. It is of course up to each of us how we will create an ethical relationship with other animals. But one thing is universally true: we can make this determination most wisely when we are not bound by culturally sanctioned ignorance.

I can't tell you how many times, well-meaning people, on learning that I am a vegetarian, have said to me: *"But you do eat fish, don't you?"*

At such times I've often been struck by the strength of our cultural conditioning, and how difficult it can be for people to free themselves from its bondage. It's as if the illusion had become lodged in our collective mind that fish are not really animals.

The catching of all kinds of fish involves killing. This is not a particularly pleasant thought, but if we are to take responsibility for the ultimate results of our choices, it is a reality we cannot avoid.

I have too much respect for the human journey to take it upon myself to tell you what you should or shouldn't eat, and where you should draw any kind of line. We are each extraordinary and unique. We have needs and emotional associations to different foods that are ours alone. We live in a wide variety of ecosystems and climates and have our individual paths to blaze. We are each responsible for our own choices and for their consequences.

There was a point in my life when I saw that what I ate could have a major impact on my consciousness, on my health and how I felt about myself, and on the world around me. It has been a joy to learn how many times the foods that are healthiest for the human body are also the healthiest for our environment and create the least suffering for other creatures. It affirms for me that nature can be trusted, and that we can yet learn to live in peace and harmony with the rest of the living Earth community.

WHAT ABOUT DAIRY PRODUCTS?

I grew up believing in dairy products the way some people believe in the Bible. My grandfather ran a dairy in Tacoma, Washington. My father and my uncle owned the Baskin-Robbins ice cream company. In my family, to question dairy products was simply unheard of. I didn't need the Dairy Council to tell me milk was nature's most perfect food; I already knew it.

When I first lived away from home and became responsible for preparing my own meals, I ate mostly so-called "convenience foods," which are in fact anything but a convenience to the human body. At that time, I suspected that I was not feeding myself very well, but I took solace from the large amounts of milk, cheese, and eggs that I consumed, for I saw them as the most nutritious part of my diet. How eagerly I looked forward to the regular deliveries of the milkman, who brought milk, butter, cottage cheese, cream cheese, yogurt, and eggs right to the door! All these products were white, simply packaged, and fresh, and in my mind they were the most wholesome and healthy things in the world.

Later, when I became less of a blind believer in the powers of dairy products and eggs, I began to question their health implications and to seek out what impartial research might reveal. For quite a while I resisted the implications of this research, because I found what was being discovered to be very unsettling. I simply could not believe that there were significant problems with these products. I remained stubbornly convinced, despite the accumulating evidence, that they were the healthiest and most pure of foods. I wanted to believe the ads, because that way I wouldn't have to change. Basing many of my meals around yogurt, cheese, and eggs, always of course with ice cream for dessert, I remained for years as loyal as could be to these products.

But time and experience have taught me that many of the things I once believed are in fact no more true than a belief in Santa Claus. The dairy industry is incredibly powerful in the United States, both in controlling our nation's food policies and in influencing what most of us think, feel, and believe about dairy products. It is difficult for any of us to stand outside the force of this cultural conditioning. But some people have tried to evaluate these products objectively.

What have they learned?

Milk: Does It Do a Body Good?

The consumption of dairy products has been found by researchers to be a leading cause of atherosclerosis, heart attacks, and strokes.[19] The highest death rate from heart disease in the world is found in Finland, a country with one of the very highest rates of dairy product consumption.[20] Compared to people in the United States, the Finnish people consume one and a half times as many dairy products—and die one and a half times as often from heart disease.[21]

The high-fat of dairy products have been implicated as the culprits in contributing heavily to heart attacks, strokes, and atherosclerosis. The high-fat dairy products are also those most likely to contain unsafe levels of environmental contaminants including pesticide residues and dangerous radioactive substances.[22] Of all the foods available to Americans, full-fat dairy products such as whole milk and cheese rank with fish as carriers of the highest levels of dangerous environmental contaminants.

As a result, many people today have come to recognize the dangers in high-fat dairy products and to view the lower-fat versions as healthier alternatives.

What About Low-Fat Dairy Products?

While lower-fat dairy products are in many ways improvements over their higher-fat counterparts, they still present major health problems that could be avoided through decreased consumption of all kinds of dairy products.

Low-fat dairy products are higher in protein than the higher-fat products. Many people assume this to be a health advantage, but as I mentioned earlier, this is not so. As a result of their higher protein concentrations, low- and especially nonfat dairy products have been shown to make an even greater contribution to osteoporosis, kidney problems, and some forms of cancer than do their higher-fat counterparts.

Dairy products are the leading culprits in food allergies, and the lower-fat versions are actually more allergenic than those higher in fat, because they are higher in protein.[23] For it is the proteins in dairy products that induce allergic reactions in humans.[24]

David Jacobs, an internist certified in nutrition, allergy, and immunology, reports:

I know hundreds of people who have spent years and thousands of dollars on tests looking for ulcers or spastic bowels. I tell them to lay off all dairy products for two weeks. The results are usually so striking that it changes their lives.[25]

The list of the most common symptoms of dairy allergies is a long one, as are the benefits often obtained by allergic people who remove dairy products from their diets. Many studies have shown allergies to dairy products to cause irritability, restlessness, hyperactivity, muscle pain, mental depression, abdominal pain, cramps or bloating, gas, diarrhea, bad breath, headaches, lack of energy, constipation, poor appetite, malabsorption of nutrients, nasal stuffiness, runny nose, sinusitis, asthma, shortness of breath, rashes, eczema, and hives.[26]

The scientific literature contains numerous accounts of dramatic improvement not just from the above problems, but also in cases of ulcerative colitis, obesity, enlarged tonsils and adenoids, and iron-deficiency anemia, with the removal of dairy products from the diet.[27]

Milk: It Sure Does Have Something for Everybody

The Dairy Council has an attractive booklet it distributes free of charge to hospitals and schools throughout the country. Entitled *Is It Safe to Be a Vegetarian?* the booklet provides the kind of remarkably self-serving answer I have come to expect from the Dairy Council. The booklet says yes, it is safe, as long as you substitute more cheese, yogurt, and milk for the "missing" meat.

In fact, the course the Dairy Council is suggesting is likely to cause food allergies and is an open invitation to the development of iron-deficiency anemia. Cow's milk is so low in iron that you'd have to drink gallons to get the iron available in a single serving of any dark green leafy vegetable.[28]

Not only do dairy products provide little or no iron, they also block its absorption. Breast-fed babies, for example, have a much higher rate of iron absorption than those fed cow's milk formulas, even when the formulas are especially fortified with extra iron.[29]

In our society, breastfeeding mothers often consume more dairy products than usual, thinking they are doing themselves and their babies a good turn. Sadly, though, they aren't. Breast-fed babies can get colic and other symptoms of cow's milk allergies if the mother consumes dairy products.[30] The dairy proteins pass into the mother's breast milk, make their way into the baby's intestine and bloodstream, and may cause persistent crying, fussing, and many other expressions of allergic reactions.[31]

The dairy industry has spent hundreds of millions of dollars to convince you and me that an absence of dairy products may lead to calcium deficiency. But, as I discussed earlier, osteoporosis and other clinical signals of calcium loss are not, in fact, signs of inadequate dietary calcium; they are signals of excess protein consumption. Citing extensive documentation in the medical literature, nutritional authority John McDougall reports:

> *An important fact to remember is that all natural diets, including purely vegetarian diets without a hint of dairy products, contain amounts of calcium that are above the threshold for meeting your nutritional needs[32] . . . . In fact, calcium deficiency caused by an*

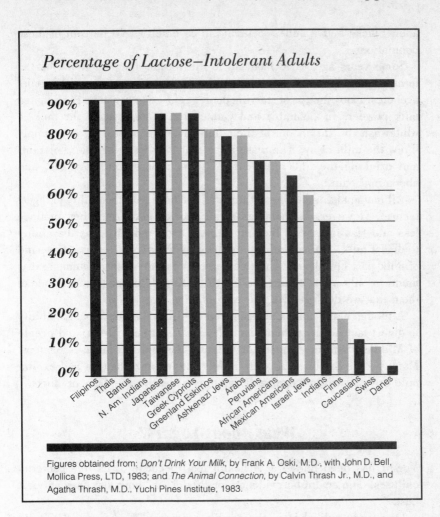

Percentage of Lactose–Intolerant Adults

Figures obtained from: *Don't Drink Your Milk*, by Frank A. Oski, M.D., with John D. Bell, Mollica Press, LTD, 1983; and *The Animal Connection*, by Calvin Thrash Jr., M.D., and Agatha Thrash, M.D., Yuchi Pines Institute, 1983.

insufficient amount of calcium in the diet is not known to occur in humans.[33]

Why the Hungry Throw Away Milk

At about the age of four, the vast majority of human beings begin to lose the ability to digest lactose, the carbohydrate found in milk. The resulting condition, known as lactose intolerance, is especially high in adult blacks and Asians, occurring in as much as 90 percent of these populations.[34]

Some years ago, U.S. food aid to the world's hungry often took the form of shipments of powdered milk. To the frustration of the relief agencies, many groups of starving people refused to consume the donated milk powder. In Colombia and Guatemala, families used the milk to whitewash the dirt floors of their huts. In other areas, people simply threw the milk away. The reason was that they were lactose intolerant, and drinking the milk only caused them illness, bloating, gas, and abdominal pain.

All mammals, including all humans, are born with the ability to digest lactose. However, as members of all species get older, they produce less and less lactase in their intestines, and gradually lose the ability to digest milk. Human beings are the only animal to consume any kind of milk past childhood. And this behavior is rare even in humans; it is found in only a few cultures on Earth.[35] It's only because ours is one of them that we don't realize how abnormal we are.

Although many adult Caucasians in the United States have the ability to digest lactose, large numbers of Native Americans, Jews, and people of Middle Eastern, African, or Oriental descent are lactase-deficient. Many people in our society are mildly intolerant of lactose and exhibit mild or less easily recognizable symptoms upon eating dairy products.[36]

What About Yogurt?

Yogurt has been hailed as a health food because of its live bacterial cultures. The scientific evidence for this claim, however, is scanty, at best.[37]

One study published in the *Annals of Internal Medicine* in 1992 did find a reduction in vaginitis in women consuming yogurt.[38] Millions of women are treated for chronic yeast problems, but drugs rarely keep yeast infections from recurring. The yogurt culture lactobacillus is found in abundance in the vagina of healthy women, and the *Internal Medicine* study suggests that the lactobacillus consumed in yogurt found a way to migrate from the intestine to the vagina.

However, a better choice for women with vaginitis, or anyone seeking to restore the presence of desirable lactobacillus bacteria in his or her system, is to take the bacterial cultures directly. Most natural food stores carry several brands (Vegedophilus, Primadophilus, Fem-dophilos, etc.) of lactobacillus that are far more concentrated, active, and usable by the human body than those that come in a dairy medium. These products are also preferable to dairy yogurt because they do not contain the cholesterol, lactose, and saturated fat found in dairy products.

Whatever benefit humans may derive from yogurt cultures is not available from the prepackaged frozen yogurts in supermarket freezers or the soft-serve frozen yogurts found in stores around the country. Researchers who have analyzed samples from many of the leading frozen yogurt producers report that the live count of the desirable bacterial cultures in these products is virtually nil.[39]

Most commercial frozen yogurt is high in fat, and some is as high in fat as ice cream. As far as the low-fat and nonfat versions go, they are often extremely high in sugar. An average medium nonfat serving contains no less than seven teaspoons of sugar.[40]

If It's Pasteurized, Then It's Safe, Isn't It?

When I was in grade school, our class took a trip to a local dairy. There we were taught the wonders of pasteurization and assured that thanks to this process we never had to worry about the bacterial contamination that "used to occur" in unpasteurized milk. After that, I always assumed that milk that had been pasteurized was safe.

But I was wrong. The largest outbreak of salmonella poisoning ever recorded in the United States came from pasteurized milk.[41] In this fatal 1985 outbreak, traced to a large Illinois milk processing plant, as many as two hundred thousand people in six states are suspected of having been infected with salmonellosis, a disease that produces severe intestinal illness.[42]

In 1985, an outbreak of infection in Southern California from a different bacteria, *listeria monocytogenes*, occurred from contamination of a soft cheese product. The outbreak killed forty-seven people, the largest number of food-poisoning deaths recorded in recent U.S. history.[43] Soft cheeses like French Brie and Camembert are the most likely to be contaminated with listeria.[44]

In 1982, an outbreak of food poisoning affecting more than fifteen thousand people in Tennessee and nearby states was caused by pasteurized milk contaminated with *yersinia enterocolitica* bacteria.[45] Infection with this organism can cause intestinal illness; infections of the skin, eye, and muscles; and long-term complications including arthritis. The first symptoms often resemble appendicitis. Many schoolchildren have had unnecessary appendectomies after they have been exposed to dairy products carrying this bacteria.

Another Thing the Dairy Council Doesn't Tell Us

Most of the milk that we drink today, and the cheese, yogurt, and ice cream that we eat, comes from cows confined on factorylike farms where conditions are nothing like the pastures and barnyards of yesteryear. The modern-day Bessie is bred, fed, medicated, inseminated, and manipulated for a single purpose—maximum milk production at a minimum cost.[46] One result of these unnatural conditions is that the modern dairy cow is highly prone to stress and disease.

These diseases, of course, present a challenge to the dairy industry, which must keep the animals producing milk in order to stay in business. Its response to this challenge has not, however, been music to the ears of people wanting to see wholesome dairy products—the industry's response has been the use of antibiotics and other drugs, including many that are illegal.

You might hope that the FDA would protect you from such shenanigans. But this is one area where the efforts of the FDA have been feeble at best. The official testing method sanctioned by the FDA and used by most states to screen milk for drugs, called the BS *(Bacillus stearothermophilus)* disc assay, is unable to detect residues from most of the medications used in the dairy industry today.[47] In fact, the FDA's efforts to undertake legitimate surveillance of the milk produced in the United States have been so inadequate as to constitute a violation of the public trust. For years, it seems that the FDA has been more concerned with telling the public how safe the milk supply is than with ensuring that safety.[48]

Four different surveys of the safety of our milk supply were conducted by independent researchers between 1987 and 1989. The results were not comforting, unless you like antibiotics and other veterinary drugs in your dairy products. The studies found between 63 and 86 percent of milk samples to contain sulfa drugs, tetracyclines, and other antibiotics.[49] These surveys embarrassed the FDA so much that the agency finally got around to conducting a survey of its own. Despite using outdated methods that cannot detect small quantities of the dangerous drug sulfamethazine, a March 1988 FDA survey found sulfamethazine in 74 percent of the samples tested.[50]

This finding was particularly disturbing. Sulfamethazine is a sulfa drug that is a suspected human carcinogen.

After this test, the FDA took steps to eliminate the use of sulfamethazine in milk production. But in December 1989, the *Wall Street Journal* published a front-page story that certainly didn't make the average dairy product consumer breathe a sigh of relief. The FDA had tried to dismiss any surveys that found widespread contamination as being isolated cases. But the survey sponsored by the *Wall Street Journal* found drug residues, including penicillin and sulfa drugs, in 38 percent of milk samples purchased in ten major cities.[51] Any pretense that the FDA was protecting the milk supply seemed to be shattered. But the FDA, showing something less than a desire to admit and learn from its mistakes, simply announced several months later that its tests showed the milk supply to be free from residues. In subsequent congressional hearings, however, the FDA revealed how farfetched this announcement had been. The FDA's own tests had actually found sulfa residues in almost 86 percent of the samples tested![52]

In 1991, the FDA, under pressure from Congress to step up its surveillance of the dairy industry, announced a new program to check milk for drug residues. The announcement came with a lot of fanfare, and the implication was made that now things would be different.

Proudly pointing to the new FDA program, the dairy industry assures the public that we can put our whole trust in the safety of our milk supply. Currently, however, the FDA tests exactly five milk samples a week. Representative Ted Weiss from New York does not find this impressive:

The FDA's attempt to describe this [testing program] as a "nationwide program" is ludicrous. To even call it a modest proposal is a wild exaggeration.[53]

Lisa Lefferts, staff scientist at the Center for Science in the Public Interest, was also not overly taken with the new program. She said it was like *"the boy who tried to stick his finger in the hole in the dike."*[54]

WHAT ABOUT EGGS?

Like chicken, today's eggs are often contaminated with salmonella and other bacteria. As a result, consumers are advised, especially if they live in New England, to avoid raw eggs and dishes made with raw eggs, to always cook eggs and egg-rich foods until the yolks are set, to avoid cracked eggs, to buy eggs only if they have been refrigerated at the store, and to refrigerate them promptly after purchase. These and similar measures can reduce, though not eliminate, the likelihood of being poisoned by salmonellosis from eggs. But such measures have no effect on the greatest health problem with egg consumption—cholesterol.

A chicken's egg yolk is 80 percent fat, most of it saturated, and is one of the most concentrated sources of cholesterol on the planet. It is certainly the most concentrated source of cholesterol in the human diet.

But as I mentioned in *Diet for a New America*, the egg industry has not been one to sit by and let a fact like that take a bite out of its profits.

In 1971, after the American Heart Association took a stand saying that dietary cholesterol caused heart disease, the egg producers countered by forming the National Commission on Egg Nutrition for the specific purpose of fighting the American Heart Association and anyone else who had the audacity to suggest that eggs weren't healthy. The newly formed Commission began its campaign by presenting a series of expensive ads in the *Wall Street Journal*, attacking what they called the "theory" that saturated fat and cholesterol promote heart disease. A typical ad stated:

There is absolutely no scientific evidence that eating eggs, even in quantity, will increase the risk of a heart attack.[55]

On seeing these ads, the American Heart Association immediately asked the Federal Trade Commission to prohibit this preposterous advertising.[56] The FTC considered both sides of the matter, and then filed a formal complaint against the National Commission on Egg Nutrition and its advertising agency, Richard Weiner, Inc.[57] Dismayed by this turn of events, the egg industry hired the best legal counsel it could find. The attorneys studied the matter in depth, then turned around and told the egg industry that its "*chances of beating the lawsuit on scientific grounds [were] almost nil.*"[58]

There followed a lengthy court battle, in which the egg producers tried to defend their ad campaign under the First Amendment guarantee of free speech.[59] But the judge wasn't convinced. In his 101-page decision, he called the statements made by the National Commission on Egg Nutrition "*false, misleading, deceptive, and unfair.*"[60] Ruled Judge Ernest G. Barnes:

There exists a substantial body of competent and reliable scientific evidence that eating eggs increases the risk of heart attacks or heart disease. . . . This evidence is systematic, consistent, strong, and congruent.[61]

Eggs on Their Faces

The egg industry was unable to convince the Federal Trade Commission, the court, or even its own attorneys that eggs do not raise blood cholesterol and promote heart disease. But this failure has not prevented it from trying to scramble the minds of the American public.

To this end, the egg industry has designed and paid for numerous studies it hoped would give the appearance that the cholesterol in eggs is harmless.[62] One of the nation's foremost authorities on clinical nutrition research, Dr. John McDougall, studied the literature and noticed something interesting:

Of the six studies in the medical literature that fail to demonstrate a significant rise in blood cholesterol level with the consumption of whole eggs, three were paid for by the American Egg Board, one by the Missouri Egg Merchandising Council, and one by the Egg Program of the California Department of Agriculture. Support for the sixth paper was not identified. . . .

The trick is in knowing how to design your experiment so you will get the results you are looking for. To get little or no increase in cholesterol results, you first saturate the subjects with cholesterol from other sources, because studies show that once people consume more than 400 to 800 milligrams of cholesterol per day, additional cholesterol has only a minor effect on blood cholesterol levels. . . . Well-designed studies by investigators independent of the food industry clearly demonstrate the detrimental effects of eggs on blood cholesterol levels.[63]

While the studies financed by the egg industry may seem to exonerate eggs, independent investigators consistently get very different results.[64] At the University of Minnesota, scientists found that a diet with 380 milligrams of egg yolk cholesterol per day caused an average blood cholesterol level 16 milligrams higher than a diet with only 50 milligrams cholesterol.[65] This is significant: It means that eating one and a half eggs a day would raise your risk of a heart attack by an incredible 32 percent![66]

At the Harvard School of Public Health, Dr. Mark Hegsted achieved similar results, finding that each 100 milligrams of egg yolk cholesterol raised blood cholesterol levels in adult men an average of 4 to 5 milligrams.[67]

Still, the egg industry continued to insist that egg consumption does not raise blood cholesterol and to claim that their studies were valid. In 1984, yet another impartial study was undertaken to resolve the issue. This study, reported in the British medical journal *Lancet*, sought to test the effects of egg consumption on blood cholesterol with as much objectivity as possible.

The experiment was imaginative. One group of subjects was fed an egg daily, disguised in a dessert. The second group of subjects was fed an apparently identical dessert, but made without the egg. Otherwise their diets were identical, and contained no other eggs or other high-cholesterol foods. In order to insure the test's objectivity, the whole thing was done double-blind: Neither the researchers nor the subjects knew who had eaten the eggs until the test was completed. The egg industry's position was dealt quite a blow when, after only three weeks, the subjects whose desserts contained eggs showed a 12 percent rise in their blood cholesterol levels, and the other group showed no such rise.[68] It is hard to overestimate the significance of this information. The 12 percent rise in blood cholesterol level that stems from eating an egg a day amounts to a 24 percent rise in heart attack risk.[69]

The egg industry, however, was not dismayed. It realized that in any struggle there are bound to be obstacles that must be surmounted. Resolutely, it continued to deny any link between eggs and heart disease.

When the Senate Select Committee on Nutrition and Human Needs, under the chairmanship of Senator George McGovern, met to establish guidelines for the nation's food choices, the egg industry presented five different research studies that they claimed took eggs off the hook. These reports, however, were so confusing that McGovern asked the National Heart, Lung, and Blood Institute to assess their validity.

The Institute carefully examined each of the five studies, then reported to Congress that the studies seemed deliberately designed to distort the facts. The Institute's impartial appraisal was that the studies were "*seriously flawed, . . . meaningless, and should be discarded.*"[70]

This news did not daunt the egg industry, however, which simply adopted new tactics in the battle to convince the American public that dietary cholesterol is benign. They proceeded to hire an advertising agency and immediately began a massive publicity campaign based on the very studies that had been so thoroughly discredited. Fliers were inserted into many millions of egg cartons reassuring egg consumers that *"eggs don't raise cholesterol."*[71]

In 1991, the industry realized that despite its efforts many Americans had by now come to understand that eggs contribute directly to heart disease. To counter this growing awareness, the California Egg Commission undertook a television advertising campaign. In the ads, viewers see an electric chair, and in it an unhappy-looking egg who has been found guilty and condemned to die. At the last moment, though, the egg is granted a reprieve, and the ad jubilantly celebrates the innocence of the egg. The ad is entertaining and persuasive. The only trouble is that there is absolutely no credible evidence that eggs are in fact anything but guilty as charged.

It goes on and on. In January 1992, *Time* magazine denounced the American Egg Board for the most deceitful advertising in the nation in 1991:

> *An ad aimed at children boasts that "eggs have as much protein as hot dogs." So what? An egg also has nine times as much cholesterol as a hot dog. And nutrition experts say most American children get more protein than they need.*[72]

The egg industry responded with a cry that it was being treated unfairly, but in informed medical circles its pleas fell on deaf ears. A few months later, the Center for Science in the Public Interest and nine other public interest organizations awarded the American Egg Board the Harlan Page Hubbard memorial award for the "most misleading, unfair, or irresponsible" ad campaign of 1991. The Egg Board's ads earned this dis-honor for proudly claiming that "there are twenty-five vitamins and minerals in just one egg," when in fact an egg is a source of only two—one of which, iodine, we already get too much of.

The public advocacy groups pointed out that the primary thing that eggs are actually a good source of is artery-clogging cholesterol.

To this day, the egg industry remains as dedicated to its purpose, which is to sell its product, as it could be. The fact that the product it sells causes enormous amounts of human suffering is seen as a public relations problem, to be solved by advertising gimmicks. The industry evidently figures that if two wrongs don't make a right, perhaps three or four might do the trick.

SIX

Into the Mouths of Babes

"In every child who is born,
under no matter what circumstances,
and of no matter what parents, the
potentiality of the human race
is born again...."
James Agee

Y ou might be surprised to hear me say this, but I believe that people who worry excessively over whether their food is sufficiently healthy are doing something that is itself unhealthy. In fact, I sometimes suspect that if they keep it up long enough, the pleasure centers of their brains may atrophy.

I love life and want to extract from it the maximum amount of happiness. I choose the food I eat with great care because I want to celebrate life, enjoy its pleasures, respond to its challenges, and appreciate all the other great gifts that come with health.

I grew up with a sweet tooth roughly the size of Mt. Everest. I'm sure it had something to do with the commercial-sized freezer we had at our house. It was always filled with many of the 31 flavors of ice cream that were featured that month in Baskin-Robbins stores. Often enough, our freezer also contained samples of the various experimental flavors that were in the process of being developed.

I believe it was at about the age of four that I took it upon myself to be the "official taster" of them all. There were certain advantages to being the son of the co-founder and co-owner of a thriving ice cream company.

As an adult I've found that mastering a sugar habit that began at such an early and formative age has not been easy. There still are times, usually when I'm under a lot of stress, that I eat more sweets than I probably should. I have found, however, that as my diet and lifestyle have become healthier and more fully in alignment with my spirit, the attraction to sweets has lessened considerably.

As for ice cream, I have not had any for many years. But please don't feel sorry for me; I've eaten enough ice cream in my life to last anyone twenty lives.

Speaking critically of sugar doesn't come easy to me. The companion animals that meant so much to me as I was growing up were given names that gave no hint that I would ever feel called to such a task. My dog was named Sugar Plum, and all of my cats were named after ice cream flavors. A black cat was named Licorice, an orange tabby was Orange Sherbet, and a white cat was Marshmallow.

Nonetheless, there are problems with sugar. For one, it provides only empty calories. An empty calorie is one that supplies virtually no vitamins, minerals, enzymes, or any of the other nutrients needed by the human body to maintain health. The more empty calories in a person's diet, the more likely he or she is to be obese, and the weaker will be his or her resistance to bacterial and viral infections.[1]

While many people are aware that sugar contributes to dental cavities, there are people and organizations spending millions of dollars to confuse the issue. The Wrigley chewing gum company finances studies that try to prove that sugared gums are beneficial to teeth. The M&M Mars candy company gives $1 million a year to an organization that sends newsletters to dentists throughout the United States. Dentists might look askance at a "dental newsletter" from a candy company, so the newsletter makes no mention of the fact that it is funded by M&M Mars. Instead, it presents itself as coming from the "Princeton Dental Resource Group," falsely implying an association with Princeton University. One 1992 issue cheerfully told dentists and dental patients that eating chocolate bars might help to fight cavities. Among others who were appalled was the scientist on whose work the claim was supposedly based. When he learned of the conclusions drawn from his work, Dr. Lawrence Wolinsky of UCLA objected vigorously: *I know that is what candy companies would love to think, but it just isn't the case.*

Despite the efforts of the sugar sellers, many dentists recognize the truth. A dentist I know has a sticker on his ceiling that patients can ponder during their appointments. It says: *"Support your local dentist. Eat more sweets."*

Then there's the notorious "sugar buzz." Studies at Yale University Medical School and elsewhere have shown that children have more dramatic hormonal reactions than adults to refined sweeteners.[2] But adults too develop anxiety, breathing difficulty, shakiness, and other signs of adrenaline response when besieged by highly concentrated simple sugars like glucose, fructose, and sucrose. These monosaccharides are rapidly absorbed, and can produce an emotional roller-coaster ride that ends up in the notorious "sugar blues."[3]

The process works like this: Simple sugars cause your blood sugar level to rise rapidly. This in turn stimulates the pancreas to churn out insulin, causing your blood sugar levels to fall. As your blood sugar levels drop, the pancreas begins to stop secreting insulin, but not fast enough to keep up. The result is that your blood sugar level may become even lower than when you began.

It's a classic vicious circle, and a classic recipe for addiction. Feeling tired and beset by a lack of energy, you feel a craving for the foods that can rapidly raise the level of sugar in your blood—more sweets.

Dramatic fluctuations in blood sugar levels lead eventually to anxiety and depression. A person who consumes sugars in excess tends to be thrown out of metabolic and emotional balance.

What constitutes "excess"? That is not always easy for members of our society to discern, for we live in a culture where it is considered "normal" to derive as much as 30 percent of our calories from sugar. Sweeteners are found not only in desserts, confections, and soft drinks. It is amazing how many of the canned, frozen, and packaged items on supermarket shelves contain sugar, corn syrup, fructose, or other refined and concentrated sweeteners.

Many parents struggle to assist their youngsters in keeping their intake of sweets within moderation. This is no simple task. When you couple the addictive nature of refined sugars with advertisements that bombard our children with sophisticated messages associating products high in sugar with cartoon characters, excitement, and fun, you have a situation wholly unprecedented in nature. Nothing in a young person's genetic inheritance enables him or her to cope with such an onslaught.

We do our children a wonderful service when we support them in maintaining healthy eating habits. We are fulfilling the genuine call of parenthood when we help them never to feel ashamed or afraid of being different, but rather to take pride in doing what they know is wholesome and good.

There is a story about Mahatma Gandhi, the great Indian leader. One day a mother brought her young son to the sage, and asked if he would please tell the youngster to stop eating sugar. Gandhi said, "Come back in a week." Puzzled, the woman departed, to return with her son a week later. Then Gandhi did what the woman had originally asked, advising the young lad to avoid sugar. Afterward, the woman asked Gandhi why he had postponed the matter for a week. "Oh," he answered, "first *I* had to give up sugar."

The deepest lessons that we teach our children come not from our advice but from our examples.

"Candy, Little Girl?"

In the summer of 1991, the Center for Science in the Public Interest analyzed the food ads on Saturday morning TV. The messages they saw being delivered were not what most people would call wholesome and uplifting:

> *Ninety-six percent of the food ads were for candy bars, sugary cereals, salty canned foods, fatty fast foods and chips, and other nutritional disasters.*[4]

The consumer advocacy group analyzed programs on five television stations, including affiliates of the ABC, CBS, NBC, and Fox networks, plus the Nickelodeon cable channel, and surveyed 222 food ads. How many of these do you think encouraged kids to eat anything resembling healthy foods?

One.[5]

Shortly thereafter, the American Academy of Pediatrics declared that the foods advertised for children are so bad that they should be banned from television. The author of the report, Dr. William Dietz of Tufts University, warned of a tightly woven net of commercialism surrounding children's television, in which some cereals are designed more to sell toys than to feed children.[6]

The processed food and cereal industry did not take kindly to this criticism from the Academy of Pediatrics. A spokesman for Ralston

Purina loyally defended the company's Teenage Mutant Ninja Turtles cereal, calling it *"nutritious and vitamin-fortified."*[7] His enthusiasm for this cereal did not seem daunted by the fact that it contains more than 40 percent sugar, nor by the list of ingredients, which reads as much like something from a chemistry laboratory as from a kitchen:

Rice, marshmallows (sugar, modified food starch, corn syrup, dextrose, gelatin, artificial and natural flavors, sodium hexametaphosphate, color added [red 40, yellow 6, yellow 5, blue 1, and other color added]), sugar, brown sugar, salt, honey, malt syrup.

In case anyone was so foolish as to listen to an organization of forty thousand pediatricians cautioning against this kind of breakfast cereal, a spokesman for Kellogg proclaimed:

It's clear the authors of the proposed ban don't understand the role of ready-to-eat cereal in providing children with a healthy breakfast. ...The sugar issue is bogus.[8]

Isn't it interesting who's calling the sugar issue "bogus"? Could it have anything to do with the fact that every morning the Kellogg company provides millions of American children with such breakfasts as Fruit Loops (45 percent sugar) and Apple Jacks (50 percent sugar)? One of Kellogg's best-selling cereals used to be called Sugar Smacks, but in response to the growing consumer awareness of the serious problems with sugar, the Kellogg company felt compelled to make a change. Its response did not, however, display much sensitivity to the public health issue involved. As public health organizations and consumer groups decried the excessive amounts of sugar in these so-called cereals, the Kellogg company did its part: It deleted the word *sugar* from the product's name. That's all that was changed, just the name. That cereal on the supermarket shelves today (always positioned exactly at kid's-eye level) is 52 percent sugar.

The Post company likes to think of itself as a manufacturer of foods that are first and foremost nutritious. The front of its Golden Crisp cereal packages announces that the product is made from *"wholesome puffed wheat*." This certainly sounds good and healthy. The truth, however, is that **this particular cereal checks in at a rather staggering 54 percent sugar.** By way of comparison, a Hershey chocolate almond candy bar is 32 percent sugar.

The Quaker Oats company also does not seem to be disturbed by little matters like the health of children. In January 1992, to promote its Cap'n Crunch (45 percent sugar) cereal, Quaker sent out media packets to teachers of kindergarten through third grade at 93 percent of the nation's public and private schools. Disguised as free educational material, the Cap'n Crunch packets were an attempt to use schools to hook kids on the product. The packets included exercises in logical reasoning and following directions, all tied into the cereal's current sales theme: "Who's the real Cap'n?"

Into the Mouths of Babes

Something has to have gone deeply awry for human beings to come to a point where they feed themselves and their young with such unnurturing foods. For many of us, sadly, the pattern of unnatural food consumption begins almost at the moment of our birth.

The food an infant receives is of tremendous importance because it is the source of nourishment for this very fragile individual during the time of peak brain development. If the brain does not receive adequate nourishment at this time, and therefore doesn't develop properly, the consequences can be irreversible, as Dr. William Connor of the Oregon Health Sciences Center makes clear:

> *The brain gets bigger right after birth. By the age of two, it's close to adult size. Man's future depends on what his food is as an infant.*[9]

For the human infant, the evidence that breastfeeding is healthier than bottle feeding is overwhelming.[10] Most of us wouldn't find this surprising, since the breastmilk of any species of mammal is obviously Nature's way of seeing to it that the species survives. Human mother's milk is perfectly designed to feed and nurture human babies. By the same token, cow's milk is the ideal food for a newborn baby calf. Nature has designed it so that human babies are born to human mothers, and

calves are born to cows, and articles in the supermarket tabloids not-
withstanding, you won't find a whole lot of exceptions to this pattern.
The nutritional needs of a baby calf, a ruminant animal that will double
its birth weight in forty-seven days, and gain as much as one thousand
pounds in its first year, are vastly different from those of a human baby,
who will take six months to double its birth weight, and gain only about
fourteen pounds in its first year. The calf takes only a few years to
become physically mature, while the human animal requires far longer
to develop the extraordinarily delicate circuitry of the human brain and
nervous system.

Speaking of the biological specificity of milk, Dr. David Reuben put
the matter colorfully:

*The digestive system of a cow is totally different from that of a
human being. Cows have several stomachs, and live on grass and
hay. If you give your baby the same diet as a baby cow, shouldn't
you, in all fairness, eat the same diet as a grown-up cow? Tonight
try a bale of hay for dinner and see how it sits on your stomach.
Then ask yourself why your baby has colic.*[11]

The Evidence Speaks

Are breastfed babies healthier than babies fed formulas? You bet your
bronzed booties they are. Bottle fed babies suffer more pneumonia,
middle-ear infections, respiratory infections, bacterial meningitis, neo-
natal septicemia, thrush, and viral illnesses, including polio and herpes
simplex.[12] In fact, the risk of influenza and spinal meningitis for bottle
fed babies is as much as sixteen times greater than the risk for breastfed
infants.[13]

A recent study published in the *British Medical Journal* analyzed the
diets that had been given to 339 infants who had to be hospitalized with
gastroenteritis. Of the 339 sick infants, it turned out that 338 of them
had been bottle fed.[14]

Citing extensive surveys published in the scientific literature, Dr.
John McDougall writes:

*Bottle feeding in the very young infant can cause hypocalcemia
(which leads to tetany), dehydration, hypernatremia (high sodium*

*level in the body, associated with permanent brain damage), and
necrotising enterocolitis (an inflammatory bowel disease seen almost
exclusively in artificially fed young infants and associated with a
high mortality).*[15]

Studies show that bottle feeding is consistently associated with the
development in later life of immune system disorders, diabetes, chronic
liver diseases, ulcerative colitis, celiac disease, Crohn's disease, food
allergies, obesity, coronary heart disease, and multiple sclerosis.[16]

In 1992, *Lancet* reported that IQs were found to be 8.3 points higher
for premature babies fed mother's milk compared to those fed formulas.

A distressingly large number of infants in modern societies today die
suddenly in their sleep, of no discernible cause. This phenomenon,
known as crib death or sudden infant death syndrome, occurs twice as
often in infants who are bottle fed than in those who are breastfed.[17]

The Love That Protects

Unlike formulas, the composition of human mother's milk is not static,
nor is it dead. It changes from day to day in response to the needs of
the baby. It is part of a living process of communication at the deepest
biological level between mother and baby. It is an expression of the
mother's love and caring and a reflection of the deep symbiotic cooperation of the mother-child bond. As Dr. H. Marano wrote in *Medical
World News*:

> *A nursing mother in close contact with her infant can make
> antibodies on demand to pathogens that challenge him [or her] and
> transfer them in milk.*[18]

By a process known as diathelic immunity, breastmilk will come to
carry antibodies to infectious agents to which the infant is exposed. Some
researchers believe that dangerous bacteria that invade the baby's body
enter into his or her saliva, and from there into the mother's breast where
they provoke the production of the needed antibodies, which the baby
then receives in the next feeding.[19]

Dr. David Reuben comments:

The human breast constantly adapts to new threats, and it functions to constantly protect the baby. Don't expect anything like that from the waxy milk carton in your refrigerator.[20]

Newborn babies are extraordinary vulnerable, and they need all the help they can get in coping with the world into which they are so suddenly plunged. In the first few days after childbirth, breastmilk contains colostrum, which carries immunoglobulins that greatly enhance the newborn's immunity against disease. Babies deprived of colostrum have much higher rates of all viral and bacterial infections.[21]

The breastfed baby has the advantage of the antibodies and immunity that the breastfeeding mother has built up throughout her life, because these are carried in her blood stream, and are hence in the milk that flows from her breasts. The baby fed on cow's milk formulas has no such benefit. Instead, the little one receives antibodies and immunities against calf scours, bovine encephalomyelitis, mastitis (udder infection), and other bovine illnesses.[22] I'm unsure what effect these antibodies have on human babies, but they certainly provide no protection against the infectious agents that pose a danger to *them.*

The Mother-Baby Bond

The psychological benefits of breastfeeding are perhaps even more profound than the purely physical ones. Some of the most important work on infant-mother bonding has been done by Dr. John Kennell at Rainbow Babies' and Children's Hospital in Cleveland. In one long-term study, he and his colleagues studied two groups of new mothers. For one of the groups, hospital policies were changed slightly to enable them to bond better with their babies. A summary of the study in *Smithsonian* magazine reported:

The Cleveland pediatricians found important differences between the two groups of mothers and babies. A month after birth, when they came back for a special office visit, the [bonded] mothers stood closer to their infants, picked up their crying babies more . . . and fondled their babies more. Interviews revealed they were more reluctant to leave their infants with someone else. And they reported that when they did go out, they found themselves constantly thinking about the baby. A year later, they still were more attentive to their babies. . . . After two years, [they] talked differently to their children, . . . used richer language constructions and more words, especially descriptive adjectives. They issued fewer commands to their children, but asked more questions. What is more, they continued to speak to their children when other adults came into the room, while the [other] mothers talked more to the adult interviewer.[23]

The bonds of affection created between mother and child in breast-feeding last throughout a lifetime. They express the most primary and essential forms of human love. They feed both mother and child in countless ways, lending meaning to the challenges each must face, and illuminating the course of all that is to follow. Dr. Kennell tells us:

The most powerful way to forge a strong bond between mother and infant is through breastfeeding.[24]

And La Leche League reminds mothers:

Each time you snuggle your hungry baby to your breast to nurse, you assure him or her of your loving presence. Through breastfeeding, babies learn about love and trust, warmth and security.[25]

In Our Society

It is a wonder that we have come to think of formula feeding as in any way equivalent to breastfeeding. But our culture does not teach us to be comfortable with our physical selves. On the contrary, we are taught that technology is more trustworthy than our bodies. Bottle-feeding grows in the soil of ignorance, body shame, and fear of intimacy.

Bottle feeding is another facet of the alienation from our physical selves and from the rest of the natural world that cries out for healing. It is another part of the pattern that leads us to buy something for our children rather than giving something of ourselves.

What must be done to a woman so that she will believe that the milk of a cow mixed with chemicals and sold to her by a multinational corporation could possibly provide better nutrition for her baby than her own milk?

We associate breasts with sex; we use them to sell everything under the sun. Bottle feeding upholds the conviction that a woman's breasts are there to attract a man, with the feeding of her babies being relegated to only secondary importance.

Breastfeeding is more acceptable in our society today than it was twenty years ago, but we are far from being a society that truly supports this fundamental human experience. If a woman should want to breast-feed her baby discreetly in a public place, she must often fear the disapproval of others.

In 1989, a nationally syndicated columnist wrote a column that exemplifies the attitudes that women who want to breast-feed may encounter.[26] The column attacked breastfeeding in restaurants, which the author called "*very '80s*." By using this phrase he implied that breastfeeding was something like hula hoops or the latest dance craze, merely a trend or the fad of a particular decade. I don't know why this man needed to speak so derogatorily about something that is as ancient as human life itself, and as central to the growing human spirit as breathing. But he ended his column with further mockery, suggesting that the trend in the 1990s will be for parents to allow their children to throw up on the carpet. How sad that he should feel a need to cast insulting aspersions on such a beautiful and important expression of human caring.

Fortunately, there is an organization called La Leche League to encourage and help mothers to enjoy fully "*the womanly art of breastfeeding*." In modern society, breastfeeding is often inconvenient, and working mothers may need all the help they can get to stay with it.

In economically less developed societies, however, the choice of whether to breast or bottle feed has another dimension to it entirely. . . .

They Call It Glamorous

Here with us now are millions upon millions of mothers. They live on every continent in the world and speak every language in the world. And they are poor.

These mothers have been the targets of the massive promotional campaigns of the companies selling infant formulas. As a result, they have come to believe their breastmilk is inferior to the purchased commercial formula.

Shortly after birth in a maternity hospital, their babies are fed free formula. As they leave the hospital, mothers are given a gift. They say "thank you" as they take home free samples of commercial infant food. Since it comes from the hospital, they assume it is the best possible food for their baby. Using the samples, they believe their little ones are being well cared for. They do not realize that the formulas lack the immunological protection their own milk would provide, and that now their babies will be subject to diseases they would not have gotten otherwise. The formula packages say to sterilize the water and the bottles, but the mothers often cannot read, and furthermore, neither clean water nor sufficient fuel to boil the water are readily available.

Soon the mothers find that their babies have become ill. At the same time, they find that they can't afford the high cost of the formulas. But if they try to go back to breastfeeding, they find they cannot, because their milk has dried up. In order to stretch the formula they can afford to buy so that it will last a little longer, they add extra water to it.

The mothers watch helplessly as their little babies get diarrhea so severe that all the tiny ones can do is cry in pain. Their fragile bodies, deprived of adequate nourishment, become progressively weaker, racked by parasitic and infectious diseases.

These mothers love their babies, and would do anything to help them. In desperation, they often go without food themselves in order to save money to buy a bit more formula for their suffering little ones. Sometimes the older children also go hungry so the infant can have more formula.

The mothers don't know that among Third World babies who are exclusively breastfed, mortality rates drop 95 percent. They think that in using the formulas they are feeding their children the modern way. They think bottle feeding is "glamorous, convenient, highly scientific, and nutritionally superior." That's what the advertisements have told them.

Not so long ago, each of these mothers was happy and proud, for she was going to have a new baby. This one was going to be different. This one was going to be healthy and strong, grow up and live a good life. Yes, this one was special. And he or she still is special and always will be. But now many of these mothers must know the unbearable pain of watching their babies suffer, waste away, and die.

The number of mothers enacting this pathetic drama every day is so enormous that it constitutes one of the great human tragedies of our time; a tragedy all the more grotesque because it is caused, in large part, by corporate greed.

Every twenty-four hours, four thousand bottle fed infants die, infants who would have lived had they been breastfed. **More than one and a half million human babies die every year from the cycle of infection and malnutrition known as Bottle Baby Disease, almost all in the Third World.**[27]

When the Australian Broadcasting Corporation's equivalent of *60 Minutes* investigated the situation, they concluded:

> *If this were the aftermath of some terrible industrial accident, the companies responsible would be paying the costs. But as it's simply the result of an international marketing exercise, it goes on unabated.*

According to UNICEF statistics, the risk of death in the less developed nations from diarrhea is **25 times higher** for children who are bottle-fed than for those who are breastfed.[28] Dr. A. Gaffar Billoo of the Pakistan Pediatrics Association explains:

> *Prescribing artificial feeding or bottle feeding in a country like this is literally prescribing a death certificate.*[29]

The Formula Pushers

The posters have said powdered milks are *"the best start in life"* for babies.[30] The radio advertisements have glowingly praised the breastmilk substitutes as *"the first choice."*[31] In many areas, the infant food companies pay health professionals to promote their products.

In Karachi, Pakistan, giant billboards and television advertisements beckon consumers to buy infant formulas. Maternity wards all over Asia are decorated with alluring pictures of beautiful and healthy babies, advertising infant formulas.

The International Baby Food Action Network (IBFAN) is composed of 148 organizations in 74 countries working for the improvement of infant health through the promotion and protection of breastfeeding. In 1991, IBFAN released the results of an extensive survey, covering 169 countries. The survey sought to determine whether or not the multinational infant formula companies were complying with the World Health Organization's International Code of Marketing of Breastmilk Substitutes.

This Code has received remarkable international support. When it was officially adopted by the World Health Assembly on May 21, 1981, the vote in its favor was 114 to 1.[32] The only dissenting vote was cast by the United States, at the insistence of President Reagan. Immediately after the vote, the U.S. representative who had been required to cast the vote emerged from the chambers in tears, and resigned in protest. Within a short time, both houses of the U.S. Congress passed resolutions overwhelmingly condemning the U.S. vote.

Today, the multinational infant formula companies claim they comply with the Code. But the IBFAN survey details hundreds of systematic violations by infant food companies who are engaged in deliberate and methodical attempts to bypass the Code's restrictions. According to the survey, the worst offenders are Nestlé, Wyeth (American Home Products), two German companies (Milupa and Hipp), and Meiji, a Japanese corporation.

One of the most important provisions in the Code is the demand for an end to the marketing strategy of providing free samples of infant formula to maternity hospitals. Free samples are a powerful marketing tool because once a mother stops breastfeeding, even if only for a few days, her milk supply dries up. The purpose of the donated formula is to create a dependence on commercial products by undermining breastfeeding.

IBFAN's extensive survey found that, despite their denials, Nestlé and American Home Products are systematically continuing this practice. In fact, these companies spend many millions of dollars every year to gain access to Third World maternity hospitals. They know that in the eyes of Third World women, free samples in the hospital imply medical endorsement. The companies' motive is simple, like that of any drug pusher on the street. The first one's free. After that, the mother's hooked. She has no other way to feed her baby.

These companies operate according to a certain set of priorities. They are interested in sales, and they know that urban slums are the fastest-growing market for infant formula. When they look at infants in the Third World, they accept no responsibility for the disease, agony, and death caused by their products. Instead, they seek to maximize the use of their products, particularly in Third World maternity hospitals. As one industry manual explains:

When one considers that for every one hundred infants discharged on a particular formula brand, approximately ninety-three infants remain on that brand, the importance of hospital selling becomes obvious.[33]

Obvious, indeed.

In Malaysia, government hospitals are not permitted to accept free supplies. This doesn't faze Nestlé or American Home Products, though. They simply "sell" formula to hospitals at prices as ridiculously low as two cents a pound.

The IBFAN survey found that Nestlé's strategy is to ingratiate itself with physicians and other medical personnel, sometimes paying them outright to pass on to new mothers the free samples that the company provides. This practice is categorically forbidden in the Code adopted by the World Health Assembly, UNICEF, the World Health Organization and every other international health organization concerned with the matter. But Nestlé is evidently not a company to let a little thing like that stand in its way. In a documentary film made by the Australian Broadcasting Corporation, a former longtime Nestlé medical representative clarifies the company's tactics:

Nestlé Representative: *"The strategy now is to . . . go around the bush . . . do it without being caught."*

ABC: *"One of those secret ways involves Nestlé representatives delivering milk formulas to hospitals, giving an invoice, but never seeking payment. It's a practice Nestlé denies."*

Nestlé Rep: *"The majority of them don't pay."*

ABC: *"So this is a way of giving free formula to [maternity] hospitals?"*

Nestlé Rep: *"Yes."*

ABC: *"Did Nestlé have a training system to teach people how to relate to doctors?"*

Nestlé Rep: *"Yes, of course. We had a lot of training including the closing or opening dialogue with the doctor. It used to be like a canned dialogue, even down to some [small talk] . . . . There are dates you have to remember, birthdates, anniversaries. . . . We do a lot of escort services for the doctors. . . ."*

ABC: *"So you are saying that pretty soon a doctor would become, as it's been called, a Nestlé doctor and promotes your product?"*

Nestlé Rep: *"Yes. Prescribe, really."*

ABC: *"Is this giving of gifts and so on a direct marketing strategy?"*

Nestlé Rep: *"Yes. . . ."*[34]

The World Health Assembly Code specifically forbids undisclosed personal gifts to health workers and hospitals. In press releases and other public statements, the infant formula companies claim that they are in full compliance with the Code.[35] But internal company documents tell a very different story. Directives are issued to company employees explaining how to give gifts without being caught. Employees are advised to deliver gifts and products *directly to the health worker without witnesses, preferably at the residence.*[36] In instructions on giving gifts to maternity hospitals, Nestlé employees are told how to avoid being traced: *Do not indicate price and source company [Nestlé] on delivery receipt.*[37]

Throughout the Third World, many babies are not born in hospitals, and so are not reached by the infant formula companies' practice of providing free infant formula samples in maternity hospitals. The companies are not about to give up on them, though, and actively seek to promote their products to the health workers who work with these mothers and infants.

Four years after the World Health Assembly adopted a resolution discouraging the use of "follow-on milks," pediatricians in Kenya received an impressive brochure telling them brightly that: *Today, medical authorities recommend follow-on formula.*[38] In a Malaysian medical journal, an American Home Products ad implies that the company's formula will help prevent disease. In the same journal, Nestlé advertises its infant formula, saying: *Your mother probably gave you the best infant formula around—Lactogen. Now, shouldn't you be doing the same for your newborn patients?*[39] In Pakistan, Bristol-Myers distributes literature to doctors, promoting Enfamil *to meet all your routine infant feeding requirements.*[40]

In some countries, attempts are made by the local authorities to enforce the Code. But Nestlé and American Home Products each spend more money on advertising than many of these nations have to spend for their entire health care budgets.

In the 1970s, due to the activities of the infant formula companies, Brazil had the lowest rates of breastfeeding in the Third World. Today, though, thanks to a nationwide campaign, things have changed. Between 1981 and 1987, the rate of breastfeeding in the first eight months of life rose over 50 percent. Death due to diarrhea in infants decreased by 46 percent.

How does Nestlé respond to these changes? Company representatives have called the doctors and health experts involved *fanatics who think it's possible for a poor mother with small breasts to breast-feed.*[41]

UNICEF states that *"virtually all women"* are able to breast-feed, even women suffering from malnutrition.[42] Despite the industry's claims, inadequate milk supply due to small breasts is unknown in humans.

Enough's Enough

On October 4, 1988, Action for Corporate Accountability formally initiated an international boycott against Nestlé and American Home Products to protest the dangerous promotion of infant formula in poor communities around the world. These two companies were chosen because they are the world's leading infant formula manufacturers and the worst violators of the 1981 World Health Assembly International Code of Marketing of Breastmilk Substitutes. According to Action for Corporate Accountability, more than half of the 1.5 million babies dying each year from Bottle Baby Disease are drinking Nestlé formulas.

You may remember there being a boycott once before against Nestlé. That one ended in 1984, when the company promised to comply with the Code. The changes believed to have been gained from that boycott were so great that Esther Peterson, Consumer Affairs Advisor to Presidents Johnson and Carter called the boycott *"the most important victory in the history of the international consumer movement."*[43]

Real gains were obtained by the boycott.

But as the evidence compiled by the International Baby Food Action Network attests, Nestlé and American Home Products have gone back on their word. As a result, informed consumers are rising up and saying that they will not tolerate this flagrant disregard for human life.

The boycott focuses on two products of the Nestlé-owned Carnation company—**Coffee Mate** and **Taster's Choice**—and on two products made by American Home Products—**Anacin** and **Advil.** Shoppers are asked not to purchase these products, and to tell the check-out clerk, pharmacist, or store manager that they are not doing so and why. The public is also encouraged to write the companies, explaining that as long as they seek to increase sale of their products by donating free samples to maternity hospitals in the Third World, and are not in full compliance with the World Health Assembly Code, consumers will find it morally impossible to buy their products.

Widespread support for the boycott continues to grow around the world. The International Nestlé Boycott Alliance has pledges of support from sixty-seven countries and from hundreds of church groups throughout the world. On July 15, 1991, the Church of England resolved to endorse and support the Nestlé boycott, the first time in its history that the Church had taken such a step.

Every so often, the media will report events that seem to indicate that the infant formula companies are changing their ways, and that the boycott and campaign against their abuses are having a positive effect. Sometimes these articles are accurate, but other times they are planted by the companies to try to give the false impression that things are all taken care of now. Appearing to work with the World Health Organization and UNICEF enables the companies to polish these tarnished images while continuing in their ways. To keep abreast of the latest developments, and to join the effort bringing an end to this crime against humanity, contact Action for Corporate Accountability (see page 140).

Beyond Denial

Uncovering the activities of the infant formula companies, and their tragic consequences to millions of human lives, has not been easy for me. I've felt sadness for the mothers who want to do the best thing for their babies, but who are conned into unknowingly feeding them preparations with disastrous results. Watching vulnerable babies live and die in agony is hardly bearable under any circumstances. But knowing that this hideous suffering wouldn't occur if it weren't for corporate greed can make it virtually impossible to tolerate.

As for the people who perpetuate and profit from these practices, what words can describe the outrage I have felt at their behavior? Or the sadness that any person could be so callous to human suffering. Sometimes, feeling overwhelmed by the seeming intractability of human greed, I've felt despair for us all.

The grief has hurt deeply, but I am nevertheless grateful for it. For through this pain, something within me has changed. A force has welled up within me in response to this tragedy. Something in the core of my humanity has awoken and called me to do what I can to turn this madness around. A determination has arisen to channel the feeling of moral outrage into sustained and constructive action.

We are not powerless in the face of this monstrous injustice. We can use our lives to make a statement that we will not condone this crime. We can join in the boycott and force these companies to pay attention to the impact of their actions. We can tell others about it, thereby raising their awareness, and also raising our own level of participation and engagement. We can set an example, both as a nation and individually, by breastfeeding and by encouraging and supporting breastfeeding. We can honor the mother-child bond, and take care that all our children are given the healthiest possible environment in which to develop.

We can educate ourselves and others about the consequences of our choices so that we act from a more informed and thus more powerful position. We can question the messages and motives of advertising, and encourage others to do the same, so that the choices we make are truly our own, not just the result of artificially implanted beliefs.

We can recognize that every time we take a step toward a world in which life is respected and cherished, something happens of immense importance. We are brought nearer to the living force of our humanity. We become stronger and more connected to our values. We become more able to bring sanity and compassion into our lives, into our families, into our societies, and into the human community.

We Are All in This Together

When I began to face the tragic consequences of the aggressive marketing of breastmilk substitutes to Third World women, I believed that nothing like this could happen in modern Western society. I assumed that we had laws to protect public health, and regulations to prohibit such merciless exploitation of human vulnerability.

But I have been disappointed to discover that the truth is otherwise. A 1991 report in the journal *Pediatrics* announced that there was "*a steep, steady decline in breastfeeding [in the United States] between 1984 and 1989.*"[44] The decline was particularly sharp among women who were enrolled in the $2 billion federal program called WIC (Women, Infants and Children), which distributes food to poor mothers. Catherine Bertini, Assistant Secretary of Agriculture for Food and Consumer Services, says:

> *There are deterrents in the WIC program to breastfeeding. We give out free formulas. When I went to a WIC center and looked at the lists of food you get if you breastfeed and if you don't . . . I almost felt breastfeeding would be giving up something for my baby.*[45]

In Canada, the largest U.S. manufacturers of infant formula bid up to $500,000.00 for the "privilege" of supplying Canada's largest maternity hospital with free formula.

In the U.S., Carnation (Nestlé) advertises formula even though this is explicitly counter to the guidelines of the American Academy of Pediatrics.

We are not separate or immune from the problems of developing nations.

In our culture, too, we are challenged by attempts to get us to make consumer choices that have life-threatening implications. In fact, we are inundated by attempts to control our eating habits in unhealthy directions for private commercial gain. Compared to the damages done by bottle feeding in the Third World, the damage here is usually more subtle, and the diseases do not manifest themselves as quickly, but we too are beset by advertisements and other marketing strategies that have been skillfully designed to hook us on products that are profoundly damaging to our health.

The number of babies killed by diseases caused by bottle feeding and inadequate diets in the Third World is staggering. But perhaps even more shocking are the numbers of people killed in our society by diseases caused by our diets. In fact, the deaths in our society from heart disease, cancer, strokes, diabetes, hypertension, osteoporosis, and the other afflictions caused in large measure by our diet make up a higher percentage of all the deaths that occur in our society than the deaths caused by malnutrition do in the Third World.

The new mothers in the Third World don't realize they're being manipulated as they lie in the maternity hospital shortly after giving birth, being given free samples of formula and encouraged to bottle-feed. But how aware are our children that they are being manipulated as they sit at home in their own living rooms, mesmerized by colorful cartoon characters who are telling them a cereal that is in fact mostly refined sugar is "*power-packed dynamite*"?

The Third World mothers have no idea they are being exploited by advertisements telling them bottle feeding will help them avoid "*bosom sag*." But do our children have any idea they are being exploited by coloring books implying that if they don't eat butter, cheese and ice cream they may end up with blue hair, red eyes, and green faces?

The Third World mothers are not aware they are being influenced by billboards presenting an image of bottle-feeding as more socially acceptable than breastfeeding. But how aware are people in our society that they are being similarly programmed when they are told that beef is "*real food for real people*"?

We object to infant formula manufacturers who imply medical endorsement of their products to Third World mothers. But tins of Similac that proudly proclaim it is the *"first choice of more physicians and used in more hospitals"* are not just found in the Third World; they can be found on the shelves of your local supermarket and drugstore.

We can see it is wrong for infant formula companies to use public maternity hospitals to promote their products. What keeps us from seeing that it is wrong for the meat and dairy industries to use public schools to promote the sale of their products?

It is not only in the Third World that vulnerable people are exploited and human health is sacrificed for commercial gain. Isn't it an exploitation of millions of Americans when industries gain control over governmental policies, and use the most sophisticated marketing tactics ever devised, in order to get us to buy and consume foods that are known to cause disease?

We do not have to look very far to find rampant greed and abuse of power in our culture. We do not have to go to the Third World to find a place where healing and love are needed.

Even the Little Steps Count

The way you help heal the world is you start with your own family.
MOTHER TERESA

Never underestimate the impact of single individuals, working sincerely to create health, understanding, and peace in their own lives. For every step we take to establish genuinely healthy food choices is a step into our own wholeness, into the power to create healthy lives for ourselves, and to contribute to the health and well-being of others.

The way we eat and the way we live have potentially enormous consequences for the quality and direction of our lives. When we acknowledge our gratitude for the food we eat, we are put in touch with something basic—that food and life are precious. In giving expression to our care for those who are without adequate food, we honor our connection to those who are in need and affirm the power of our common humanity.

Each time we recognize the reality of those who suffer, we become a little more human and the world becomes a little less lonely. Each time we acknowledge how interwoven we are with one another and with the Earth, we break free from the alienation that otherwise might hold us separate. We become alive with a power to bring joy, healing, and compassion into a world that is starving for this blessing.

When we take time to bless our food and the land on which it grew, and to appreciate the many who have labored that we might be fed, something important occurs. We become more aware of the implications of our choices. In upholding the Earth we are moved closer to its powers. In recognizing and honoring what nurtures life, we become more responsible citizens of this marvelous planet. We become ever more capable of making choices that are consistent with our true purpose and love.

Every time we say "yes" to foods that nourish our bodies and spirits, and every time we say "no" to foods that aren't good for us, we are saying "yes" to life.

We are afforded an extraordinary opportunity today. By choosing to eat more healthfully and more consciously, we can take a stand on behalf of ourselves and our interconnectedness with the rest of humanity. At a personal level we may be simply saying that we do not want to cause ourselves to suffer a heart attack. But at the same time we can add our voice to the mounting chorus calling for a world in which our land, our water, our energy, and our labor are used to grow food for people to eat, rather than feed for livestock.

The same food choices that are healthiest for each of us are also votes for a world in which all people are fed, rather than one in which a privileged few eat meat while others starve. By eating with awareness and gratitude, we not only bring more health into our lives, we also join hands with one another to build a world in which basic human needs are respected.

We do not yet know what it would be like to live in a truly healthy and compassionate society. But there are some things that are available to us now: We can know the fulfillment of working toward such a world. We can know the liberation of freeing ourselves from habits that are not natural and do not serve us, but have come to pass for normal in our society. We can know the power of uniting with others in working to bring understanding and clarity where it is so greatly needed.

The task that lies before us cannot be accomplished overnight. It will take a lifetime of patient persistence. But, to my heart at least, it is a challenge more than worth the struggle.

Thank you for being part of it with me.

MAY ALL BE FED,
MAY ALL BE HEALED,
MAY ALL BE LOVED.

SEVEN

What You Can Do

"I shall tell you a great secret, my friend.
Do not wait for the last judgement;
it takes place every day."
Albert Camus

"The test of a first-rate intelligence is the ability to hold two opposed
ideas in mind at the same time and still retain the
ability to function. One should, for example, be able to see that
things are hopeless and yet be determined
to make them better."
F. Scott Fitzgerald

Just because we can't instantly make the world perfect doesn't mean that we can't do something to make it a little better. What follows is a list of possible actions.

Addresses and phone numbers for the specific organizations mentioned in this list can be found on pages 160 to 163.

What You Can Do
About the Infant Formula Scam

1. You can contact Action for Corporate Accountability, 129 Church Street, New Haven, CT 06510 (203-787-0061) for further information on the Nestlé and American Home Products boycott.

2. You can write Tim Crull, President, Nestlé USA, 800 North Brand Ave., Glendale, CA 91203, and John Stafford, President, American Home Products, 685 Third Ave., New York, NY 10017. Let them know that you support the boycott, and why. Be prepared to receive a standard form answer that will make it seem that the company is innocent of all wrongdoing, and that the problem doesn't exist. Send a copy of your correspondence to Action for Corporate Accountability.

3. You can conduct a campaign to get Nestlé and AHP products out of the local shops. You can target several products, such as the Nestlé-owned Carnation Company's Taster's Choice and Coffee Mate Non-Dairy Creamer and the products Anacin and Advil (which are made by AHP even though the packages don't say so).

4. You can work to keep your children's school from selling Nestlé candy in vending machines or for fund-raising drives.

5. You can call Nestlé (1-800-637-8537) and let them know you are going to boycott all Nestlé products until the company comes into compliance with the WHO Code, including stopping free formula supplies to hospitals. Don't worry if the response is public relations fast talk; the phone calls add up.

6. You can tell pregnant women you meet about La Leche League and the support networks it provides to help mothers breast-feed.

7. You can support efforts to allow mothers to nurse their infants at work and in other public places.

What You Can Do
to Help Children Eat Well

8. You can set a good example by preparing and eating foods from the new four food groups—grains, legumes, fruits, and vegetables.

9. You can talk with children about the foods advertised on television.

10. You can explain to children that the people they see touting products in commercials are paid to do so, and are acting.

11. You can have a variety of nutritious foods in the house, and not keep junk food around.

12. You and your child can use a hot air popcorn popper to make your own chemical-free popcorn.

13. You can explain patiently, simply, and consistently why you choose to eat as you do.

14. You can prepare healthy food in attractive ways.

15. You can involve your children in preparing food.

16. You can use the excellent sprouting kit and sprout teaching aids for children as young as three years old that are available from Natural Food Systems, Inc. (1-800-U-SHARED).

17. You can have a special section in the refrigerator where you keep cut-up vegetables, fruit, and other healthy snacks.

18. You and your child can make sandwiches in advance, and keep them in air-tight containers in the refrigerator as ready-to-eat healthy snacks.

19. You and your children can prepare homemade soup, which older children can learn to heat up for themselves.

20. You can encourage children to make drawings or pictures about healthy foods they enjoy eating, and place their artistic creations in prominent spots around the house.

21. You can have each family member create a poster expressing his or her sense of gratitude and reverence for food, and display these in the kitchen.

22. You can write poems, songs, or stories with children to bring to life their (and your) feelings and thoughts about different foods.

23. You can create a "stuffed animal" game in which a child gets to play out the food dynamics of the household through stuffed animals, and gets to help a stuffed animal learn how to eat better.

24. You can remember to include your children's food preferences in all your meal planning.

25. If you have a child who's going to a party where food will be served that isn't healthful, you can encourage him or her to pass up such foods, and pack him or her a better substitute to make it easier.

26. You can help children grow and take responsibility for a food plant. Indoors, a pot of parsley near a window works well; outdoors, try a pumpkin or winter squash plant.

27. You can pack your child's school lunch rather than depending on the school cafeteria (studies show that fresh fruit packed in children's lunchboxes is more likely to be eaten than any other food).

28. You and your child can make healthful pizzas, muffins, cupcakes, and other foods.

29. You can raise healthy children without relying on animal products. An excellent book on the subject is *Pregnancy, Children and the Vegan Diet*, by Michael Klaper, M.D., available from EarthSave (see page 160).

30. You can make your own baby food. The best solid foods to add first to an infant's diet are puréed and strained vegetables and fruits, including mashed bananas. Nonallergenic infant cereals made from rice, barley, or oats can be added soon thereafter. Legumes should not be added until a bit later, and then only after they have been thoroughly cooked, had their skins removed, and been puréed.

What You Can Do for Better School Nutrition

31. You can encourage schools to obtain a "salad-a-day" machine, which produces twelve pounds of fresh sprouts a day and takes up less space than a dishwasher (for further information, call Natural Food Systems, Inc. at 1-800-U-SHARED).

32. You can call your local school district's child nutrition services director and urge a meat-free day in honor of Earth Day, the Great American Meat-Out, or World Vegetarian Day. You can obtain from EarthSave a *Healthy People, Healthy Planet* manual designed to help this endeavor succeed.

33. You can demand that schools replace candy and other junk food in vending machines with apples, oranges, and other healthy foods.

34. You can insist that school bake sales involve healthy whole-grain products, and protest when schools are involved in candy sales. And you can provide wholesome products for the bake sales.

35. You can convince your school board to refuse to allow into the classroom any "educational materials" that promote particular

brands or high-fat, high-sodium, high-sugar, or high-cholesterol foods.

36. You can bring the YES! (Youth for Environmental Sanity) Tour to your community. This is a talented and committed group of young people who tour the country entertaining and educating at school assemblies about the environment, food choices, and what young people can do to make a positive difference. They reach two hundred thousand young people in person each year through their school assemblies and summer workshops. YES! is entirely youth-run, and is an extremely successful project of EarthSave.

37. You can order a copy of the New Four Food Groups chart from The Physicians Committee for Responsible Medicine (see page 160) and ask your child's teacher to put it on the wall.

What You Can Do To Help Fight Hunger in Your Own Community

38. In late summer and fall there are often garden and orchard surpluses of certain foods, such as zucchini and apples. You can collect these and contribute them to local free food programs. The contact phone numbers can be obtained from local food banks or churches.

39. You and your family can grow a garden to help feed your selves and others.

40. You can help to set up a May All Be Fed program. Organize with other volunteers to pick up surplus food from food businesses such as bakeries, fruit and vegetable stands, supermarkets, and restaurants, and deliver these to free food centers. For details on how to organize a May All Be Fed program, contact EarthSave (see page 160).

41. You can volunteer an hour or week or more to help with local programs that already exist. You can call your local food bank or soup kitchen, and offer:

   • *to pick up donated food,*
   • *to donate kitchen equipment,*
   • *to donate food,*

- *to help out in the office (answering phones, writing letters, making calls),*
- *to provide any special skills or connections you might have (public relations, computers, fundraising, printing, advertising, transportation, food service, etc.), or*
- *to help serve or cook food.*

What You Can Do About Pesticides

42. You can be aware that pesticides, waxes, fungicides, and sprays are often used on fruits and vegetables for purely cosmetic reasons. You can avoid many of these contaminants by selecting your food according to taste, safety, and nutritional value instead of merely by appearance.

43. You can ask the produce manager at your local grocery store to display the origins of all produce, as well as any pesticides, fumigants, or waxes that have been used. If the store carries organic produce, let them know that you are grateful; if not, encourage them to do so.

44. You can buy produce from farmers' markets and roadside stands. Even if the food isn't organically grown, it is less likely to have been heavily sprayed or waxed because it most likely has not travelled a great distance to get to you and is being sold soon after harvest.

45. You can show your appreciation to the farmers and other workers who have helped to grow your food by recognizing that pesticides and other poisons are not only bad for your body, but also represent serious dangers to workers when they are continuously exposed to these toxic chemicals. You can join César Chavez and the United Farm Workers (UFW) in boycotting fresh table grapes from California until grape growers stop using the five pesticides that cause the most danger to workers (captan, parathion, phosdrin, methyl bromide, and dinoseb).

46. You can buy foods grown by low-input sustainable agriculture (LISA), integrated pest management (IPM), organic agriculture, and other methods that rely on crop rotation, soil building through com-

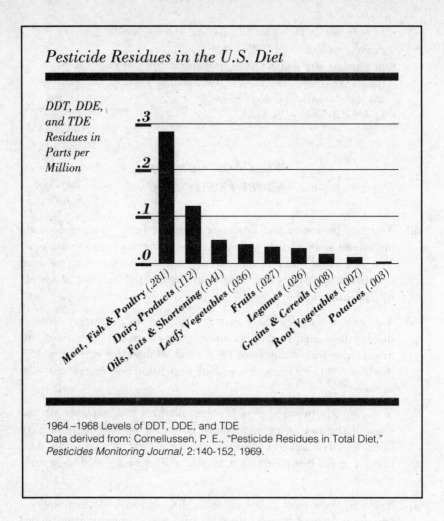

Pesticide Residues in the U.S. Diet

DDT, DDE, and TDE Residues in Parts per Million

1964–1968 Levels of DDT, DDE, and TDE
Data derived from: Cornellussen, P. E., "Pesticide Residues in Total Diet," *Pesticides Monitoring Journal*, 2:140-152, 1969.

post, and natural methods rather than on poisons and synthetic fertilizers. These forms of agriculture do not only produce healthier food. They also conserve natural resources like soil, water, and energy; protect wildlife and species diversity; reduce the use of dangerous chemicals in the food chains; and provide a better living and better health for farmers and farm workers.

47. You can get to know the growers at your local farmers' markets, learn about the methods they use, and thank them for their efforts.

What You Can Do
to Make Your Voice Heard

48. You can protest any presumption that meat is an indication of abundance or wealth, remembering that an increase in meat consumption means increased destruction and hardship for the world's ecosystems and people.

49. You can point out advertisements that encourage bad eating habits, raising awareness among your family and friends. When these ads are targeted at kids, you can report them to the Children's Advertising Review Unit of the Council of Better Business Bureaus, 845 Third Avenue, New York, NY 10022.

50. You can be alert to the tendency of advertisements from the meat industry to obscure the real issues, and you can draw attention to the real price we pay for meat—heart attacks, cancers, ecological havoc, and starvation.

51. You can participate in the Great American Meat-Out, which occurs one day each March. Contact the Farm Animal Reform Movement (see page 161) for information.

52. You can participate in the celebration of World Vegetarian Day on October 1 of every year. Contact the North American Vegetarian Society (see page 160) for information.

53. You can offer educational programs or cooking or food demonstrations to schools, service and religious groups, health clubs, scouts, and other organizations.

54. You can obtain packages of audio cassettes of John Robbins' talks from EarthSave (1-800-362-3648), and give these as gifts to others.

55. You can become vocal about the enormous influence livestock industries have had over our nation's food policies. You can lobby for the new basic four food groups, as suggested by the Physicians Committee for Responsible Medicine, EarthSave, and other public interest groups.

56. You can contact congressional representatives and editors of relevant publications and educate them about the connections between

a meat-centered diet, the depletion of our resources, and the spread of world hunger.

57. You can contact the World Bank and other international lending institutions and ask them to stop promoting and subsidizing cattle projects. Ask them instead to promote labor-intensive sustainable vegetable and grain farming that will provide jobs, food, and an ecologically sound agriculture.

58. You can write television and movie producers, asking them to stop presenting unhealthy food and drink as part of a desirable lifestyle. You can point out where programs associate unhealthy habits with glamor or power. Ask them to incorporate into their scripts the awareness of the real human and environmental costs. Remind them of the far-reaching influence they have. When TV programs portray healthful eating habits in a positive light, you can write letters of thanks and support.

59. You can participate in a nationwide campaign that has been launched to prompt the nation's major fast food chains to provide low-fat, no cholesterol, meat-free, fish-free, dairy-free, low-sodium entrées. Contact the North American Vegetarian Society (see page 160) for information.

60. You can put bumper stickers on your car and wear T-shirts that speak for your values and life direction.

61. You can join EarthSave and other worthy organizations, helping to spread the message of *May All Be Fed* and *Diet for a New America* to an ever-growing number of people (see page 159).

62. You can get copies of *Our Food, Our World*, the powerful booklet of facts based on *Diet for a New America* and *May All Be Fed*, and share them widely. EarthSave provides *Our Food, Our World* inexpensively in bulk quantities specifically for this purpose (see page 160).

63. You can prominently display the very popular and humorous poster of the full-page *New York Times* ad *How to Win an Argument with a Meat Eater* (available from EarthSave, see page 160) at libraries, supermarkets, natural food stores, co-ops, and other appropriate public places.

64. You can sponsor a healthful dinner, potluck supper, or a tasting party, providing literature (and great food!) to help educate others.

65. You can set up exhibits or pass out leaflets at public events, shopping malls, supermarkets, or fairs.

66. You can ask local restaurants and other meal suppliers to offer meat-free dishes, and thank them when they do.

67. You can host a dinner or luncheon for local legislators, religious leaders, teachers, and other educators, providing an educational presentation along with the food.

68. You can create a skit, rap song, piece of theater, or music to entertain and educate others about the implications of their food choices.

69. You can hire a plane to fly a banner over large public events, creating more awareness and discussion about important issues.

70. You can get "We serve vegetarian meals" window stickers from People for the Ethical Treatment of Animals (see page 161), and offer them to restaurants to put on their windows. These small yet eye-catching stickers are a great way to advertise to anyone who is looking for meat-free option that here is the place.

71. You can ask public, high school, and college libraries to set up displays featuring information and books about creating a healthy, sane, and compassionate society.

72. You can arrange for, or create and exhibit educational displays or banners in high-traffic public areas, such as bus signs and billboards.

73. You can give copies of *May All Be Fed* and *Diet for a New America* as gifts. Contact EarthSave (see page 160) for bulk and case prices.

74. You can make use of the PBS special "*Diet for a New America.*" Obtain a VHS videocasette of the program from EarthSave and show it to your family. EarthSave can also provide you with a *How to Host a Video Night* manual. Show the program at your school, church, or the next appropriate meeting of any social or civic organization. Donate a copy to your public library or arrange a public screening. Call your local PBS station program manager and tell him the documentary received a very high rating (3.5) in Los Angeles, was an extraordinarily successful pledge show, and that you feel it is an important story for your community. Station managers can call Jim Tabasz at KCET (213-666-6500) to schedule "*Diet for a New America.*"

What You Can Do at the Store

75. You can watch out for unhealthful products that claim to be sugar-free. They may still contain dextrose, corn syrup, fructose, high-fructose corn syrup, brown sugar, molasses, honey, or other sweeteners. While some of these alternatives may be slight improvements over sugar, they still provide only empty calories and virtually no nutrients, cause tooth decay, jar blood sugar levels, and contribute to overweightness.

76. You can remember that just because a product is sold in a health food store doesn't mean it is healthful. Many health food stores, for example, carry candies that are high in saturated fat from tropical oils (palm, palm kernel, coconut, and chocolate), and loaded with refined sweeteners (fructose and corn syrup).

77. You can emphasize vegetables, fruits, and whole grains in your shopping cart, knowing that these are the best sources of vitamins, minerals, complex carbohydrates, and dietary fiber.

78. You can reduce your risk of cancer by:

    • *Eating less fat and fewer animal products.*
    • *Eating dark green and yellow vegetables, which contain beta-carotene and other carotenoids and help protect against cancers of the breast, bladder, mouth, larynx, and esophagus.*
    • *Eating vegetables in the cabbage family, including Brussels sprouts, kale, turnips, broccoli, and cauliflower. They contain flavones, indoles, and other substances known to exhibit anti-cancer activity.*

79. You can eat plenty of fruits and vegetables. They contain Vitamin C, which has many benefits, including lowering the risk for many cancers.

80. You can try the various alternatives to cow's milk. Laws supported by the dairy industry do not allow the producers of other products to call them "milks," so soy, almond, rice, and potato-based substitutes have to be labeled "beverages" or "drinks."

81. You can tell your supermarket manager that you will not buy foods that have been exposed to radiation, nor will you shop in a store that sells them. Tell him or her that radiation-exposed foods receive

the equivalent of ten to thirty million chest X rays. Exposing foods to this kind of radiation depletes essential nutrients, including Vitamins A, C, E, K, and some Bs. It also makes foods unsafe, leaving residues that may cause cancer. (Contact Food and Water for more information; see page 160.)

82. You can maximize freshness and nutrition by:

- *Finding out what day your favorite bread is delivered to the store, and buying it then.*
- *Buying oils in small quantities, and keeping them in a cold, dark place.*

83. You can encourage the supermarket manager to handle organically produced commodities, locally grown when possible.

84. You can urge the produce manager at your local grocery or supermarket not to buy waxed fruits and vegetables. Fungicides, insecticides, and pesticides are often found in the waxes.

85. You can ask your supermarket to carry organic coffee, thereby doing a favor both to coffee drinkers, who won't be ingesting high levels of pesticides in their coffee, and to the organic coffee growers in the Third World.

86. You can buy environmentally benign and cruelty-free cleaners, laundry detergents, hand soaps, and personal care products. For a free catalog of cruelty-free products, contact The Compassionate Consumer, P.O. Box 27, Jericho, NY 11753 (718-445-4134), or Beauty Without Cruelty, 175 W. 12th St., New York, NY 10011.

What You Can Do in the Kitchen

87. You can cut back on fat by:

- *Limiting fried foods.*
- *Eating more vegetables, breads, beans, and fruits, and less meat and fewer dairy products.*
- *Sautéing onions and other vegetables in just a small amount of oil, or even using water instead of oil.*
- *Using mustards, tomato sauces, or vegetable spreads rather than fatty gravies, butter, mayonnaise, or margarine.*

• *Using apple butter or all-fruit jams on bread instead of butter, margarine, or cream cheese.*

88. You can be aware that saturated fats are the worst culprits. These include tropical oils (coconut, palm and palm kernel oil, and chocolate), all meats, dairy fats (ice cream, cheese, cream, butter, whole and low-fat milk), and eggs.

89. You can increase your fiber intake by:

• *Using whole wheat pastas instead of those made from white flour.*
• *Eating whole-grain cereals.*
• *Adding bran to cereals and pancake or muffin batters.*
• *Using whole wheat flour in baking.*
• *Choosing whole wheat or other whole-grain breads and crackers.*
• *Consuming more fresh fruit and vegetables.*

90. You can save yourself a lot of time and get optimum nutrition by:

• *Buying huge quantities of the finest and freshest organically grown vegetables at local farmers' markets in the fall and making great quantities of wonderful vegetable soups and stews from them to freeze for the rest of the year.*
• *Making big pots of soups, stews, and casseroles on the weekend, then keeping them in the refrigerator both for dinners during the week and to take for lunches to school and work.*

91. You can reduce pesticide exposure by:

• *Buying unsprayed or organic food whenever possible.*
• *Discarding the outer leaves of commercially grown leafy vegetables like lettuce and cabbage, and washing the inner leaves.*
• *Washing all the leaves of commercially grown greens like chard, kale, or collards, discarding any that are discolored.*
• *Peeling or very thoroughly scrubbing commercially grown potatoes, carrots, cucumbers, apples, peaches, tomatoes, and pears.*
• *Washing commercially grown eggplants, peppers, green beans, cherries, grapes, strawberries, cauliflower, broccoli, and spinach thoroughly.*
• *Avoiding commercially grown imported produce, because toxic*

*chemicals are often found at notoriously high levels on these
products.*

92. You can save the cooking water from cooking vegetables. This liquid
    is rich with the water-soluble flavors and nutrients. You can use it
    as the base for soups or broths.

93. You can grow a kitchen sprout garden. This takes no soil, and is
    especially useful in the winter when locally grown fresh produce
    may be scarce.

94. You can eat a healthier baked potato by leaving off the sour cream
    and butter, and instead topping it with steamed vegetables, or a
    sauce made with tamari, lemon juice, and olive oil. Once in a while,
    try a baked potato plain.

95. You can preserve vitamins and other nutrients by:

    * *Eating whole-grain rather than refined breads and cereals, and
      brown rice instead of white.*
    * *Steaming or pressure-cooking vegetables, rather than boiling
      them.*
    * *Using fresh fruits and vegetables in season, frozen as a second
      choice, and canned less often.*
    * *Storing perishable items like bread, flour, produce, seeds, nuts,
      and oils in sealed containers in your refrigerator (or freezer).*
    * *Avoiding prolonged soaking of fresh vegetables.*
    * *Preparing salads just before they are to be eaten.*
    * *Not overcooking vegetables.*

96. You can try the delicious recipes in this book.

*What You Can Do
to Learn More*

97. You can carefully read the ingredients lists on packaged foods in
    supermarkets and other food stores.

98. You can conduct a personal awareness exercise by keeping a food
    diary, writing down *everything* you eat for a week.

99. You can attend events, seminars, workshops, and other gatherings
    where activists in the health, environmental, and vegetarian move-

ments come together. EarthSave (see page 160) puts on excellent workshops, seminars, and wilderness outings. The North American Vegetarian Society (see page 160) puts on an annual four-day Summerfest.

100. You can get books, tapes, and other educational merchandise from EarthSave (see page 160) and other groups to further your awareness and effectiveness. As you become more educated, you can more confidently educate others, raising public awareness and deepening your commitment.

101. You can take advantage of the North American Vegetarian Society's offer for free rental of VHS videocassettes on related issues (see page 160).

102. You can get your blood pressure or cholesterol checked, avoid all animal products for a few weeks, and then get it checked again. You can then announce your discoveries and discuss them with family and friends.

103. You can notice how often people speak of specific foods as being "high in protein" as if this were an obvious good, and when possible speak out about this outdated cultural programming.

104. You can visit a slaughterhouse. This is an extremely eye-opening experience for many people. To find one near you, ask a local butcher.

How to Survive Creatively in a Meat-Based Culture

105. You can prepare your lunch at home, and take it with you, even to business meetings.

106. You can order vegetarian meals on all major airlines, if you or your travel agent call at least twenty-four hours in advance of your flight.

107. Before going to a party or other social gathering where you know the food will not be what you'd prefer, you can eat a good meal at home. This will help you to feel more comfortable at the activity and to avoid eating something you'd regret.

108. In restaurants, you don't have to choose only from what you see on the menu. You can tell them what you want, being clear and consistent about your preferences, and those restaurants who want to serve their customers will be glad to prepare it for you. Stick with simple things like baked potatoes, rice, spaghetti, salads (without eggs, ham, fish, etc.), or steamed vegetables. Sometimes several side dishes can make up a meal quite well.

109. You can go to restaurants that serve the kind of food you are happiest eating. Italian restaurants always have pasta dishes. Chinese restaurants are good for noodles and vegetable dishes. The better Mexican restaurants will be happy to make tacos, burritos, and enchiladas (you may want to make sure they don't use animal fat for cooking) to your preferences. East Indian restaurants are good places for rice curries. Natural food restaurants are good places to get meals based on tofu, tempeh, and other wholesome ingredients.

110. If you are the houseguest of someone who eats differently from the way you would like, you can offer to help out with the shopping and cooking.

111. If you eat in a cafeteria that offers nonmeat options, you can be very public about your appreciation. If they don't have any, you can tell them how much you and many others would like to see this changed.

112. When family members make healthy choices, you can tell them that you appreciate them for doing so. When they make unhealthy choices, you can tell them with all respect that you love them, and that you hate to see them hurting themselves.

113. You can bring a feeling of beauty and quiet to your dinners by sometimes having them by candlelight.

114. If you are eating a meal where it's not appropriate to ask others to share a moment of silence or to take time to give thanks, you can make it a point to pause for a few seconds before you eat, to slow down. Taking time to relax and bless the food will help you deal more gracefully with the social realities as well as aid your digestion.

115. When you want to give a gift to someone outside your immediate family, rather than buying them something, you can prepare whole-

some and delicious meat-free food and take it to them. How about a fruit basket that you arrange yourself? Or several containers of homemade soup?

116. You can write a letter of thanks to someone who has been a model to you or has in some other way helped you to move in a healthier and more conscious direction.

117. You can realize that we have come a long way in a short time. Not too many years ago the average American mother would have been more concerned to learn that her son or daughter was becoming "a vegetarian" than to learn that he or she was taking up smoking. But today the many positive benefits of a meat-free diet are gaining ever-wider recognition.

118. You can remember that people can change. One hundred thirty years ago, slavery was legal in this country. Only seventy years ago, women couldn't vote.

119. You can take pride in the steps you take personally to reduce or eliminate meat consumption, knowing that every move you make in this direction is a step toward a future that is healthy and sustainable. You can be an example to others by reducing your personal consumption of animal products.

120. You can invite friends and family to a special celebration meal, to inform them in a positive way about changes you are making in your food awareness and choices.

121. You can organize a meat-free Thanksgiving or Harvest Feast. For a truly memorable (and newsworthy) celebration, you can even find and invite a real live turkey to come and share the meal with you!

122. You can celebrate Thanksgiving by eating the same foods and feeling the same gratitude that were at the core of the meal when people originated the holiday. A Thanksgiving feast originally meant corn, beans, pumpkin, squash, berries, nuts, herbs, and maple syrup. For the pilgrims, the holiday started as a celebration of survival, of gratitude to the local natives who saved their lives, and of thankfulness for their first bountiful harvest of the lifesaving crop, corn. Native words for this grain translate as "our life," "it sustains us," and "giver of life."

123. You can refuse to be discouraged by the many signs that the Earth is the lunatic asylum of the solar system, and rejoice in the many signs that things are changing for the better. For example, even the fast food chains are becoming aware of the increasing concerns about health and nutrition. McDonald's is experimenting with a meat-free burger. Wendy's and Taco Bell have taken the animal fat out of their beans. Pizza Hut opened a test unit in Wichita, Kansas, that offers pasta. KFC (formerly Kentucky Fried Chicken) has been test marketing pasta dishes at its restaurants in Nevada. A chain in Chicago named Brown's Chicken started test marketing pasta in 1990. By 1991, various pasta dishes had been added in all 100 of its Chicago-area stores. The response was so over-whelmingly positive that the chain is now known as Brown's Chicken and Pasta. Burger King now broils its sandwiches, no longer uses animal fats for frying, has Paul Newman "natural ingredient" salad dressings, and is testing Weight Watchers brand vegetarian entrées. It's also considering offering a nonmeat burger in its U.S. outlets, similar to the Spicy Bean Burger it sells in the United Kingdom (made from red kidney beans, carrots, onions, peppers, green chilies, chili powder, mixed herbs, bread crumbs, potato flakes, garlic, white pepper, salt, wheat flour, and corn flour). How does it sell there? Corporate officials say "extremely well."

124. You can be an encouraging force, bringing love and awareness into the lives of all you meet.

EarthSave and Other Resources

EarthSave

If you feel touched by the message of *May All Be Fed,* you may well be interested in the work of **EarthSave,** the nonprofit organization I founded.

EarthSave is people of all kinds taking informed and significant action to heal our lives and our planet. Our "Healthy People, Healthy Planet" program works to get unbiased nutritional information taught in schools and low-fat, high-fiber plant-based options available in school cafeterias.

EarthSave believes that food is a basic and universal human right and ought not to be treated as just another commodity. We work to create a society built upon the certainty that all humanity is connected.

EarthSave invites people to live with a healthy respect for themselves and the interdependence of all life.

EarthSave's outstanding newsletter provides up-to-date information on the issues discussed in *May All Be Fed*. In addition, EarthSave offers substantial bulk discounts for ordering quantities of *Diet for a New America* and/or *May All Be Fed*. For information on a wide and excellent selection of related books, audio and video tapes, my speaking tours, seminars, workshops, wilderness outings, local support and action groups, school nutrition and environmental programs, and other activities, contact:

EarthSave, P.O. Box 68, Santa Cruz, CA 95063-0068

Organizations Concerned with Food and Health

Physicians Committee for
    Responsible Medicine
5100 Wisconsin Avenue,
    Suite 404
Washington, D.C. 20016
(202) 686-2210

North American Vegetarian
    Society
P.O. Box 72
Dolgeville, NY 13329
(518) 568-7970

American Vegan Society
501 Old Harding Highway
Malaga, NJ 08328

Beyond Beef
1130 17th Street,
    Suite 300
Washington, D.C. 20036
(202) 775-1132

Center for Science in the Public
    Interest
1875 Connecticut Avenue,
    N.W., Suite 300
Washington, D.C. 20009-5728
(202) 265-4954

Vegetarian Resource Group
P.O. Box 1463
Baltimore, MD 21203

Food and Water (food
    irradiation)
225 Lafayette Street, Suite 612
New York, NY 10012
(212) 941-9380;
    1-800-EAT-SAFE

Vegetarian Union of North
    America
P.O. Box 9710
Washington, D.C. 20016

Sprouts and Sprouting Information

Natural Food Systems, Inc.
P.O. Box 1028
Pagosa Springs, CO 81147
1-800-U-SHARED

Sprouting Publications
Box 62
Ashland, OR 97520

Organizations Concerned with the Treatment of Livestock

Farm Animal Reform Movement
P.O. Box 70123
Washington, D.C. 20088
(301) 530-1737

Humane Farming Association
1550 California Street, Suite 6
San Francisco, CA 94109
(415) 485-1495

Humane Society of the United
  States
2100 L Street, N.W.
Washington, D.C. 20037
(202) 452-1100

Compassion in World Farming
20 Lavant Street
Petersfield, Hants
England

People for the Ethical
  Treatment of Animals
P.O. Box 42516
Washington, D.C. 20015
(202) 726-0156

Progressive Animal Welfare
  Society
P.O. Box 1037
Lynnwood, WA 98046
(206) 743-3845

Farm Sanctuary
P.O. Box 150
Watkins Glen, NY
  14891-0150
(607) 583-2225

United Poultry Concerns
P.O. Box 59367
Potomac, MD 20859
(301) 948-2406

The Fund for Animals
850 Sligo Avenue
Suite LL2
Silver Spring, MD 20901
(301) 585-2591

Organizations Concerned with World Hunger

Food First
145 Ninth Street
San Francisco, CA 94103
(415) 864-8555

Oxfam America
115 Broadway
Boston, MA 02116
(617) 482-1211

American Friends Service
   Committee
1501 Cherry Street
Philadelphia, PA 19102
(215) 241-7000

Institute for Agriculture and
   Trade Policy
1313 5th Street, S.E., #303
Minneapolis, MN 55104
(612) 379-5980

Environmental Organizations

Greenhouse Crisis Foundation
1130 17th Street, N.W.,
   Suite 630
Washington, D.C. 20036
(202) 466-2823

Youth for Environmental Sanity
   (YES!)
706 Frederick Street
Santa Cruz, CA 95062
(408) 459-9344

Greenpeace USA
1611 Connecticut Avenue,
   N.W.
Washington, D.C. 20009
(202) 462-1177

Rainforest Action Network
301 Broadway, Suite A
San Francisco, CA 94133
(415) 398-4404

Earth Island Institute
300 Broadway, Suite 28
San Francisco, CA 94133-3312
(415) 788-3666

Friends of the Earth
530 7th Street, S.E.
Washington, D.C. 20003
(202) 543-4312

National Coalition against the
   Misuse of Pesticides
701 E Street, S.E., #200
Washington, D.C. 20003
(202) 543-5450

United Farm Workers (UFW)
P.O. Box 62
La Paz Street
Keane, CA 93531
(805) 822-5571

Public Lands Action Network
P.O. Box 712
Placitas, NM 87043
(505) 867-3062

Rest the West
P.O. Box 10065
Portland, OR 97210
(503) 645-6293

Breastfeeding

La Leche League
P.O. Box 1209
Franklin Park, IL 60131-8209
(708) 455-7730

Action for Corporate
   Accountability
129 Church Street
New Haven, CT 06510
(203) 787-0061

Recommended Magazines

World-Watch
1776 Massachusetts Ave.,
   N.W.
Washington, D.C. 20036

Earth Island Journal
300 Broadway, Suite 28
San Francisco, CA 94133-3312

Vegetarian Times
P.O. Box 446
Mt. Morris, IL 61054-9894
1-800-435-0715

Nurture
The Center to Prevent
   Childhood Malnutrition
3333 K Street, #101
Washington, D.C. 20007
(202) 338-6465

Natural Health
17 Station Street
Box 1200
Brookline, MA 02147

Health and Fitness Resorts

National Institute of Fitness
   (very reasonable rates)
P.O. Box 938
Ivins, Utah 84738

Rancho La Puerta
P.O. Box 69
Tecate, CA 91980
(619) 744-4222

We Care Health Center
18000 Long Canyon Road
Desert Hot Springs, CA 92240
1-800-888-2523

Hippocrates Health Institute
1443 Palmdale Court
West Palm Beach, FL 33411

PART TWO

KITCHEN PRAYER

May this kitchen be so filled with peace
  that all who eat food prepared here receive peace.
May this kitchen be so filled with happiness
  that all who eat food prepared here receive happiness.
May this kitchen be so filled with good will
  that working here is a joy.
Bless this kitchen.
Bless all who work here.
Bless the food that is prepared here.
May this kitchen and the work done here be a blessing to all
  who live.

EIGHT

Choosing Where You Shop

T he ambience, selection, convenience, quality, and costs vary so greatly from one food store to the next that one of the most important things you can do to help create a more healthy life is to choose carefully where you shop for food.

Supermarkets often have names that speak of security, centralization, and uniformity: *Safeway, Value-Mart, A & P, Grand Union.* Natural food stores, on the other hand, usually have names that speak of diversity and respect for the Earth: *Staff of Life, Whole Foods Market, Nature's Harvest, Nature's Pantry.*

You may be a bit apprehensive about shopping at stores with such eccentric names. But it is worth a try. In recent years, natural foods stores have taken a huge step forward. They are no longer a fringe phenomenon. Most of them are clean, well lit, accessible, and friendly.

Who shops in natural food stores? Sensible people who are willing to take action to create healthier and more wholesome alternatives to the junk food culture. These aren't people who have dropped out of society. They tend to be people who care about themselves and about the environment, and who are working responsibly for positive change.

Many supermarkets as well are expanding their selection of natural and vegetarian foods, and are likely to do so even more in the future. But these foods are not their specialty, and if your only experience of purchasing natural foods has been in a supermarket, you have a great treat in store for yourself.

To find the natural food stores in your area, ask for recommendations from friends who are vegetarians or health aficionados. Or, look in the yellow pages under "Health Food Stores." Which brings up the obvious question . . .

How to Recognize a Good Natural Food Store

The best natural food stores emphasize food. They often carry vitamins, supplements, and many other nonfood items, but they neither look nor feel like drugstores. Food is the priority. The store should be clean and well lighted. If the items on the shelves are dusty, this is a sign of slow turnover, and perhaps a signal to shop elsewhere. The store should be at least reasonably spacious, and the items clearly marked.

The best natural food stores have a large selection of "bag-it-yourself" foods that you can buy in bulk from bins. Bulk buying saves you money, and also saves on unnecessary packaging and waste.

The best natural food stores are dependable. They have clear policies and standards for freshness, quality, and wholesome ingredients. They maintain solid criteria for what they will and will not carry. For example, Mrs. Gooch's, a thriving chain of natural food stores in southern California, never carries anything with chemical additives, harmful preservatives, artificial flavorings and colorings, refined sugar, white flour, hydrogenated oil, or irradiated foods. Bread and Circus, a chain of natural food stores in New England, announces on every shopping bag that the store does not carry items containing preservatives, artificial colors and flavors, refined or synthetic sugars and sweeteners (including fructose), irradiated foods, and so forth. Each store has different standards and policies concerning what it will and will not sell. The important thing is that the standards are clear, and that they are upheld.

The best natural food stores are proud of their produce sec-

tions. They realize that at any given time of year the freshest produce is what is grown locally, and strive to carry as much as they can from local growers. They will often carry produce that's not specific to the region and season in order to provide as wide a selection as they can. But they go out of their way to provide produce from local farmers, including many small family farms.

That is one of the really special things about natural food stores. Most supermarkets can't take advantage of locally grown produce: It is too variable in availability and quantity, and they need uniformity. But although the bananas from Honduras, the tomatoes from Mexico, and the iceberg lettuce from California may be large and look pretty, they are likely to be weeks old and sprayed with poisons not only in the growing but in transit. Good natural food stores grab every chance they get to offer fresh local produce. Some of it may be only hours from the garden, tree, or vine.

The best natural food stores are part of a growing awareness about the ecological realities of food. They make it clear which items are organically grown and carry as many of these as they can. They recognize that organically grown food means more than the absence of detectable chemical residues. It means that the food was grown in an environmentally responsible way, with methods that conserve the quality of water, energy, and soil resources. They recognize, too, that petrochemical-based fertilizers supply only nitrogen, phosphorous, and potassium to the soil. Foods grown by organic methods, on the other hand, come from soil that has been replenished by the addition of organic materials rich in the full spectrum of minerals. Organically grown food is more healthful, not only because it is grown without poisons, but because it provides a complete range of minerals and other micronutrients.

The best natural food stores are at the vanguard of the emerging awareness of the diet-health-environment connection. They do not carry irradiated food, and they minimize products with unnecessary quantities of plastic and foam packaging. If they sell nonfood items, these also reflect a consciousness that respects the environment. They often sell napkins, toilet paper, and tissues that are made without artificial colors and scents, from recycled materials. They have household cleaning products that are phosphate-free and biodegradable. They provide cosmetics and personal care products that have not been tested on animals.

The best natural food stores provide services that cater to the specific needs of their clientele. They know that the people who shop in their store are special: They are not passive consumers; they are people who are taking active responsibility for their lives, and they want to be informed. The best stores provide educational programs and resources that recognize the interests of the people who shop there. These may include cooking classes, food and cooking demonstrations, community bulletin boards, and in-store recycling centers.

The best natural food stores are run by people who love what they are doing. They believe in their products. They are informed and eager to share their knowledge. You may find tofu at Safeway, but you won't find anyone there who can tell you what to do with it. Some natural food stores have people on staff who shepherd first-time shoppers through the aisles, sharing recipes and cooking tips.

Other Food Shopping Options

Local farmers' markets are often wonderful places to get fresh fruits and vegetables, and they usually provide not only the freshest of foods, and sometimes substantial savings, but also the special treat of buying directly from the people who grew the food. I treasure the opportunity to make friends with the people who grow the food my family eats. Knowing them, I feel more connected to the Earth that sustains us all.

Of course, just because you buy from a friendly farmer doesn't mean the food is organically grown. You must ask. At many farmers' markets, the farmers post signs saying whether their products are unsprayed and organically grown, in some cases even saying how many years the soil has been treated organically.

Co-ops are another alternative. They differ from natural food stores in that they are owned and managed by consumers. The investment and involvement of the community often allow co-ops to reflect and serve the needs of the community in special ways. Shoppers are encouraged to become members, and all key decisions, including electing and serving on the co-op board of directors, are made by the consumer/owners. Co-ops purchase directly from wholesalers and can sometimes offer significant savings.

Another option is to buy a share in the harvest of an organic farm. Subscription farming programs allow consumers to pay organic farmers in advance for a portion of the annual harvest.

Farmers' markets and co-ops aside however, the primary access most of us have to whole food is through natural food stores. Many people think these are wonderful places to shop **if** you happen to have an unlimited amount of cash. The truth, though, is there is a secret to buying at natural food stores that can save you bundles of money.

Saving Money

When I was young I thought that money was the most important thing in life; now that I am old I know that it is. (Oscar Wilde)

Supermarkets carry vast amounts of packaged items, which they buy in freight-car quantities. Natural food stores can't compete with the buying power enjoyed by the large chain supermarkets, and so if you compare the prices of packaged goods in supermarkets with the prices of packaged goods in natural food stores, it is likely that it will appear that shopping in a supermarket will be less expensive. You still may prefer the items in natural food stores, though, for they usually do not contain the sugar, preservatives, and other artificial additives and chemicals typical of much supermarket fare. Additionally, some of the items in the aisles of natural food stores are made from organically grown ingredients, a major plus for both your body and the ecosystems on which our lives so intimately depend.

Where natural food stores outshine supermarkets in terms of price is in selling bulk foods. Supermarkets usually don't have significant bulk-food sections, and if they do the products they sell in bulk are rarely the kind of wholesome and healthful foods to base a diet around. Natural food stores virtually all have basic food staples like rice, beans, oats, whole wheat flour, raisins, pastas, sunflower seeds, and many other items in bulk, at significantly lower prices than if they were prepackaged. If a health food store doesn't have bulk staples, it is probably more of a "supplement" store, and not the best of places to shop for food.

The primary rule of saving money in a natural food store is simple: Buy in bulk.

Once through the door of the store, pick up your shopping cart and head directly for the bulk bins, and from there to the produce department. These are the areas where your dollars will be most productively spent.

You will be amazed at how much money you can save by buying beans, grains, vegetables, fruit, seeds, and just about anything else by the pound, compared to buying the same items prepackaged.

A corollary to the primary rule of saving money is: Move away from processed and refined foods and toward foods in their more natural state.

By eating this way you take in fewer chemicals and more natural nutrients. This means eating more baked potatoes and fewer potato chips, more homemade cookies and fewer of the packaged variety, more soups made by you from fresh vegetables and fewer soups made by multinational companies from the cheapest thing they could find. It means opening fewer cans and being more creative in the kitchen. It means saving yourself the privilege of paying extra to have the food you eat mangled by corporations that try to make up for their lack of skill in food preparation by dosing almost everything they sell with excessive quantities of salt, sugar, and various fats.

The Test

Can you really save money by buying whole foods in bulk at a natural food store? To find out, I take pen and paper in hand and make a trip to my local Safeway, and then to my local natural food store, Staff of Life. (Since Santa Cruz, California, is something of a natural food heaven, the prices at Staff of Life may be lower than they would be in natural food stores in other parts of the country.)

I compare prices for a number of staple items, going to the bulk bins at Staff of Life and pricing out the same items, packaged, at Safeway. I figure out the price of the various packaged items per pound or per pint. Items in smaller-sized packages usually cost more, of course. Here is a representative sample of what I find:

Raisins: Safeway sells three different-sized packages of Sun Maid brand raisins, ranging from $1.70/pound to $3.41/pound. Staff of Life offers organically grown raisins in bulk for $1.59/pound.

Almonds: Safeway has Azar brand almonds in 2-ounce packages for $.97 ($7.76/pound). Staff of Life has organically grown almonds in bulk for $3.25/pound.

Olive oil: Safeway has several different brands of extra virgin, ranging from $2.82/pint to $6.71/pint. They also sell pure olive oil, an inferior product, for similar prices. Staff of Life has extra virgin on tap at $2.90/pint, does not carry lesser-quality oil.

Sesame oil: Safeway's least expensive is Dynasty brand in 12-ounce bottles for a price that comes to $7.59/pint. Staff of Life has sesame oil on tap for $3.47/pint.

Soy sauce: Safeway sells Kikkoman soy sauce, an inferior product made with the preservative sodium benzoate, in several sizes, ranging from $1.92/pint to $2.72/pint. They also sell tamari (a Japanese soy sauce made without wheat, a much better product) for $4.32/pint. Staff of Life has tamari on tap for $1.17/pint.

Buckwheat groats: Safeway's best buy is Wolff's brand toasted buckwheat groats for $2.70/pound. Staff of Life sells organically grown toasted buckwheat groats in bulk for $2.28/pound.

Tahini: Safeway's only tahini is Joyva brand for $3.62/pound. Staff of Life has tahini in bulk for $3.25/pound.

Brown rice: Safeway sells packaged brown rice in several sizes, the least expensive of which comes to $.86/pound. Staff of Life sells brown rice in bulk for $.40/pound, and organically grown brown rice in bulk for $.79/pound.

Pinto beans: Safeway sells dried pinto beans in several package sizes, the least expensive for $.99/pound. Staff of Life sells organically grown pinto beans in bulk for $.89/pound.

Oats: Safeway sells Quaker old-fashioned oats for $1.56/pound. Staff of Life sells organically grown rolled oats in bulk for $.79/pound.

NINE

Stocking a Healthy Pantry

Because there are ingredients used in *May All Be Fed* that you may not be familiar with, we have compiled the following information.

Agar-Agar, sometimes called *kanten,* is a natural gelling agent made from seaweed and rich in iron. Tasteless and colorless, agar-agar can be used in place of animal gelatin in any recipe (although less agar-agar is required). It comes in powder, flakes, bars, and sticks. The powder, which dissolves most easily and is the most concentrated, is sold loose by the ounce in natural food stores. The flakes are sold in small packages. Bars and sticks are harder to find but both are sold packaged and are available at large natural food stores.

A teaspoon of agar-agar powder or two teaspoons of flakes firmly gels one cup of liquid. For a softer gel, use less agar-agar, and for a less rubbery end result, use one part agar-agar powder to three parts arrowroot powder. Add agar-agar to a cool liquid, bring the mixture to a boil, lower the heat, and simmer for about two minutes. As it cools, the mixture will gel. At room temperature this takes from twenty to thirty minutes, depending on the amount of food; in the refrigerator, the process takes about half as long.

Almond Milk is made from almonds soaked in water. It can be substituted directly for cow's milk (or goat's) in most recipes. Almond milk, along with rice beverage and soy milk, is recommended for use in drinks, pancakes, breads, soups, sauces, main dishes, and desserts. A cup of soaked or blanched almonds makes a quart of almond milk (page 209) or one cup of more intensely flavored almond cream (page 382).

You can buy an excellent commercial product called White Almond Beverage in natural food stores. It's made by Wholesome and Hearty Foods in Portland, Oregon, and can be used in place of cow's milk with very good results. Sold in quart-size, shelf-stable, recyclable aseptic containers. It should be refrigerated after opening and used within a week or so.

Apple Juice (unfiltered) is the next best thing to juicing your own apples. Unlike clear, pasteurized apple juice, unfiltered juice looks cloudy, and sediment often collects at the bottom of the bottle. It contains a higher volume of whole fruit and therefore tastes more of the apple. The best apple juice is made without added preservatives, artificial colors, or added sweeteners. It is readily available at natural food stores and some supermarkets. After opening, it should be refrigerated and consumed within several days. Unfiltered apple juice is also called apple cider, depending on where it is made and how the manufacturer decides to label it. In the fall, apple orchards in the Northeast, northern Midwest, and Northwest often make their own cider. If possible, buy it from organic orchards.

Arrowroot Powder is made from the West Indian arrowroot plant. This digestible starch is used to thicken desserts, soups, sauces, and Oriental dishes. Arrowroot, which can be substituted for cornstarch and is preferred because it is a whole food and relatively unprocessed, makes transluscent sauces with no floury aftertaste. It is especially good for fruit desserts and other preparations that require little or no cooking, and a light dusting is recommended for vegetables to be stir-fried. Arrowroot does not have to reach the boiling point to thicken. It is easy to find on the spice shelf in supermarkets and natural food stores. Store arrowroot in a cool, dry cupboard. It keeps almost indefinitely, although it is recommended that you use it within a year of purchase.

As a general guideline, a tablespoon of arrowroot powder thickens a cup of liquid. For a thicker mixture, use two tablespoons per cup. Dissolve the arrowroot powder by stirring it into an equal amount of cool liquid before adding it to the dish you are preparing, then stir the mixture in during the last minute or so of cooking time.

Baking Powder should be the nonaluminum type, such as Rumford. Rumford is available in supermarkets and natural food stores and is actually slightly less expensive than other brands. It reacts in recipes just as any baking powder does. Natural food stores also sell sodium-free baking powders, which are less powerful than Rumford, and so twice the amount of regular baking powder called for in most recipes should be used.

You can make your own baking powder by combining two parts cream of tartar, one part baking soda (sodium bicarbonate), and two parts arrowroot.

Barley Malt Syrup is a grain-based sweetener made by cooking the liquid extracted from fermented, partially sprouted barley to a syrup consistency. It has a distinct flavor, similar to molasses but somewhat less intense. Barley malt syrup contains some complex carbohydrates and has less impact on the body's metabolism than most refined sweeteners, causing less of a sugar high. Buy barley malt syrup in natural food stores and store it in a cool, dry place.

Bran is the outside shell of a whole grain, which protects the germ so that it can sprout. Bran is well known for its high fiber content and is a healthful addition to diets high in processed foods, although it is usually not necessary in vegetarian diets. The most common type of bran is made from wheat, but oat and rice are also available. Bran sold in natural food stores is referred to as unprocessed bran or bran flakes. It's used in baking and cooking to bolster the fiber content of the finished dish.

Buckwheat Flour has a distinctive hearty flavor. Despite its name, buckwheat is a plant that is related to sorrel and rhubarb, with no relation to wheat. Whole buckwheat groats, sometimes called *kasha*, are usually toasted before sold for consumption and cooking. Buckwheat flour is gluten-free and therefore must be combined with wheat flour in recipes requiring rising. Buckwheat flour is most commonly used in pancakes. We export buckwheat flour to Japan, where it is made into soba and buckwheat noodles. When buying buckwheat flour, look for the stone-ground product, which is called dark buckwheat flour, made from un-hulled buckwheat and containing small, dark flecks. Store buckwheat flour in the refrigerator and use within a few weeks; it keeps in the freezer for about two months.

Bulgur is a precooked, nutty-flavored grain made from steamed, dried, and cracked wheat. Traditionally featured in Balkan and Middle Eastern cooking, it is used in tabouleh and other dishes in place of rice. Bulgur is available in bulk and packaged in natural food stores and packaged in supermarkets. It requires little or no cooking and will soften to a palatable consistency after it is steamed or soaked in hot water. Store bulgur in cool, dry cupboards and use within a month.

Canola Oil is made from a strain of rapeseed developed in Canada (which explains its name). It is primarily mono-unsaturated fat and a good source of Omega-3 fatty acids. The oil is light colored and prac-tically flavorless, and it has a high smoking point making it a good choice for cooking. El Molino Canola Mist, an oil spray propelled from a non-aerosol can without aid of harmful chemicals, is used as any cooking oil spray is used. Both canola oil and El Molino Canola Mist are sold in supermarkets and natural food stores, although the mist is often harder to locate. Canola oil should be stored in a cool, dark, place. Keep it tightly capped and use it within a few months.

Cardamom is used in Indian, Middle Eastern and Scandinavian cook-ing. It is especially compatible with such vegetables as winter squash, sweet potatoes, and pumpkins. It is used in custards, cakes, and cookies as well as in the Indian spice blend called *garam masala* and in curry powder. It is sold ground or whole, in the pod. Like other spices, cardamom should be stored away from direct light in a cool, dry place. Use it within three or four months.

Carob Powder is a dark brown powder made from the dried pods of the honey locust tree, which grows primarily in Mediterranean countries. It is a delicious, healthful alternative to chocolate, which is highly sweetened to counteract its natural bitterness, is high in fat, and contains caffeine. In contrast, carob is naturally sweet, low in fat, and caffeine-free. What is more, carob is high in fiber and calcium. Carob is available in powder and chip form, although the chips may contain partially hydrogenated palm kernel oil or coconut oil, milk products, soya, lec-ithin, and malted corn or barley. Sweetened chips may also contain refined sugar—it's important to read the label carefully. Carob can usually be substituted in equal measure for cocoa in beverages, candies, and desserts. Add some instant roasted grain beverage for a coffeelike flavor. Store carob in a cool, dark cupboard and use within several months.

Catsup is most familiar as a bottled condiment, notorious for being loaded with refined sugar. However, fruit-sweetened and unsweetened brands are available at natural food stores. These tend to be lower in sodium as well and contain no preservatives or chemicals. Although catsup does not have to refer to a tomato-based sauce, most versions are. Store catsup in the refrigerator after opening.

Cornmeal is ground more coarsely than flour; for improved texture, some recipes call for it to be mixed with wheat flour. Most often it is used in muffins and breads or cooked for a hot cereal. Cornmeal is made from dried corn kernels; stone-ground meal is preferable to other kinds. Its shelf life is shorter than that of wheat flour and, unless you plan to use it within a week or two, it should be stored in the refrigerator well wrapped in plastic or in a tightly sealed container. Refrigerated, it will keep for several months.

Couscous is made from precooked cracked millet or from coarsely ground semolina, a flour made by highly refining durum wheat, and some is made from whole wheat. Couscous made from whole wheat flour is the most healthful; a more nutritious choice is to buy bulgur, which can be substituted for couscous in nearly any recipe.

Couscous is sold in bulk and packaged in natural food stores, and packaged couscous is frequently available in supermarkets. Store it in a cool, dry, dark place and use it soon after opening or purchase. Couscous also refers to a traditional dish served in North Africa (where the grain is made from millet or from coarse semolina) with vegetables and meats. It can be used to make nutritious vegetable salads and many other grain-based dishes.

Dried Beans, sold in packages in supermarkets and in bulk in natural food stores, are good sources of calcium and protein. Regardless of where you buy them, pick them over and rinse them well before soaking. All dried beans, or legumes as they are also known, should be soaked before they are cooked to soften their tough, insoluble fiber. Depending on the type of beans, soak them for four to eight hours; then drain and proceed according to the recipe. Another way to soften beans is to quick-soak them: Put them in water to cover, bring to a boil, and boil for one minute; then remove from the heat, cover, and let stand for an hour. Drain and proceed with the recipe.

Dried beans can be stored in a cool, dry place for many months without loss of nutritional value.

Dried Fruit offers concentrations of nutrients, fiber, and fruit sugars. Beware of bright-colored dried fruits for they may be treated with sulphur dioxide, which prevents discoloring, and potassium sorbate to suppress the growth of fungi and molds; many imported and domestic dried fruits are fumigated to kill insects. Unsulphured dried fruits are available in natural food stores and by law must be so labeled. These usually are pesticide-free as well. For a sweet snack, dried fruits are a satisfying alternative to cookies and candies. They also are delicious in baked goods, cereals, and stuffings. They are available all year and, with the exception of dates, do not require refrigeration. Keep them in an airtight container or plastic bag to prevent further drying, and keep in a cool, dark place.

Dried Herbs and Spices are best stored in small glass jars, although many manufacturers package them in plastic. Store them in a cool, dark, dry cupboard, as heat and humidity accelerate deterioration. Home-dried herbs often freeze well (basil is an exception), although they lose their bright color once dried. Ground and powdered herbs and spices lose flavor and potency more quickly than whole spices and seeds and should be used within three to four months. Whole spices, such as cinnamon sticks and mustard seeds, will keep for up to a year. It is a good idea to date the jars and replace them regularly. If a recipe calls for a tablespoon of fresh herb, use a teaspoon of dried (or a third as much). For the best flavor, rub the dried herb between your fingers or in the palm of your hand for a few seconds before adding it to the food to release the aromatic oils.

Dulse is a purplish leafy sea vegetable that is used to flavor food. Purchased as dried leaves or granules, it can be eaten as a snack or added to vegetable and grain dishes, soups, stews, salads, and sandwiches. Because it contains only 2 to 4 percent sea salt, it adds a briny, but not fishy, flavor to food rather than an unpleasantly salty one. For milder flavor, soak dulse leaves in water for about ten minutes and rinse them well. Dulse leaves are soft and chewy.

Filo or Phyllo Dough is a paper-thin pastry dough that figures prominently in Greek cuisine. Traditionally used for making vegetable pies such as spanakopita and desserts such as baklava, filo has numerous culinary uses. When baked, it produces a crisp, flaky crust. Filo is similar to strudel dough and, like strudel, is extremely hard to make at home. Most cooks buy it frozen in supermarkets or specialty shops. It keeps in the freezer for months. Filo dough dries out quickly at room temperature, so keep it covered with a damp dishcloth during food preparation. Nearly all filo is made from white flour, although some companies now are making whole wheat filo. It is still hard to find, even in natural food stores.

Flours are made from the finely ground berries or seeds of grasses. Unrefined flours made from whole grains are better tasting and more nutritious than refined flours, and of these, flours made from organic grains are the best.

Most Americans equate flour with refined white flour, which is valueless from a nutritional standpoint. Almost anything you can make from refined flour can be made from whole-grain flour. Wheat flour is best for making light breads and puffy desserts because of its high gluten content. Gluten is an elastic protein that, when heated to a certain temperature, expands like thousands of little balloons to hold the carbon dioxide released by yeast or baking powder and causes the dough to rise. Other flours have little or no gluten and so are frequently combined with wheat flour in recipes. The less wheat flour, the denser the baked good.

Stone-ground whole wheat flour is the best for bread. It has plenty of gluten for good rise and the nutrition of the whole kernel. Whole wheat pastry flour is more finely milled than bread flour and has less gluten, making it more desirable for cakes, cookies, and pie crusts.

All flour is best stored in a tightly sealed container in a cool, dry place. Refrigeration increases their shelf life somewhat, but also adds moisture, which must be taken into consideration in preparing a recipe. The humidity of the day, the heat of the kitchen, and the moisture content of the flour always affect the final product, which is why most bread recipes list a varying measure of flour. If well wrapped, flour will keep in the freezer for a month or two—a good idea in the summer, when the humidity is high and most people do less baking than usual.

Fresh Herbs are becoming more and more widely available all year round in supermarkets, green grocers, specialty shops, and natural food stores. Parsley is so readily available that there is no reason ever to use dried. Thyme, tarragon, chives, basil, mint, and rosemary are often available in the markets, and during the summer months the variety increases. Buy small bunches of herbs with bright green leaves. Rinse them under cold running water and shake dry. When completely dry, wrap the herbs in paper or cloth towels and store in the refrigerator. (If you store them damp, they will spoil more rapidly.) Use the herbs within a week—sooner if possible.

Chop or tear the leaves and add to soups, casseroles, sautés, stews, salads, breads, sauces, and spreads. Depending on the recipe, it is usually best to add herbs toward the end of cooking. If you must substitute dried herbs for fresh, use a third as much, as the flavor of dried herbs is more concentrated and intense.

If you have a sunny kitchen window, try growing your own herbs in pots. Most do well with minimal care and, you can snip what you need any time. Your kitchen will smell lovely, too. In the summertime, move the "herb garden" to the porch or deck.

FruitSource® is a new commercially available sweetener made from grape juice and whole rice syrup. It is 35 percent complex carbohydrates. FruitSource is about 20 percent less sweet than cane sugar, and its pleasant taste works well in many recipes. To use it in a recipe, mix it with the liquid ingredients and let sit for two to three minutes before combining with the dry ingredients. FruitSource is available in granules and liquid form in many natural food stores, or it can be ordered from FruitSource Associates, 1803 Mission Street, Suite 404, Santa Cruz, California 95060.

Gingerroot is available all year round in supermarkets, green grocers, and natural food stores in the produce section. Fresh ginger should be plump and firm and show no evidence of dryness or mold. The small greenish knobs growing from the root are new growth and have a milder taste. Gingerroot should be stored in a dry place. It will keep for several weeks. Unless especially tough, fresh ginger does not need to be peeled before cooking.

Grain Beverages and Grain Coffees are made from roasted grains and seeds such as barley, rye, and/or wheat. They are sometimes flavored with malt, beet root, figs, chicory, and/or acorns. The quick-to-dissolve powders produce a hot beverage with a rich, coffeelike flavor and no caffeine. These instant powders are the most popular, but coarser grinds for brewing are also available. The best known brands, such as Cafix, Inka, and Pero, are readily available in natural food stores. Stored in a cool cupboard, they keep for months.

Liquid Amino is a seasoning liquid made from soy beans with a salty taste similar to soy sauce. Not fermented, and containing no additives or preservatives, it adds a rich, savory flavoring to salads, soups, sauces, potatoes, rice, and tofu dishes. Often used to replace salt, one tablespoon of liquid amino is the equivalent of one teaspoon of salt. The product is sold under the brand name Bragg Liquid Aminos and is available in two sizes in natural food stores or from its distributor, Live Food Products, Box 7, Santa Barbara, California 93102.

Maple Syrup is made by tapping the sap from maple trees and then boiling the clear, almost tasteless liquid until it is concentrated, full flavored, amber colored, thick and syrupy. Approximately forty gallons of sap are necessary to make a single gallon of syrup. Fortunately, the distinctive flavor of maple syrup means that a little goes a long way. Maple syrup has more nutrients and less concentrated sucrose then white sugar, but should still be used in moderation, as should all sweeteners. Syrups labeled "maple flavored" are likely to be pure sugar or corn syrup with artificial maple flavoring and coloring added. Newly-made maple syrup is available in the spring shortly after sugaring season, but sold year round, and keeps in the refrigerator for up to a year. Unhappily, overtapping and maple tree blight are making supplies limited and expensive.

Mayonnaise is a condiment that most health-conscious people avoid as it is made from eggs and oil and is high in cholesterol. However, natural food stores carry "mayonnaises" that are made from tofu and are cholesterol-free. These are priced competitively with supermarket brands. They must always be refrigerated.

Millet is an ancient grain that is still a major food source in Asia and North Africa (see Couscous). In India, the grain is ground into flour for a flat bread called *roti*. In this country we use most of our millet crop for birdseed; that destined for human consumption is hulled and sold primarily in natural food stores. The tiny round yellow grain may be eaten as a breakfast cereal or used in soups and main courses, much as you would use rice. It is slightly crunchy and nutty in flavor. To cook millet, combine one part millet with two parts water, bring to a boil, and simmer (covered) for thirty-five to forty minutes. Store millet in a cool, dry place or the refrigerator for several months.

Miso is a traditional Japanese food made from fermented soy beans, rice, barley, and other grains. It is used primarily as a salty seasoning and as a base for dips, dressings, sauces, and soups. Different types of miso vary in flavor, aroma, and color. Light, sweet, creamy miso is a good dairy substitute in mashed potatoes and soups and can be used in place of sour cream in dips, spreads, sauces, and salad dressings. Dark miso is saltier and should be used sparingly in bean, and grain dishes and in hearty soups and stews. Dark miso is fermented for as long as three years; it's sold as barley miso, brown rice miso, and red miso. Miso is high in B-complex vitamins. Avoid boiling miso which destroys some of its nutritional value and its digestive properties. Stored in the refrigerator in a tightly sealed container, miso will keep for months.

Molasses is a by-product of sugar refining and, like sugar, is mostly empty calories. It contains some nutrients, but the amount is negligible. Its distinctive taste makes molasses a desirable sweetener for some preparations, particularly bread and bean dishes such as Boston baked beans. If possible, buy unsulphured molasses. Avoid blackstrap molasses; it tastes very bitter. Whenever possible, substitute barley malt syrup for molasses.

Mustard is a popular condiment used to flavor sauces, salads, vegetables, and other dishes. It ranges from mild to hot and often is flavored with spices, herbs, wine, and/or vinegar. Yellow mustard is mild tasting and is made from ordinary yellow mustard seeds. Dijon mustard is made from brown mustard seeds and most varieties are imported from France. Chinese mustard, made from both brown and yellow seeds, is very hot and should be used sparingly. If preparing mustard from powdered mustard, mix it with water no more than thirty minutes before using, as its flavor diminishes as it stands.

Mustard Seeds have a mild, tangy flavor that adds good taste to pickles, salad dressings, and other preparations. Most Americans are familiar with yellow mustard seeds. Stored in a cool, dark place, mustard seeds will keep up to a year.

Nori is a mild-flavored cultivated sea vegetable that is commonly used for wrapping steamed rice to make sushi. It is also used to garnish grain and vegetable dishes. Nori comes dried in paper-thin black sheets about seven inches square. Use nori as it comes from the package for making sushi. For garnishing, toast it lightly over an open flame or in a moderate oven until it turns shiny green and crisp. (This takes only about a minute, so watch carefully.) Crumble or cut the toasted nori and sprinkle it over salads, soups, pasta, rice, potatoes, and even air-popped popcorn. Dried nori sheets keep for months in a cool, dry cupboard.

Nut and Seed Milks can be directly substituted for cow's milk in most recipes. Any nut or seed can be blended with water to make "milk." Among the most commonly used are cashews, pecans, walnuts, sesame seeds, and sunflower seeds. You can find nut and seed milks in natural food stores, but because it's difficult to stabilize the product, it is usually advisable to make your own if possible (see page 209). Some natural food stores and health bars do make these milks fresh and sell them as a perishable item. Nut and seed milks should always be refrigerated. (See Almond Milk for information on White Almond Beverage.)

Nutritional Yeast is a food supplement rich in the B-vitamin complex, with a delicious cheesy flavor. It should not be confused with brewer's yeast, which tastes bitter, or the yeast used for leavening. Use nutritional yeast to add flavor and nutrients to salads, sauces, soups, and main dishes. It is even good sprinkled over popcorn. Add nutritional yeast toward the end of cooking, as prolonged heating, and boiling in partic- ular, diminish its nutritional value. Be sure you buy the product grown for supplemental nutrition purposes, not one that is a by-product of brewing. It is inexpensive and readily available packaged or in bulk in natural food stores.

Nuts are high in unsaturated fats. Sold both packaged and loose, nuts are available shelled or not, roasted, raw, salted, unsalted, and flavored. A good rule of thumb is to buy nuts closest to their natural form. Nuts in the shell keep the longest; packaged chopped nuts may already be rancid. Their oil content causes nuts to turn rancid easily, so it's a good idea to store them in the refrigerator in a tightly covered container. Some nuts, such as pecans and walnuts, do very well frozen for several months. In general, buy nuts only as needed, from a reputable store with good turnover.

Olive Oil is made by pressing the oil from the soft pulp of olives. The best olive oils come from the first pressing and are labeled "extra virgin." "Virgin" olive oil is next best. Oils labeled "pure" are from later press- ings and are often extracted at high temperatures and/or with chemical solvents.

Olive oil has an exquisite flavor and fragrance and is excellent in salad dressings. Its relatively low smoking point (375°F) makes it less acceptable for sautéing and stir frying. Unless you use it frequently, it is advisable to buy olive oil in small quantities. Store it in a cool, dry place. It lasts longer in the refrigerator but will cloud up and develop hard, milky particles when cold; these, however, disappear at room temperature and the oil returns to its natural clear state.

Olives come in a variety of colors, sizes, and flavors. We recommend using imported olives from the Mediterranean, which include brownish-black Greek Kalamatas, black French *niçoise* olives, and large Sicilian green olives. They keep indefinitely in the refrigerator. Canned ripe olives are comparatively tasteless.

Pasta is made from flour and water and, sometimes, salt. Some pastas include vegetables, such as spinach, carrots, and tomatoes, to provide color and subtle flavor. Some pastas also contain eggs. Products called "noodles" usually contain 5½ percent egg product.

Dry pasta keeps for months stored in a cool, dry place. It stands up to hearty sauces but can also complement more delicate toppings. Many shoppers prefer fresh pasta, which is sold in the refrigerator sections of a growing number of supermarkets and in specialty shops. Fresh whole wheat and vegetable pastas frequently are available in natural food stores. Fresh pasta should be stored in the refrigerator and used as soon as possible. Fresh pasta cooks faster than dried pasta, usually needing only a minute or two in boiling water.

Quinoa, pronounced "keen-wa," is a nutritious grain with a delicate, pleasant flavor. It is quick to prepare and easy to digest. The plant has been cultivated in Peru for thousands of years and is now being grown in Colorado and elsewhere with good results. Quinoa seeds, which are yellowish and slightly larger than mustard seeds, are covered with a substance called saponin that protects them from insects and birds. Because saponin tastes bitter, quinoa should be rinsed well in hot water before using. If desired, toast the seeds briefly before further cooking to help bring out their nutty flavor.

Rice is the staff of life for more than half the world's population. More than 98 percent of the rice grown in the United States is milled into white rice, which means the germ and bran are removed, and with them much of the nutrients. Brown rice is more nutritious than white and tastes better, too. There are several sorts of brown rice, all are best if organically grown.

Basmati brown rice, native to the foothills of the Himalayas, is the rice traditionally used in Indian cooking. Recently introduced domestic varieties are thriving in the United States due to their full flavor and delicious aroma. Basmati brown rice is available in some supermarkets and in specialty stores, Indian and Pakistani markets, and natural food stores.

Brown rice is the whole grain with only the indigestible hull removed. It is available as short-, medium-, and long-grain rice, with the short tending to be stickier and denser and best for croquettes, patties, and sushi. Long-grain brown rice is the most commonly consumed and is available in supermarkets, specialty stores, and natural food stores.

Sweet brown rice is relatively unknown. Its sweet flavor and sticky consistency make it ideal for croquettes and patties, sushi, rice puddings, and other confections. It is sold in natural food stores and some specialty shops.

To cook brown rice, brings two parts water to a boil, then add one part brown rice. Cover, bring to a boil, and simmer for forty-five to fifty minutes. Remove the pot from the heat and let the rice stand, covered, for ten minutes. (The secret is to leave the pot covered the entire time.) Rice does not require stirring while cooking.

Rice Beverage is a commercially available product made from fermented rice. It can be directly substituted for dairy milk in most recipes. It is made by Imagine Foods in Palo Alto, California, which sells the beverage under the Rice Dream label. It is sold in natural food stores in eight-ounce and one-quart shelf-stable, recyclable aseptic containers. It must be refrigerated after opening; use it within a week or less.

Rice Flour has no gluten and is of value to people with wheat allergies and gluten intolerance. Rice flour produces dense-textured baked goods; it is particularly good for thickening sauces and gravies. Brown rice flour is better tasting and more nutritious than white rice flour; organically grown is best. Rice flour does not behave as wheat flour and therefore cannot be directly substituted in recipes. Rice flours are available at natural food stores. Store in a tightly sealed container in a cool, dry place or in the refrigerator.

Rice Syrup, also known as rice malt, is a sweetener made by cooking the liquid from fermented rice until it thickens to syrupy consistency. Brown rice syrup has a mild flavor that blends well with other ingredients. It is about 50 percent complex carbohydrates and as such has the gentlest effect on blood sugar levels of any sweetener. It's very easy to digest. Additionally, rice syrup is made from only slightly polished whole-grain rice and so benefits nutritionally from all the components of the rice: hull, bran, and germ. It is hypoallergenic and contains no fructose or sucrose. Rice syrup is generally available at natural food stores. If you cannot find it, substitute two-thirds as much maple syrup.

Rolled Oats are hulled and then scoured to remove most of the bran. They next are steamed, then flattened into flakes between rollers to make the familiar oatmeal sold as cereal and used in baking. The difference between quick-cooking oatmeal and old-fashioned oatmeal is the thickness of the flake: One simply cooks faster than the other. Instant oatmeal, on the other hand, often contains such ingredients as added salt, calcium carbonate, caramel flavor, and guar gum. Steel-cut or Scotch oats are groats that have been cut rather than rolled. They tend to be crunchier than rolled oats. Store them in a cool, dry place in a tightly sealed container.

Rye Flour is the second most popular flour (after wheat) for bread baking. It gives bread chewiness and denseness as well as unique flavor. Because it's a low-gluten flour, it usually is combined with wheat flour in a proportion of one cup rye for every two to three cups of wheat flour. Dark rye flour contains the most bran and therefore is most nutritious. Buy it in small quantities from natural food stores, as it turns rancid in a few weeks. It is best stored in airtight containers in a cool, dark cupboard or in the refrigerator.

Safflower Oil has a mild flavor that blends with nearly anything. It also has a high smoking point and so is recommended for sautéing and wok cooking. Because it contains nearly 95 percent highly unsaturated fats, safflower oil has a short shelf life. Buy it in small quantities and store it in the refrigerator, where it will keep for several months.

Sea Salt is made from evaporated sea water, and may contain trace elements of the rich minerals of the ocean. So-called "table salt" is mined from the earth. Additives are often added to table salt to prevent clumping and moisture absorption. These additives are not added as often to sea salt. Sea salt is sold in supermarkets and natural food stores and is available finely or coarsely grained. Sea salt is the salt used in the recipes in this book.

Sea Vegetables have been eaten in coastal areas throughout the world since ancient times. Sea vegetables are exceptionally high in minerals and aid in the digestion of many foods. When possible, try sea vegetables gathered or cultivated in unpolluted waters. They should be stored in airtight containers in a cool, dark place, and will keep for months.

Sesame Oil has a rich, distinctive taste and aroma that makes it a favorite flavoring for Oriental dishes. Regular, or light, sesame oil has a high smoking point and so is good for sautéing and wok cooking. Toasted sesame oil is a dark, strongly flavored oil that is used in moderation in Chinese cooking. It is made from seeds that are roasted before being pressed, and is sometimes called dark sesame oil. It can be used in dressings and flavoring, rather than for cooking. Light sesame oil is milder tasting and good for both salad dressings and cooking. Hot sesame oil is oil infused with hot chiles for a fiery flavor. Unless you use it frequently, buy sesame oil in small bottles, and store in a cool, dark place.

Shoyu and Tamari are high-quality soy sauces that are vastly superior to most commercial soy sauces (see Soy Sauce). Shoyu typically is made with equal parts soy beans and cracked roasted wheat, while Japanese tamari is made from soy sauce with no added wheat. However, some companies call shoyu "tamari" and so it is important to read the label carefully if you have wheat allergies. Both have added salt and are fermented for up to three years. Either can be substituted for salt in recipes, using one tablespoon for one teaspoon of salt. Both should be added to a dish during the last few minutes of cooking or at the table. Shoyu and tamari are available at natural food stores and many Asian markets.

Soba Noodles are dried Japanse noodles made either entirely from buckwheat or from various combinations of buckwheat and wheat flour. They are sold in Asian markets and at natural food stores in a variety of sizes, including square cut and thin cut, similar to but thinner than udon noodles. They should be stored like any dry pasta, in a cool, dry place, well wrapped and away from direct light.

Soy Milk is a commercially available beverage. All soy milk is made from ground soy beans that are boiled in water and then strained. It is rich in iron, calcium, and phosphorous. Plain soy milk is a good alternative to cow's milk in baking and dessert making. The flavored milks, meant to be consumed as is, not for baking and cooking, have varying degrees of sweetness from the addition of barley malt syrup, honey, and/or maple syrup. Soy milk is sold in shelf-stable, recyclable, eight-ounce and quart-size aseptic packages. Refrigerate after opening.

Soy Sauce is a dark, salty seasoning made from soybeans. Most soy sauces are made from soy products, salt, water, caramel coloring, hydrolyzed vegetable protein, corn syrup, and other chemicals. These soy sauces are unfermented, inferior, and inexpensive. Shoyu and tamari are excellent alternatives (see Shoyu and Tamari).

Spices, see Dried Herbs and Spices.

Sprouts are grown from seeds, grains, or beans that have been soaked from six to twelve hours and then rinsed periodically as they germinate. Sprouts are easy to digest and are high in nutritional value. They are also inexpensive and delicious when added to salads and sandwiches. Almost any seed, grain, or bean can be sprouted. The most popular sprout is alfalfa, but other favorites include adzuki bean, cabbage, clover, garbanzo bean, green pea, kale, lentil, mung bean, mustard, radish, and sunflower. You can buy sprouts at natural food stores, supermarkets, and greengrocers—or grow your own at home.

To grow your own, begin with organically grown sprouting seeds and beans from a natural food store or reputable catalog. Feed and seed stores are not good sources, as their products are intended for planting and often have been sprayed with poisonous chemicals. Each type of sprout grows slightly differently, but in general the procedure is as follows: Put the seeds (or beans or grains) in a quart jar and add water to cover well. The sprouts will expand a lot, so start with a small amount—a quarter cup for most seeds and beans, two tablespoons for tiny seeds, a half cup for lentils. Cover the jar with a screen or cheesecloth and secure with a rubber band or screw-on canning ring. Let the seeds soak for six to twelve hours, then pour off the water, and rinse the seeds well. Set the jar of rinsed, still-wet seeds at a 45-degree angle in a place with good air circulation (a dish drainer is good for this) and leave it there for three to five days, rinsing and draining the seeds at least twice a day. Once the seeds have sprouted, store them well covered, in the refrigerator. (Do not let them sit in water or they will rot.) Eat them within a few days or so; they sometimes keep for up to a week.

Tahini is an excellent and versatile paste made from ground hulled sesame seeds, which are sometimes roasted. (Sesame butter, on the other hand, is made from crushed and roasted unhulled seeds and has a thicker consistency and more bitter flavor.) Tahini, a staple in Middle Eastern cooking, is becoming increasingly popular because of its nutty flavor and creamy consistency. The product made from roasted seeds is stronger tasting than the mild paste made from raw seeds. If possible, buy tahini from natural food stores, where it is more likely that the hulls have been removed without the aid of chemicals; otherwise, you can find it where Oriental products are sold. Store in the refrigerator.

Tamari, see Shoyu and Tamari.

Tempeh has its roots in Indonesian cooking and traditionally is made from fermented whole soybeans, although some commercially available varieties are made from soybeans combined with grains or other beans. Like tofu, tempeh is low in fat and calories, but it is richer in nutrients because it is made from the whole soybean; it's also more flavorful. The flavor is often compared to beef or chicken but it is in fact distinctive and comes to life with the appropriate seasonings, marinades, and/or cooking. Tempeh is sold in solid off-white cakes and can be found in the refrigerator or freezer section of natural food stores. It is perishable and if stored in the refrigerator, should be eaten within a week of purchase; it can be frozen for two to three months.

Tofu, made from soybeans, has been a staple of Chinese and Japanese cooking for centuries. Today, it is popular as an ingredient in many kinds of vegetarian diets. Its neutral taste renders it extremely versatile, allowing it to pick up a rich variety of flavors from herbs, spices, and other ingredients. Tofu can be baked, broiled, dried, grilled, marinated, scrambled, steamed, or crumbled raw into salads. It can be used as the basis for salads, salad dressings, spreads, soups, main dishes, and desserts. Although tofu may be substituted for cheese in some dishes, it does not melt.

Tofu is sold in firm and soft forms. The firmer the tofu, the higher its nutrient density because there is less water per ounce. Soft tofu is recommended for dressings, sauces, and dips; firm tofu cakes are best for cooking and stir-frying. Soft tofu is white and malleable and usually sold in tubs; firm tofu is sold as blocky, off-white cakes. It is inexpensive and easy to find in supermarkets, Asian markets, and natural food stores. It is sold in bulk or packages in the refrigerator section and is kept covered with water. Tofu will keep in the refrigerator for up to a week if the water is changed daily to help keep it fresh.

Wheat Germ is to the grain what a seed is to a fruit—the plant sprouts from the germ, which holds its most precious nutrients. Wheat germ is high in fiber, iron, vitamin E, and the entire B complex (except for B_{12}). It is sold raw or toasted and can be sprinkled or spooned on cereals and added to soups, stews, breads, and other dishes. Wheat germ should always be refrigerated or frozen, as it is highly perishable. Raw wheat germ can turn rancid very quickly; toasted wheat germ lasts a little longer, but toasting destroys some of its nutritional value. Jars of wheat germ are easy to find in supermarkets and natural food stores.

White Almond Beverage, see Almond Milk.

Udon Noodles are flat Japanese noodles made from whole wheat flour or from a combination of whole wheat and unbleached white flour or whole wheat and brown rice flour. The noodles, which are thicker than soba noodles, are delicious in cold noodle dishes. They are sold in natural food stores and Asian markets.

Umeboshi Plum Paste is a distinctive sour-salty Japanese seasoning that is used in dressings and in sushi. (Use it sparingly.) It is made from green, immature umeboshi plums, and its purple color derives from the shiso leaves added to the mixture during processing. It is available at natural food stores and Asian markets and should be stored in the refrigerator once opened.

Unbleached White Flour is white flour that has not been chemically bleached. Its color is not quite as white as bleached white flour. It is the one exception to our rule about using only unrefined, whole grain flours. Although most nutrients are removed from the flour during processing, unbleached white flour contains more gluten than whole wheat flour and therefore is useful in bread recipes that need a really good rise. Always combine it with whole wheat or another whole-grain flour. Unbleached white flour is easy to find in supermarkets and will keep, if properly stored, for up to six months. Store it in an airtight container in a cool, dry place or in the refrigerator. See Flour for more information.

Vinegar is made from fermented grains and/or fruit. Each kind has a distinctive flavor. Oriental vinegars are made from rice and have a gentle, tart flavor. (Umeboshi plum vinegar, which is not really a vinegar because it is not fermented, is salty tasting.) More robust red wine vinegars are typical of the Mediterranean countries, and subtle white wine vinegar is often used in French cooking. Apple cider vinegar is a kitchen staple in the United States. Vinegars are essential ingredients in salad dressings, pickling recipes, and sauces. The best are made from organic ingredients, without additives, and are unfiltered and unpasteurized. These may look cloudy but they taste wonderful. Buy organic vinegar at natural food stores and keep it in a cool, dry cupboard. It lasts for months.

Wild Rice is actually the seed of an aquatic grass with a distinctive long, dark brown kernel. Long a staple of the Native American diet in certain parts of the country, wild rice is still harvested from shallow lakes in the northern parts of the country where it grows wild. Some cultivated wild rice is grown in paddies. Wild rice is never ground into flour; the whole kernel is always cooked. To cook, put one part wild rice and three parts water in a large pot, bring to a boil, and simmer for an hour, or until the rice is tender. True wild rice is expensive and usually is sold in specialty shops and in some natural food stores. Hybrid and cultivated strains are less expensive and easier to find.

TEN

Breakfast

Don't let lack of time be the reason you don't eat breakfast. Many breakfast foods can be prepared in advance: Fruit for salad can be cut up the night before, granola can be made ahead and stored in an airtight container for several weeks, muffins can be baked, frozen, and reheated as needed.

HEARTY THREE-GRAIN CEREAL

Makes 4 servings

This hearty, thick cereal has a great wholesome taste. Most health food stores carry a six- or nine-grain cereal, but this simpler version uses just three grains—cracked wheat, cut oats, and cornmeal. Most any combination of grains will make a flavorful cereal.

4 cups water

¼ teaspoon fine sea salt, optional

½ cup chopped pitted dates

½ cup cracked wheat

½ cup cut oats

⅓ cup yellow stone-ground cornmeal

3 tablespoons sesame seeds

Ground cinnamon to taste

Pure maple syrup, for serving

Rice beverage, almond beverage, soy milk, or Almond Milk (page 209), for serving

In a medium heavy-bottomed saucepan, bring the water and salt to a boil over medium-high heat. Stir in the dates, cracked wheat, oats, and cornmeal and return to the boil, then reduce the heat to low and simmer, stirring often to avoid scorching, until thickened, about 5 minutes. Remove from the heat, cover, and let stand for 5 minutes.

Spoon into individual bowls and sprinkle with the sesame seeds and cinnamon. Serve with maple syrup and rice beverage on the side.

Praise to the Earth,
Praise to the Sky,
Praise to all the plant and animal beings
Who have helped create this food for us.

> *"Our food system takes abundant grain, which people can't afford, and shrinks it into meat, which better-off people will pay for."*—Frances Moore Lappé

WASTE-NOT BROWN RICE-AND-RAISIN BREAKFAST PUDDING

Makes 4 servings

This cereal is a great way to use leftover cooked grains. Serve hot for breakfast or cold as a pudding dessert. Almost any leftover grain will work; try couscous with almonds and dates, or millet with dried blueberries and walnuts. Keep some extra cooked grains in the refrigerator just for this recipe.

3   cups cooked brown rice

½   cup raisins

¼   cup pure maple syrup

1   cup rice beverage

½   cup coarsely chopped raw almonds or other nuts, toasted, optional

1   teaspoon ground cinnamon

½   teaspoon ground cardamom

Additional rice beverage, for serving

Put all the ingredients into a medium saucepan and stir together. Bring to a boil over medium-high heat, then immediately reduce the heat to low and simmer, stirring often to avoid scorching, until thickened, 5 to 8 minutes.

Spoon into individual bowls, and serve immediately with rice beverage on the side.

Toasted Nuts and Seeds

We recommend lightly skillet- or oven-toasting nuts and seeds to bring out their flavor. To toast seeds or small amounts of nuts, cook in a dry skillet over medium heat, stirring often, until toasted, 3 to 5 minutes. To toast large amounts of nuts, bake in a preheated 350°F oven on a baking sheet, stirring occasionally, until toasted, 10 to 15 minutes.
Store toasted nuts and seeds in an airtight container in the refrigerator for up to one week.

CREAMY CORNMEAL AND RAISIN CEREAL

Makes 4 servings

Hot cooked cornmeal is smooth and comforting.

- 4 cups water
- ¼ teaspoon fine sea salt, optional
- ¾ cup raisins
- 1 cup yellow stone-ground cornmeal
- ½ cup coarsely chopped raw almonds or other nuts, toasted, optional
- ¼ cup raw sunflower seeds, toasted, optional

Ground cinnamon to taste

Pure maple syrup, for serving

Rice beverage, almond beverage, soy milk, or Almond Milk (page 209), for serving

Put the water, salt, raisins, and cornmeal into a medium saucepan and stir together. Bring to a boil over medium-high heat, then immediately reduce the heat to low and simmer, stirring often, until thickened, 3 to 5 minutes.

Spoon into individual bowls. Sprinkle the almonds, sunflower seeds, and cinnamon over the top. Serve with maple syrup and rice beverage on the side.

HOT APPLE SPICE OATMEAL

Makes 4 servings

This good cereal is made with rolled oats, an old-fashioned favorite. Try using other rolled grains like wheat or rye flakes. They take a little longer to cook, so increase the cooking time to 15 to 20 minutes.

1½ cups unfiltered apple juice

1½ cups water

¼ teaspoon fine sea salt, optional

1⅓ cups rolled oats

1 cup chopped dried apples

½ cup coarsely chopped raw walnuts, optional

Ground cinnamon to taste

Pure maple syrup, for serving

Rice beverage, almond beverage, soy milk, or Almond Milk (page 209), for serving

Put the apple juice, water, and salt into a medium saucepan and bring to a boil over medium-high heat. Add the rolled oats and dried apples and return to the boil, then immediately reduce the heat to low and simmer until thickened, about 5 minutes. Remove from the heat, cover, and let stand for 5 minutes.

Pour into individual bowls and sprinkle with the walnuts and cinnamon. Serve with maple syrup and rice beverage on the side.

NUTTY SUNNY GRANOLA

Makes 6 cups

Homemade granola is surprisingly easy to prepare. It will keep for two to three weeks in an airtight container.

3 cups rolled oats

½ cup wheat or oat bran

½ cup wheat germ

1 cup coarsely chopped raw walnuts

½ cup raw sunflower seeds

1 cup raisins

½ cup coarsely chopped pitted dates

1 teaspoon ground cinnamon

¼ cup pure maple syrup

Preheat the oven to 275°F.

In a large bowl, combine the oats, bran, wheat germ, walnuts, and sunflower seeds and stir together. Spread the mixture evenly on a baking sheet. Bake for 15 minutes. Stir the mixture and again spread it out evenly. Bake for another 15 minutes.

Transfer the toasted mixture to a large bowl. Immediately add the raisins, dates, and cinnamon and stir together. Slowly pour in the maple syrup and stir to distribute evenly.

Let cool completely before storing in an airtight container.

Our father, hear us, and our grandfather...
Listen to us, Father, Grandfather.
We ask thought, heart, love, happiness.
We are going to eat.

—Arapaho grace

Dried fruits of any kind—apples, raisins,
apricots—can be added to hot
cereals as they cook.

VEGETABLE TOFU SCRAMBLE

Makes 4 servings

This colorful vegetable and tofu scramble is delicious with Ocean's Blueberry Orange Muffins (page 229) and "Home-Fried" Potatoes (page 200).

2   tablespoons olive oil

1   pound soft tofu, cut into ½-inch cubes

1   medium onion, chopped

1   medium zucchini, cut into ½-inch-thick rounds

1   ear corn, kernels cut off the cob, or ¾ cup (thawed) frozen corn

4   ounces asparagus, trimmed and cut into 1-inch pieces

2   garlic cloves, minced

2   medium tomatoes, cut into ½-inch cubes

½   cup finely chopped fresh basil or parsley

2   tablespoons tamari

1   teaspoon ground cumin

½   teaspoon turmeric

⅛   teaspoon cayenne pepper

In a wok or large skillet, heat the oil over medium-high heat. Add the tofu, onion, zucchini, corn, asparagus, and garlic and stir-fry until crisp-tender, about 3 minutes. Add the tomatoes, basil, tamari, cumin, turmeric, and cayenne pepper, and stir-fry until the tomatoes are heated through, about 1 minute. Serve immediately.

"HOME-FRIED" POTATOES

Makes 4 servings

4 medium boiling potatoes, unpeeled
3 tablespoons olive oil
1 medium onion, chopped
1 medium green bell pepper, seeded and chopped
1 teaspoon fine sea salt
¾ teaspoon paprika
¼ teaspoon freshly ground black pepper
¼ cup finely chopped fresh parsley

In a large saucepan with enough lightly salted boiling water to cover, cook the potatoes until just tender when pierced with the tip of a sharp knife, 15 to 20 minutes. Drain, rinse under cold water, and cool. Cut into ½-inch cubes.

In a large skillet, preferably cast iron, heat 1 tablespoon of the oil over medium heat. Add the onion and bell pepper and cook, stirring often, until softened, about 5 minutes. Transfer to a plate and set aside.

Increase the heat to medium high and add the remaining 2 tablespoons oil to the skillet. Add the potato cubes, salt, paprika, and pepper. Cook, stirring occasionally, until the potatoes are browned, about 10 minutes. Stir in the cooked onion/pepper mixture and the parsley and cook stirring, for 1 minute. Serve hot.

If you take the time to make yourself a breakfast that fits your mood and needs, and the kind of day you have ahead of you, you set in motion a wave of self-care and responsibility that remains with you throughout the day.

ORANGE–POPPY SEED PANCAKES

Makes twelve 4-inch pancakes

Poppy seed pancakes are deliciously light and ideal when making a special morning feast for family or friends.

1 cup soy milk

⅔ cup water

1 cup whole wheat pastry flour

1 teaspoon nonaluminum baking powder

½ teaspoon baking soda

¼ teaspoon fine sea salt

½ cup rolled oats

½ cup sunflower seeds, toasted

¼ cup poppy seeds

1 teaspoon finely grated orange zest

Canola or safflower oil

Chunky Fruit Sauce (page 204), maple syrup, jam, applesauce, or fresh fruit, for serving

Preheat the oven to 200°F.

Put the soy milk and water into a small bowl and stir until combined.

Whisk the flour, baking powder, baking soda, and salt together in a large bowl. Add the oats, sunflower and poppy seeds, and orange zest. Add the soy milk mixture and stir to combine, using as few strokes as possible so you do not overmix the batter. Let sit for 5 minutes to allow the batter to thicken.

Lightly oil a frying pan or griddle and heat over medium heat. Using a measuring cup, pour ¼ cupfuls of the pancake batter into the hot pan or onto the hot griddle. Cook until the pancakes are bubbly on top and the edges are slightly dry, 2 to 3 minutes. Turn and cook until the pancakes are light brown on the bottom, 2 to 3 minutes. Transfer the pancakes to a baking sheet and keep warm in the oven while continuing with the remaining batter, oiling the pan between each batch of pancakes.

Serve immediately with Chunky Fruit Sauce, maple syrup, jam, applesauce, or fresh fruit.

BANANA-PECAN BUCKWHEAT PANCAKES

Makes about fourteen 5-inch pancakes

The combination of banana, pecans, and buckwheat makes unusually flavorful pancakes.

1⅓ cups rice beverage
1 cup water
2 tablespoons freshly squeezed lemon juice
1 cup whole wheat pastry flour
½ cup buckwheat flour
½ teaspoon ground cinnamon
1 teaspoon nonaluminum baking powder
½ teaspoon baking soda
½ teaspoon fine sea salt

1 ripe banana, finely chopped
½ cup coarsely chopped pecans, toasted
Canola or safflower oil
Chunky Fruit Sauce (page 204), maple syrup, jam, applesauce, and/or fresh fruit, for serving

Preheat the oven to 200°F.

Put the rice beverage, water, and lemon juice into a small bowl and stir until combined.

Whisk the flours, cinnamon, baking powder, baking soda, and salt in a large bowl until combined. Add the rice beverage mixture and stir to combine, using as few strokes as possible so you do not overmix the batter. Fold in the banana and pecans. Let sit for 5 minutes to allow the batter to thicken.

Lightly oil a frying pan or griddle and heat over medium heat. Using a measuring cup, pour ¼ cupfuls of the pancake batter into the hot pan or onto the hot griddle. Cook until the pancakes are bubbly on top and the edges are slightly dry, 2 to 3 minutes. Turn and cook until the pancakes are light brown on the bottom, 2 to 3 minutes. Transfer the pancakes to a baking sheet and keep warm in the oven while continuing with the remaining batter, oiling the pan between each batch of pancakes.

Serve immediately with a choice of toppings.

BLUEBERRY CORNMEAL PANCAKES

Makes twelve 4-inch pancakes

1 cup soy milk

½ cup water

1 cup whole wheat pastry flour

½ cup yellow stone-ground cornmeal

1 teaspoon nonaluminum baking powder

½ teaspoon baking soda

¼ teaspoon fine sea salt

1 cup fresh or (thawed) frozen blueberries

Canola or safflower oil

Chunky Fruit Sauce (page 204), maple syrup, jam, applesauce, or fresh fruit, for serving

Preheat the oven to 200°F.

Put the soy milk and water into a small bowl and stir until combined.

Whisk the flour, cornmeal, baking powder, baking soda, and salt in a large bowl until combined. Add the milk mixture and stir to combine, using as few strokes as possible so you do not overmix the batter. Fold in the blueberries. Let sit for 5 minutes to allow the batter to thicken.

Lightly oil a frying pan or griddle and heat over medium heat. Using a measuring cup, pour ¼ cupfuls of the pancake batter into the hot pan or onto the hot griddle. Cook until the pancakes are bubbly on top and the edges are slightly dry, 3 to 4 minutes. Turn and cook until the pancakes are light brown on the bottom, about 3 minutes. Transfer the pancakes to a baking sheet and keep warm in the oven while continuing with the remaining batter, oiling the pan between each batch of pancakes.

Serve immediately with Chunky Fruit Sauce, maple syrup, jam, applesauce, or fresh fruit.

CHUNKY FRUIT SAUCE

Makes about 2¹/₂ cups

This fruit sauce combines the rich flavor of maple syrup with the goodness of fresh fruit and juice. It will keep up to two weeks in the refrigerator.

 1 **tablespoon arrowroot powder**
 1 **tablespoon water**
 1 **cup unfiltered apple juice or freshly squeezed orange juice**
 1 **cup pure maple syrup**
 Pinch of ground cloves, optional
 1 **cinnamon stick**
 1 **cup fresh or (thawed) frozen blackberries, blueberries, raspberries, strawberries, cranberries, or other berries**

In a small dish, dissolve the arrowroot in the water.

In a medium saucepan, combine the juice, maple syrup, cloves, cinnamon, and berries and bring to a boil over medium-high heat. Immediately reduce the heat to low and simmer, stirring occasionally, for 2 to 3 minutes. Whisk in the arrowroot and cook just until thickened, about 30 seconds. Remove the cinnamon stick.

Serve warm over pancakes.

Average cholesterol level of people eating a meat-based diet:
210 mg/d
Chance of dying from heart disease if your blood cholesterol level is 210 mg/d: **40 to 50 percent**
Average cholesterol level of people consuming no animal products: **150 mg/d**
Chance of dying from heart disease if your blood cholesterol level is 150 mg/d: **virtually zero**

The art of breakfast has to do with creating a relationship with yourself that lasts throughout the whole day, spreading feelings of wellness and satisfaction into all that you do.

MOCHA-BANANA BREAKFAST SMOOTHIE

Makes 2 servings

This creamy breakfast smoothie is mildly sweet. Light and easy to digest, it will sustain you through the busiest of mornings.

½ cup sunflower seeds (preferably soaked in water to cover for at least ½ hour or overnight, then drained, rinsed, and drained again; see page 235)

2 ripe bananas

2 heaping teaspoons roasted grain beverage powder

¾ cup vanilla soy milk, rice beverage, or almond beverage (or more, if desired), well chilled

2 teaspoons pure maple syrup

1 teaspoon pure vanilla extract

Put all the ingredients in a blender and blend for 1 to 3 minutes, until smooth. (For a thinner shake, add more soy milk.) Serve immediately.

Modern "cowboys" no longer run five hundred head on ten thousand acres of open prairie. Today, they are more likely to run ten thousand head on five acres of concrete.

ELEVEN

Beverages

In our culture, people tend to associate drinking alcoholic
beverages with having a good time, with "happy hours," with
taking a break from work and stress, and with relaxation,
play, and self-expression. But what would happen if we were to
take time for all these things without depending on substances
that can be harmful? The journey from addictive beverages
that undermine our health to delightful ones that support our
freedom leads to greater health and self-esteem.

BANANA MILK

Makes about 4¹/₂ cups

Like nut and seed milks, banana milk is a healthful alternative to cow's milk. It is a delicious beverage especially appreciated by young children. Use overripe bananas for a naturally sweet taste. Banana milk does not keep well and should be served within an hour of preparation.

3 ripe bananas

¼ cup pure maple syrup

3 cups cold water

¾ teaspoon pure vanilla extract

Put all the ingredients into a blender and blend until smooth.

Almond Body Scrub

Leftover almond pulp makes an invigorating body scrub. Mix the pulp with some water and liquid soap, such as Dr. Bronner's Peppermint Pure-Castile Soap. Rub it all over your body while showering.

ALMOND MILK

Makes 2³/₄ cups, unstrained,
or 2¹/₄ cups, strained

Almond Milk, like other nut milks, seed milks, soy milks, and rice beverages, is good in shakes and over cereals and can be substituted for cow's milk in most recipes. Almonds are the nuts most commonly used to make nut milk because their neutral taste can be easily flavored. However, most any nut or seed can be used—for example, cashews, walnuts, sesame seeds, or sunflower seeds—with resulting differences in color and taste.

½ **cup raw almonds or other nuts or seeds**

2 **cups water**

1 **to 2 tablespoons pure maple syrup or rice syrup, if using as a beverage (omit if the Almond Milk is to be used in cooking)**

Put the almonds or other nuts or seeds into a jar, cover them with water, and soak the nuts for 12 to 24 hours or seeds for 6 to 12 hours. Drain off the soaking water and thoroughly rinse the nuts or seeds.

Blanch the almonds in boiling water for 30 seconds. Drain off the water and plunge the almonds into cold water; drain. Squeeze the almonds between your fingertips to remove the skins. (Compost or discard the skins.)

Put the almonds or other nuts or seeds, ½ cup of the water, and the syrup, if using, in a blender, and blend until smooth, about 1 minute. With the machine running, slowly add the remaining 1½ cups water, and continue to blend for 1 more minute.

The nut or seed milk can be used as is; if you prefer a smoother texture, separate out the pulp: Just pour the nut or seed mixture into a fine strainer and press out the liquid with a rubber spatula. (Compost or discard the pulp.)

Nut and seed milks keep 2 to 3 days, covered and refrigerated.

STRAWBERRY ALMOND SHAKE

Makes 4 cups

This shake, made from strawberries, bananas, and almond milk, is a heavenly way to start the day or a nutritious snack anytime. For a special treat, pour the shake over fresh fruit salad or make frozen ice pops.

- 2 **cups Almond Milk (page 209) or almond beverage, chilled**
- 2 **ripe bananas**
- ½ **pint fresh strawberries or 1½ cups loosely packed unsweetened (thawed) frozen strawberries**
- 4 **pitted dates**
- 1 **teaspoon pure vanilla extract**

Put all the ingredients into a blender and blend until smooth. Serve immediately, or refrigerate for up to 4 hours, and blend again until smooth before serving.

ALMOND LASSI

Makes 2 servings

This recipe uses Almond Milk to create the traditional flavor of lassi, a sweet and spicy yogurt drink from India. You can make a banana lassi by adding a ripe banana before blending.

- 2 **cups Almond Milk (page 209) or almond beverage, chilled**
- 3 **pitted dates**
- 1 **teaspoon ground cardamom**
- ¼ **teaspoon freshly ground black pepper**

Put all the ingredients in a blender and blend until smooth, about 2 minutes. Refrigerate for at least 30 minutes. Serve cold.

BANANA CAROB SHAKE

Makes 4 cups

This delightfully simple fruit shake is made with carob powder, bananas, dates, and sunflower seeds. The shake is best served immediately, but it will keep several hours refrigerated.

½ cup raw sunflower seeds

4 pitted dates

1 cup ice water

1 cup Almond Milk (page 209), soy milk, or almond beverage, chilled

2 ripe bananas

2 tablespoons carob powder

1 teaspoon pure vanilla extract

Put the sunflower seeds, dates, and water in a blender and blend until smooth, about 1 minute. With the machine running, slowly add the Almond Milk. Add the bananas, carob powder, and vanilla, and blend until smooth. Serve chilled.

SUNBURST SMOOTHIE

Makes 4½ cups

Rain or shine, fresh fruit juice and fresh ginger make this Sunburst Smoothie a great way to get your day going. It is best served immediately, but will keep several hours refrigerated.

3 cups freshly squeezed orange juice, chilled

3 ripe bananas

4 pitted dates

¾ teaspoon finely grated fresh gingerroot

Put all the ingredients into a blender and blend until smooth. The smoothie may be refrigerated for up to 4 hours before serving.

CANTALOUPE COOLER

Makes about 3 1/2 cups

Sweet melon and fresh mint leaves make this a refreshing morning drink or a cool afternoon pick-me-up. Try using different melons to make this cooler.

- 1 cantaloupe, honeydew, or Crenshaw melon, or a combination, peeled, seeded, cut into large chunks, and chilled
- ½ cup ice water
- ¼ cup tightly packed fresh mint leaves
- 8 ice cubes
- 2 tablespoons freshly squeezed lime juice
- ⅛ teaspoon fine sea salt, optional

Put all the ingredients into a blender and blend until smooth. Serve immediately, as the cooler will separate upon standing.

ORANGE LIMEADE

Makes about 5 cups

- 3 cups water
- 1½ cups freshly squeezed orange juice
- ¼ cup freshly squeezed lime juice
- 3 tablespoons pure maple syrup

Put all the ingredients in a large jar, cover, and shake until well mixed. Serve over ice.

APPLE MINT COOLER

Makes 6 cups

A very refreshing iced mint tea naturally sweetened with apple juice. For a less sweet beverage, just add less apple juice.

2 cups boiling water
4 peppermint tea bags or 2 teaspoons loose peppermint tea
4 cups unfiltered apple juice
4 teaspoons freshly squeezed lemon juice
Lemon slices, for garnish

In a heatproof pitcher, combine the boiling water and tea. Let steep for 3 to 5 minutes; the longer you leave it, the stronger the tea will be. Remove the tea bags or strain out the loose tea.

Stir in the apple juice and lemon juice. Refrigerate for at least 30 minutes. Serve over ice and garnish with lemon slices.

GINGER TEA

Makes 4 cups

Herbalists tell us that ginger aids digestion and relieves head colds. True or not, this spicy tea tastes great. It keeps for several days in the refrigerator and is good reheated.

5 cups water
1 4-inch piece fresh gingerroot, thinly sliced
¼ cup freshly squeezed lemon juice
Pure maple syrup, for serving

Put the water and gingerroot in a medium saucepan. Cover and bring to a boil over high heat, then immediately reduce the heat and simmer for 10 minutes. Strain out the gingerroot and compost or discard it. Stir in the lemon juice. Serve hot, or chill and serve over ice. Let each person add maple syrup to taste.

CHAI

Makes 4 cups

Chai is the traditional hospitality beverage of India and other Asian countries. Made with peppermint tea and whole spices, it's a refreshing alternative to caffeinated tea.

4 cups water

1 tablespoon cardamom pods

1 tablespoon finely grated fresh gingerroot

1 teaspoon whole cloves

1 teaspoon black peppercorns

1 3-inch cinnamon stick

4 peppermint tea bags or 4 teaspoons loose peppermint tea

Pure maple syrup, for serving

Vanilla or plain soy milk, for serving

In a medium saucepan, combine the water, cardamom, ginger, cloves, peppercorns, and cinnamon stick. Cover and bring to a boil over high heat, then immediately reduce the heat and simmer for 5 minutes. Remove from the heat and add the peppermint tea. Cover the pan and let steep for 3 to 5 minutes; the longer you leave it, the stronger the tea will be.

Strain out the spices and tea and compost or discard them. Serve immediately, and let each person add maple syrup and soy milk to taste.

Together, Pepsi and Coca-Cola spent the equivalent of $1.14 per person on marketing in the United States last year— more than most African governments can spend on health care for their citizens.

May we be filled with peace.
May we be filled with love.
We give thanks for peace.
We give thanks for love.

HOT ALMOND NOG

Makes 2 servings

This wholesome version of an old favorite holiday treat is so flavorful you will want to drink it year around. An unusual variation is a hot banana nog; just add a sliced ripe banana before blending.

   2 cups Almond Milk (page 209) or almond beverage
   6 pitted dates
   ½ teaspoon pure vanilla extract
   ½ teaspoon ground cinnamon
   ¼ teaspoon grated nutmeg

Put all the ingredients into a blender and blend until smooth. Transfer to a medium saucepan and warm over low heat. Do not allow to boil, as the beverage will separate. Serve immediately.

> *To make nut or seed "milks," use nuts and seeds as they are,
> or for a smoother, more digestible drink, soak them
> in water first.*

HOT ALMOND
CAROB DRINK

Makes 5 cups

Carob gives this delicious beverage a naturally sweet chocolatey flavor, and the grain beverage adds an even richer mocha flavor.

    4 cups Almond Milk (page 209) or almond beverage
    6 tablespoons pure maple syrup
    5 teaspoons carob powder
    5 teaspoons roasted grain beverage powder

Put all the ingredients into a blender and blend until smooth. Pour into a saucepan and warm over low heat. Do not boil, as the beverage will separate. Serve immediately.

TWELVE

Breads and Muffins

Quick breads and muffins use baking soda and baking powder instead of yeast to leaven, or raise, the bread. Unlike yeast breads, quick breads and muffins will deflate and suffer from vigorous beating. Stir the dry and wet ingredients just until they are combined; do not overbeat.

OCEAN'S BOMBS OF LOVE BREAD

Makes 2 loaves

When John's son, Ocean, was just ten years old he started a very successful enterprise called Ocean's Bakery. He had more than one hundred regular customers and sold all the breads and muffins as quickly as he could bake them because they were so delicious, healthy, and baked with such loving care. Ocean's Bombs of Love Bread is a basic bread recipe and one of his customers' favorites. Each time Ocean baked it, he surprised his customers by adding different combinations of nuts, seeds, herbs, spices, vegetables, and raisins or other dried fruit.

> 1 **cup lukewarm water (100° to 110°F)**
> 2½ **teaspoons (1 package) active dry yeast**
> ¼ **cup pure maple syrup (at room temperature)**
> 2 **cups water**
> ¼ **cup canola or safflower oil**
> 2 **teaspoons fine sea salt**
> 7 **cups whole wheat flour**
> **Canola oil for brushing the loaves, optional**

Make the sponge: In a small bowl, combine the lukewarm water, yeast, and 1 tablespoon of the syrup; let stand until creamy, about 10 minutes.

In a large bowl, combine the yeast mixture, the remaining 3 tablespoons maple syrup, the 2 cups water, the oil, and salt and stir until well blended. Using a wooden spoon, stir in 4 cups of the flour, one cup at a time, and then stir vigorously in one direction until the batter is thick and smooth, about 150 strokes. The dough will be sticky. Using a rubber spatula, scrape down the sides of the bowl. Cover the bowl with a damp cloth, put it in a warm place, and let rise until the sponge is doubled in size and tiny holes appear on the surface, 1½ to 2 hours.

Make the dough: If desired, add nuts, seeds, herbs, spices, grated vegetables, fresh fruits, raisins, and/or dried fruits to the sponge. Then add the remaining 3 cups flour, a little at a time, mixing first with a spoon and then with your hands, until the dough is firm and holds together.

Turn the dough out onto a lightly floured work surface, shape the dough into a ball, and knead the dough until smooth and elastic, 10 to 15 minutes. (To knead, pick up the far edge of the dough, fold it over in half, and press down the center of the dough with the heels of your hands. Turn the dough a quarter turn and repeat.) Add more flour to the work surface as needed, to keep the dough from sticking.

First rise: Shape the dough into a ball, put into a lightly oiled bowl, and turn once to coat it. Cover the bowl with a damp cloth, put it in a warm place, and let the dough rise until it is doubled in size, about 1 hour.

Lightly oil two 8½- by 4½-inch loaf pans.

Shaping the loaves and final rise: Punch the dough down ten to fifteen times by pushing your fist into the center of the dough. Divide the dough in half. On a floured surface, knead half the dough for 5 minutes. Press the dough flat with your hands, roll up into a log shape, and pinch the seam closed. Repeat with the remaining dough. Put the loaves, seam side down, into the prepared pans, press the dough gently into the corners of the pans. Cover the pans with a damp cloth, put them in a warm place, and let the dough rise until it is just above the sides of the pans, about 30 minutes.

Preheat the oven to 350°F.

Bake the bread for 40 to 50 minutes, until it tests done. To test for doneness, remove a loaf from its pan by turning the pan upside down and tapping on the bottom of the pan. Then tap the bottom of the loaf. If done, it will sound hollow. If you want a softer crust, lightly brush the tops of the loaves with oil as soon as the bread is removed from the oven. Allow the bread to cool in the pans for 5 minutes, then remove from the pans and cool completely on wire racks before slicing.

Peace.
We ask for peace.
We give thanks for peace.
Let there be great peace.

CHAPATIS

Makes eight 6-inch chapatis

Popular unleavened flatbreads from India that are easy to make and versatile. Serve chapatis instead of a loaf of bread, or use them as a wrap for beans, rice, and vegetables.

> 2 cups whole wheat flour
> 1 cup water
> ½ teaspoon fine sea salt

Put the flour and water into a large bowl and stir to form a soft dough. Shape the dough into a ball and turn out onto a lightly floured work surface. Knead the dough for 5 minutes. (To knead, pick up the far edge of the dough, fold it over in half, and press down the center of the dough with the heels of your hands. Turn the dough a quarter turn, and repeat.) Add more flour to the work surface as needed, to keep the dough from sticking.

Shape the dough into a ball, put into a lightly oiled bowl, and turn once to coat it. Cover the bowl with a damp cloth, put it in a warm place, and let the dough stand at room temperature for 30 minutes.

Lightly flour a work surface and a rolling pin. Divide the dough into 8 pieces and shape each one into a ball. On a lightly floured work surface, roll each ball into a 6-inch circle, about ⅛ inch thick. Shake each chapati to remove excess flour.

Heat a dry frying pan or griddle over medium-high heat. Add a chapati to the hot pan and cook until the underside is spotted and lightly browned, about 1 minute. Turn over and cook for 1 more minute. Repeat with the remaining chapatis. Then, if you have a gas stove, place each chapati directly on the burner over a low flame, and heat until puffy, about 3 seconds on each side. Skip this step if you have an electric stove.

Chapatis are best cooked just before serving.

> *"Our wholeness as human beings depends upon the depth of our awareness of the fact that we are a part of the wholeness of nature."*—Ashley Montagu

WHOLE WHEAT SESAME CRACKERS

Makes about 6 dozen crackers

Surprise your family or guests with freshly baked crackers. For special occasions, use cookie cutters to make them into imaginative shapes. Serve them with a dip for an appetizer or pack them in a lunch. Crackers will keep for two to three weeks stored in an airtight container. If the crackers lose some of their crispness, heat them at 250°F for about 5 minutes.

 6   tablespoons plus ½ cup sesame seeds
 1   cup water
 3   tablespoons canola or safflower oil
 1   teaspoon fine sea salt
2½ cups whole wheat flour
 ½   teaspoon nonaluminum baking powder

Position two racks in the center and the bottom third of the oven, and preheat the oven to 350°F.

Spread 2 tablespoons sesame seeds on each of three unoiled baking sheets. This will prevent the crackers from sticking and will give them a delicious crisp bottom.

Put the water, oil, and salt in a small bowl and stir together. Whisk the flour and baking powder in a large bowl until combined. Stir in the ½ cup sesame seeds. Add the water-oil mixture and mix to form a rough dough. Knead the dough in the bowl to form a ball, and turn out onto a lightly floured work surface.

Lightly flour a rolling pin. Roll the dough out into a 22- by 14-inch rectangle, about ⅟₁₆ inch thick. Using a fork, prick the dough all over to release trapped air and keep the dough flat. With a pizza wheel or sharp knife, cut the dough into 2-inch squares or other shapes, or cut shapes with a 2-inch cookie cutter.

Using a spatula, transfer the crackers to the prepared baking sheets. Bake until the crackers are light brown and firm to the touch, 15 to 20 minutes, switching the positions of the sheets halfway through the baking time. When the first two sheets are finished, remove them, and bake the third one as directed. Cool completely.

CURRANT BISCUITS

Makes about 15 biscuits

The sweet taste of currants makes these biscuits sconelike. Serve them with a dab of fruit-sweetened jam and a cup of tea.

½ cup currants

½ cup water

⅔ cup soy milk

¼ cup canola or safflower oil

3 tablespoons pure maple syrup

1 teaspoon ground cinnamon

2 cups whole wheat pastry flour

1½ teaspoons nonaluminum baking powder

½ teaspoon baking soda

½ teaspoon fine sea salt

Preheat the oven to 350°F.

Put the currants and water in a small saucepan, and bring to a simmer. Remove from the heat, cover, and let stand for 5 minutes. Drain well.

In a medium bowl, combine the soy milk, oil, maple syrup, and cinnamon.

Whisk the flour, baking powder, baking soda, and salt in a large bowl until combined. Add the soy milk mixture and currants and combine, using as few strokes as possible so you do not overmix the dough.

Turn the dough out onto a lightly floured work surface. Shape the dough into a ball and pat out with your fingers to a thickness of ½ inch. Use a lightly floured 2-inch round cookie cutter to cut out the biscuits. Gather up the scraps, pat out again, and cut out more biscuits; you should have about 15 in all.

Transfer the biscuits to an ungreased baking sheet. Bake until lightly browned, 20 to 25 minutes. Serve hot.

VEGETABLE RYE BREAD

Makes two 1¹/₂-pound loaves

The abundance of root vegetables available in the fall and winter makes this bread a natural for serving with hearty soups and vegetable stews. This recipe is adapted from the well-known Moosewood Restaurant in upstate New York.

- 1 **cup lukewarm water (100° to 110°F)**
- 2½ **teaspoons (1 package) active dry yeast**
- 3 **tablespoons unsulphured molasses**
- 1½ **cups water**
- 3 **tablespoons canola or safflower oil**
- 4½ **cups unbleached white flour**
- 2 **cups whole wheat flour**
- 2 **cups rye flour**
- 1 **medium carrot, grated**
- 1 **medium baking potato, grated**
- 1 **small beet, grated**
- 3 **tablespoons finely chopped fresh dill**
- 1 **tablespoon fine sea salt**
- 2 **teaspoons caraway seeds**

Canola oil, for brushing the loaves

Make the sponge: In a small bowl, combine the lukewarm water, yeast, and 1 tablespoon of the molasses. Let stand until creamy, about 10 minutes, then stir to blend well. Transfer to a large bowl and stir in the 1½ cups water, the remaining 2 tablespoons molasses, and the oil.

In a large bowl, whisk the flours until combined. Using a wooden spoon, stir 4 cups of the flour mixture into the yeast mixture, one cup at a time, to form a thick batter and then stir vigorously in one direction until smooth, about 150 strokes. Using a rubber spatula, scrape down the sides of the bowl. Cover the bowl with a damp kitchen towel, and let stand in a warm place until the sponge has doubled in bulk and tiny holes appear on the surface, 1 to 2 hours.

Stir in the grated carrot, potato, and beet, dill, salt, and caraway seeds. *(continued)*

Make the dough: Using a wooden spoon at first, and then your hands, work 2 cups of the remaining flour mixture, or more if necessary, into the sponge until a soft, kneadable dough is formed.

Sprinkle a work surface with ¼ cup of the remaining flour mixture. Gather the dough into a ball and turn out onto the work surface. Knead the dough, adding more of the flour mixture as necessary, until firm, smooth, and elastic, 10 to 15 minutes. The dough should be slightly moist, but not sticky; the amount of flour needed depends on the moisture in the vegetables.

First rise: Form the dough into a ball and place in a lightly oiled bowl. Turn to coat, and cover with a damp kitchen towel. Let stand in a warm spot until the dough doubles in bulk, 1 to 1½ hours. (If you poke your finger 1 inch into the dough, the indentation should remain.)

Lightly oil two 9½- by 5½-inch loaf pans.

Shaping the loaves and second rise: Punch down the dough, and knead on a lightly floured work surface for 5 minutes. Cut the dough in half. Roll each half into a log shape, pinch the seams closed, and place, seam side down, in the prepared pans. Cover the pans with a damp cloth, and let stand in a warm place until the dough has risen above the top of the pans, 30 to 45 minutes.

Preheat the oven to 350° F.

Bake the bread for 40 to 50 minutes, until it tests done. To test, invert a pan to remove one of the loaves, and tap the bottom of the loaf. If the bread is done, it will sound hollow. Lightly brush the tops of the loaves with oil to glaze, and cool the bread completely on wire racks before slicing.

Pounds of grain and soybeans needed to produce one pound of edible food from:

Beef	*16*
Pork	*6*
Turkey	*4*
Chicken	*3*
Egg	*3*

Number of children who die as a result of malnutrition every day: **40,000**

GARLIC HERB BREAD

Makes 8 slices

Garlic and herbs make this bread a tasty addition to most any meal.

¼ cup olive oil
½ teaspoon dried basil
¼ teaspoon dried oregano
1 large garlic clove, minced
8 slices whole-grain bread

Preheat the oven to 350°F.

Put the olive oil, basil, oregano, and garlic into a small bowl and stir together. Brush the mixture over one side of the bread slices. Re-form the slices into a loaf shape, and wrap tightly in aluminum foil.

Bake until thoroughly heated, about 15 minutes. Serve immediately.

HERBED BREAD CRUMBS

Makes about 2 cups

Keep homemade bread crumbs on hand. Store them in a plastic bag in the freezer.

4 slices stale whole wheat bread
1 teaspoon dried basil
½ teaspoon dried thyme
1 garlic clove, minced

Put all the ingredients into a food processor fitted with the metal blade, and process until the bread is chopped into crumbs.

If your recipe calls for toasted bread crumbs, preheat the oven to 350°F. Spread the bread crumbs evenly on a baking sheet. Bake for 3 to 5 minutes, stir the crumbs, and bake until light brown and crisp, 2 to 3 minutes.

BOSTON BROWN BREAD

Makes 1 large loaf (8 to 10 servings)

Boston brown bread has its roots in New England, where it is paired with baked beans. While it is traditionally steamed in a coffee can, we suggest using a 2½-quart-lidded pudding mold, because no coffee company could assure us that their cans were lead-free. This recipe comes to us from Ocean's Bakery.

- 2 cups soy milk
- ½ cup canola or safflower oil
- ½ cup unsulphured molasses
- ¼ cup freshly squeezed lemon juice
- 2 cups whole wheat pastry flour
- 1 cup yellow stone-ground cornmeal
- 2 teaspoons nonaluminum baking powder
- 1 teaspoon baking soda
- 1 teaspoon fine sea salt
- 1 cup raisins
- 1 cup sunflower seeds

Preheat the oven to 350°F. Lightly spray the inside and the lid of 2½-quart tube pudding mold with canola oil pan spray (El Molino Canola Mist), and dust with cornmeal, tapping out the excess.

Put the soy milk, oil, molasses, and lemon juice into a bowl and stir together.

Whisk the flour, cornmeal, baking powder, baking soda, and salt together in a large bowl until combined. Add the soy milk mixture and combine, using as few strokes as possible so you do not overmix the batter. Fold in the raisins and sunflower seeds.

Spoon the batter into the prepared mold. Cover with the lid.

Put the mold into a large pot, and add enough hot water to come 2 inches up the side of the mold. Bring to a boil over high heat, reduce the heat, cover tightly, and simmer until a toothpick inserted in the center of the bread comes out clean, 1½ to 2 hours. Do not be concerned if the bread sinks slightly in the center.

Let the bread cool for 5 minutes before removing it from the mold. Then run a thin, sharp knife around the sides and the center tube to release the bread, and invert onto a serving platter.

This bread is best served warm, cut into wedges with a serrated knife.

HERBED CROUTONS

Makes about 2 cups

Homemade croutons, seasoned with herbs and garlic, are easy to make and preservative-free. Float them in soups or toss in salads. Croutons can be made with different herbs and any leftover whole-grain bread.

¼ **cup olive oil**

1 **teaspoon tamari**

¼ **teaspoon** *each* **dried basil, thyme, oregano, and marjoram, or 1 teaspoon of any combination of these herbs**

1 **garlic clove, minced**

½ **teaspoon finely grated lemon zest**

4 **slices stale whole-grain bread, cut into ½-inch cubes**

Preheat the oven to 350°F.

In a medium bowl, stir together the olive oil, tamari, dried herbs, garlic, and lemon zest. Add the bread cubes and toss to coat.

Spread the bread cubes on a baking sheet. Bake for 5 minutes, stir, and continue baking until crisp, about 5 more minutes. Cool completely.

The croutons will keep, stored at room temperature in an airtight container, for up to 2 days.

We who are about to eat
Know that more than our bodies will be fed
Through the food we are about to eat.
Fill us with beauty.
Fill us with joy.
Fill us with peace.

SPICY CORN BREAD

Makes 9 servings

This corn bread has a hint of hotness from the chile pepper and crunchiness and color from the corn and red bell pepper. Serve with soups, salads, pastas, and main dishes. Be sure to wash your hands well after mincing the chile pepper.

> 5 tablespoons olive oil
> 1 medium red bell pepper, seeded and finely chopped
> 1 fresh hot chile pepper, seeded and minced
> 1 cup soy milk
> 2 tablespoons freshly squeezed lemon juice
> 1 cup whole wheat pastry flour
> 1 cup yellow stone-ground cornmeal
> 1 teaspoon nonaluminum baking powder
> 1 teaspoon baking soda
> 1 teaspoon fine sea salt
> 1 ear corn, kernels cut off the cob, or ¾ cup (thawed) frozen corn

Preheat the oven to 350°F. Lightly oil an 8- by 8-inch baking pan with olive oil and dust with cornmeal, tapping out the excess.

Heat 1 tablespoon of the olive oil in a frying pan over medium heat. Add the bell pepper and chile pepper and cook, stirring, until tender about 5 minutes. Remove from the pan and cool completely.

Put the soy milk, the remaining ¼ cup olive oil, and the lemon juice into a small bowl and stir together.

Whisk the flour, cornmeal, baking powder, baking soda, and salt together in a large bowl until combined. Add the soy milk mixture and combine, using as few strokes as possible so you do not overmix the batter. Fold in the peppers and corn.

Spread the batter evenly in the prepared pan. Bake the bread until a toothpick inserted into the center comes out clean, 20 to 25 minutes.

Cool the bread for 5 minutes. Cut into squares and serve hot or warm.

OCEAN'S BLUEBERRY ORANGE MUFFINS

Makes 1 dozen muffins

1½ cups freshly squeezed orange juice

⅓ cup canola or safflower oil

⅓ cup pure maple syrup

2 tablespoons raw tahini

Grated zest of 1 orange

2 cups whole wheat pastry flour

1 cup rolled oats

1 teaspoon nonaluminum baking powder

1 teaspoon baking soda

½ teaspoon fine sea salt

1 cup fresh or (thawed) frozen blueberries

Preheat the oven to 350°F. Lightly oil a 12-cup muffin pan with canola oil.

Put the orange juice, oil, syrup, tahini, and orange zest into a medium bowl and whisk until well combined.

Whisk the flour, oats, baking powder, baking soda, and salt together in a large bowl until well combined. Add the orange juice mixture and combine, using as few strokes as possible so you do not overmix the batter. Fold in the blueberries.

Spoon the batter into the prepared muffin pan, filling each cup about three quarters full. Bake until a toothpick inserted into the center of a muffin comes out clean, 20 to 25 minutes.

Let the muffins cool for 5 minutes before removing from the pan.

"Your choice of diet can influence your long-term health prospects more than any other action you might take."
—Former Surgeon General C. Everett Koop

QUICK AND SIMPLE BANANA BREAD

Makes 16 1-inch squares

¼ cup soy milk, rice beverage, or almond beverage

6 tablespoons canola or safflower oil

6 tablespoons pure maple syrup

2¼ cups mashed ripe bananas (about 5 medium bananas)

2 cups whole wheat pastry flour

2 tablespoons roasted grain beverage powder

1 teaspoon baking soda

1 teaspoon nonaluminum baking powder

½ teaspoon fine sea salt

1 cup chopped walnuts

Preheat the oven to 350°F. Lightly oil an 8- by 8-inch cake pan and dust with flour, shaking out the excess.

Put the soy milk, oil, maple syrup, and bananas in a blender and blend until smooth.

In a large bowl, whisk the flour, beverage powder, baking powder, baking soda, and salt until well combined. Add the banana mixture and combine, using as few strokes as possible so you do not overmix the batter. Fold in the walnuts. Scrape into the cake pan and smooth the top. Bake until a toothpick inserted into the center of the bread comes out clean, 30 to 35 minutes.

We give thanks to all who have come before us,
We give thanks to those who dug the wells from which we drink,
We give thanks to those who built the houses in which we live,
We give thanks to those who grew the food which we eat,
May our lives be a blessing to those yet to come.

One teaspoon of soil can contain more living creatures than there are people in the world.

ORANGE MARMALADE MUFFINS

Makes 1 dozen muffins

When these moist muffins with the zesty taste of orange were served at an EarthSave board meeting, they disappeared immediately.

- ¾ cup freshly squeezed orange juice
- ½ cup fruit-sweetened orange marmalade
- ⅓ cup canola oil
- ¼ cup pure maple syrup
- Grated zest of 1 orange
- 2 cups whole wheat pastry flour
- 1 teaspoon nonaluminum baking powder
- 1 teaspoon baking soda
- ½ teaspoon fine sea salt

Preheat the oven to 350°F. Lightly oil a 12-cup muffin pan with canola oil and dust with flour, tapping out the excess flour.

Put the orange juice, marmalade, oil, syrup, and zest into a small bowl and stir together.

Whisk the flour, baking powder, baking soda, and salt together in a large bowl until well combined. Add the orange juice mixture and combine, using as few strokes as possible so you do not overmix the batter.

Spoon the batter into the prepared muffin pan, filling each cup about three-quarters full. Bake until a toothpick inserted into the center of a muffin comes out clean, 20 to 25 minutes.

Let the muffins cool for 5 minutes before removing from the pan.

BANANA-GINGER MUFFINS

Makes 1 dozen muffins

⅔ **cup mashed ripe banana (about 2 medium bananas)**

⅓ **cup pure maple syrup**

⅔ **cup freshly squeezed orange juice**

⅓ **cup canola or safflower oil**

2 **teaspoons finely grated fresh gingerroot**

1 **teaspoon finely grated lemon zest**

2 **cups whole wheat pastry flour**

1 **teaspoon nonaluminum baking powder**

1 **teaspoon baking soda**

½ **teaspoon fine sea salt**

1 **cup coarsely chopped walnuts, toasted**

Preheat the oven to 350°F. Lightly oil a 12-cup muffin pan with canola oil and dust with flour, tapping out the excess.

In a medium bowl, combine the banana, maple syrup, orange juice, oil, ginger, and lemon zest.

Whisk the flour, baking powder, baking soda, and salt together in a large bowl until combined. Add the banana mixture and combine, using as few strokes as possible so you do not overmix the batter. Stir in the walnuts.

Spoon the batter into the prepared muffin pan, filling each cup about three-quarters full. Bake until a toothpick inserted into the center of a muffin comes out clean, 20 to 25 minutes.

Let the muffins cool for 5 minutes before removing from the pan.

Rise in blood cholesterol from consuming one egg per day:
12 percent
Rise in heart attack risk from 12 percent rise in blood cholesterol: **24 percent**

PINEAPPLE-DATE BRAN MUFFINS

Makes 1 dozen muffins

- 1½ cups pineapple juice
- ½ cup pure maple syrup
- ¼ cup canola or safflower oil
- 1 teaspoon pure vanilla extract
- ⅓ cup pitted dates, finely chopped
- 2 cups whole wheat pastry flour
- 1½ teaspoons nonaluminum baking powder
- ½ teaspoon baking soda
- ½ teaspoon fine sea salt
- 1½ cups wheat or oat bran
- ½ cup raisins
- 1 6-ounce can crushed unsweetened pineapple in juice, drained
- ½ cup coarsely chopped unsalted macadamia nuts

Preheat the oven to 350°F. Lightly oil a 12-cup muffin pan with canola oil and dust with flour, tapping out the excess flour.

Put the pineapple juice, maple syrup, oil, vanilla, and dates into a medium bowl and stir together.

Whisk the flour, baking powder, baking soda, and salt together in a large bowl until combined. Stir in the bran and raisins. Add the pineapple juice mixture and combine, using as few strokes as possible so you do not overmix the batter. Fold in the pineapple and nuts.

Spoon the batter into the prepared muffin pan, filling each cup about three-quarters full. Bake until a toothpick inserted into the center of a muffin comes out clean, 20 to 25 minutes.

Let the muffins cool for 5 minutes before removing from the pan.

Looking at a piece of bread, may we be touched
By the clouds and the rain that enable the wheat to grow;
Strengthened by the fertile Earth
In which the great waving fields are rooted;
And reminded of the glorious sun
Whose warmth and light are converted by plant life
Into the energy on which we all are sustained.

Holding a piece of fruit, may we be grateful
To the men and women who dug the wells,
Planted the seeds and seedlings, tended the plants,
Harvested the fruit, and in so many other ways
Brought forth the bounty of the Earth.
May we be aware that human effort
Built and maintains the roads, trucks, markets, and delivery
    systems
That help carry this fruit to our hands.

In eating, may we remember to give thanks
To all the countless people,
Each with his or her own name and spirit,
Who have labored that we might eat.

THIRTEEN

Dips and Spreads

Some dips and spreads use nuts or seeds, which benefit from being soaked to achieve a more desirable taste and texture. Soaking the seeds before adding them to a recipe starts the sprouting process and makes them easier to digest. Soak seeds in water for six to twelve hours, nuts for twelve to twenty-four. Discard the soaking water and rinse the seeds well. Soaked nuts and seeds will keep for two to three days in the refrigerator.

KEFFI'S PÂTÉ

Makes 2 cups

This delectable pâté comes from Restaurant Keffi in Santa Cruz. It is uncooked and is made from pumpkin and sunflower seeds that are soaked for six to twelve hours to achieve the desired taste and texture. More important, soaking starts the sprouting process, which improves the nutritional value of the seeds. Spread a tortilla with the pâté, top with lettuce and tomato, and roll up.

1 **cup raw pumpkin seeds**

1 **cup raw sunflower seeds**

½ **medium red onion**

2 **tablespoons tamari**

½ **cup coarsely chopped fresh basil**

¼ **teaspoon freshly ground black pepper**

Put the pumpkin and sunflower seeds in a medium bowl and cover with water. Allow to soak for 6 to 12 hours. Drain, rinse thoroughly, and drain again.

Put the soaked seeds and all the remaining ingredients in a food processor fitted with the metal blade. Process until smooth. Mound the pâté in the center of a serving dish, cover, and refrigerate for at least 1 hour before serving.

The pâté keeps up to 3 days in the refrigerator.

Amount of U.S. corn consumed by people: **20 percent**
Amount of U.S. corn consumed by livestock: **80 percent**
Amount of U.S. soybeans consumed by people: **10 percent**
*Amount of U.S. soybeans consumed by
livestock:* **90 percent**
*How frequently a child on Earth dies as a result of
malnutrition:* **Every 2.3 seconds**

Most dips, spreads, and pâtés are made with high-fat animal products loaded with calories. Try some of the tasty dips and spreads in this chapter, and you'll see that they don't have to be high in fat to be good.

WALNUT-MUSHROOM PÂTÉ

Makes about 3 cups

Serve this pâté at your most festive occasions. It is a delicious blend of walnuts, mushrooms, onion, and tofu.

1 tablespoon olive oil
1 medium onion, finely chopped
½ pound mushrooms, sliced
2 cups walnuts, toasted
½ pound firm tofu, crumbled
2 tablespoons nutritional yeast flakes
2 tablespoons Bragg Liquid Aminos

Heat the olive oil in a large frying pan over medium heat. Add the onion and cook, stirring, until golden, about 6 minutes. Add the mushrooms, cover, and cook for 3 minutes. Uncover and cook, stirring occasionally, until the mushrooms have given off their liquid and are lightly browned, about 5 minutes.

Put the cooked vegetables in a food processor fitted with the metal blade, and process until smooth. Add the remaining ingredients and process until smooth. Put into a serving dish, cover, and refrigerate for at least 1 hour before serving.

The pâté keeps for up to 1 day in the refrigerator.

GARBANZO AND CUCUMBER SPREAD

Makes 4 cups

A close relative of *hummis bi tahini,* the Mid-Eastern garbanzo purée, this spread is sensational in a whole wheat pita bread pocket, topped with sliced tomatoes and sprouts. It's also a tasty appetizer, served with toasted pita wedges.

1½ cups dried garbanzo beans (chickpeas), picked over and rinsed

2 medium unwaxed cucumbers

1¾ teaspoons fine sea salt, or more to taste

½ cup plus 1 tablespoon freshly squeezed lemon juice, or more to taste

½ cup tahini

3 garlic cloves, crushed

3 tablespoons water

⅛ teaspoon cayenne pepper, or more to taste

⅓ cup olive oil

2 tablespoons chopped fresh dill, optional

Place the garbanzo beans in a large bowl and add enough cold water to cover by 2 inches. Let stand at room temperature overnight. Drain well.

Place the beans in a large pot, add enough fresh cold water to cover by 2 inches, and bring to a boil over high heat. Reduce the heat to low, cover, and simmer, stirring occasionally, until the beans are tender, 1 to 2 hours. (The exact cooking time will depend on the age of the beans.) Drain the beans well.

Meanwhile, halve the cucumbers lengthwise and scoop out the seeds with the tip of a spoon. Finely chop the cucumbers, place in a bowl, and toss with 1 teaspoon of the salt. Let stand for 1 hour to draw out excess moisture. Rinse well, drain, and pat the cucumbers dry with kitchen towels.

Place the cooked garbanzo beans in a food processor fitted with the metal blade. Add the lemon juice, tahini, garlic, water, the remaining ¾ teaspoon salt, and the cayenne and process until the garbanzo beans are finely chopped. With the machine running, slowly add the oil and process until puréed and fluffy. (You may have to add a little more water.) Taste the spread, and season, if desired, with additional lemon juice, salt, and cayenne.

Transfer the spread to a bowl and stir in the cucumber and dill. The spread will keep up to 2 days, covered and refrigerated.

Note: Two 16-ounce cans of garbanzo beans, drained and rinsed, can be substituted for the cooked dried beans.

SUNNY ALMOND SPREAD

Makes 3 cups

Serve this delicious spread on crackers or rolled in warmed tortillas with sprouts and tomatoes.

1 **cup raw almonds**
1 **cup raw sunflower seeds**
1 **small carrot, grated**
2 **tablespoons freshly squeezed lemon juice**
¼ **cup Vegetable Stock (see page 250) or water**
¼ **cup tofu mayonnaise**
¼ **cup chopped fresh parsley**
2 **tablespoons Bragg Liquid Aminos**
2 **garlic cloves, peeled**
⅛ **teaspoon cayenne pepper**

Put the almonds and sunflower seeds in a medium bowl and cover with water. Allow to soak for 6 to 12 hours. Drain, rinse thoroughly, and drain again.

Put the soaked almonds and sunflower seeds in a food processor, fitted with the metal blade, and process for 30 seconds. Add the remaining ingredients and process until smooth. Cover, and chill before serving.

The spread keeps up to 3 days in the refrigerator.

> *"There will never be any peace in the world so long as we eat animals."*—Isaac Bashevis Singer

EGGPLANT, VEGETABLE, AND TAHINI SPREAD

Makes 4 cups

Roasted eggplants give an elusive smoky character to this chunky sandwich stuffer. It's just the thing to spread between slices of Ocean's Bombs of Love Bread (page 218) for a nutritious lunch.

- 2 medium eggplants
- 6 tablespoons tahini
- 6 tablespoons freshly squeezed lemon juice
- ¼ cup olive oil
- 1 teaspoon fine sea salt
- ⅛ teaspoon cayenne pepper
- 2 medium carrots, grated
- 2 ribs celery, finely chopped
- 1 small red onion, minced
- 2 garlic cloves, minced
- 2 medium tomatoes, seeded and finely chopped

Preheat the oven to 400°F. Lightly oil a 9- by 13-inch baking pan.

Prick the eggplants all over with a fork. Place in the baking pan and bake until soft, about 45 minutes. Cool completely.

Halve the eggplants and remove the soft eggplant pulp from the skin, scraping it off with the dull side of a knife. Place the pulp in a medium bowl and discard or compost the skin. Add the tahini, lemon juice, oil, salt, and cayenne and beat well with a wooden spoon until light. Stir in the carrots, celery, onion, and garlic, then stir in the tomatoes. The spread will keep up to 2 days, covered and refrigerated.

TAHINI MISO SPREAD

Makes 1 cup

Serve with toasted pita bread or warmed bagels.

¾ **cup raw tahini**

¼ **cup white miso**

2 **tablespoons nutritional yeast flakes**

3 **tablespoons hot water**

1 **teaspoon dried basil**

½ **teaspoon dried oregano**

Put all the ingredients into a bowl and stir until blended well. Transfer to a serving dish. The spread will keep up to 2 weeks in the refrigerator.

The meat, dairy, and egg industries claim:
We need animal products to be healthy.
Fact: The diseases and conditions that can be commonly prevented, consistently improved, and/or sometimes cured by a low-fat diet free from animal products include: **strokes, heart disease, osteoporosis, prostate cancer, breast cancer, colon cancer, hypertension, salmonellosis, hypoglycemia, peptic ulcers, obesity, diabetes, hemorrhoids, diverticulosis, asthma, constipation, gallstones, and irritable bowel syndrome.**

O Thou, the sustainer of our bodies, hearts, and souls,
Bless all that we receive in thankfulness.
Amen.

—Sufi grace

TEMPEH SANDWICH SPREAD

Makes about 3 cups

This spread is made from colorful little bits of vegetables in a tempeh mixture. Like tofu, tempeh is made from soybeans, but unlike tofu, tempeh uses the whole bean, and it contains more nutrients.

½ **pound tempeh**

2 **ribs celery, with leaves, finely chopped**

3 **green onions, with tops, finely chopped**

1 **small carrot, grated**

½ **green bell pepper, seeded and finely chopped**

¼ **cup tofu mayonnaise**

1 **tablespoon soy sauce**

2 **teaspoons Dijon mustard**

1 **teaspoon celery seeds**

Fine sea salt to taste

Pour 1 inch of water in a large saucepan with a steamer basket, cover with the lid, and bring to a gentle boil. Put the tempeh in the steamer basket, cover and steam for 15 minutes. Let the tempeh cool.

Crumble the tempeh into small pieces, and put it in a large bowl. Add all the remaining ingredients and stir to mix. Store, well covered in the refrigerator, for up to 2 days.

SPICY TOFU DIP

Makes 2¹/₂ cups

Serve this spicy dip with raw vegetables.

- 1 **pound firm tofu**
- 6 **green onions, with tops, chopped**
- 1 **rib celery, with leaves, chopped**
- ¹/₃ **cup tofu mayonnaise**
- 2 **tablespoons tamari**
- 1¹/₂ **tablespoons Dijon mustard**
- 1 **teaspoon celery seeds**
- 1 **teaspoon turmeric**
- 1 **garlic clove, minced**
- ¹/₈ **teaspoon cayenne pepper**

Using your hands, squeeze the excess water from the tofu.

Put the tofu and all the remaining ingredients in a food processor fitted with the metal blade, and process until smooth. Cover and refrigerate for at least 1 hour before serving.

The dip will keep up to 2 days in the refrigerator.

---

*Enzyme inhibitors are found in the skins of almonds,
so removing their skins, a technique known
as "blanching," makes them easier to digest.
To blanch almonds, put the almonds into boiling water
for thirty seconds. Drain, plunge the almonds into cold
water, and then drain again. Use your fingertips to rub
the skin from the almonds.*

TOFU CHIVE SPREAD

Makes 2 1/2 cups

1   **pound firm tofu, crumbled**
3   **tablespoons rice vinegar**
1   **teaspoon onion powder**
1   **teaspoon fine sea salt**
¼   **cup olive oil**
½   **cup finely chopped fresh chives**

Using your hands, squeeze out the excess moisture from the tofu.

Put the tofu, vinegar, onion powder, and salt in a food processor fitted with the metal blade, and process until smooth. With the machine running, slowly add the oil and blend until mixed.

Transfer the tofu mixture to a bowl, add the chives, and stir until mixed. The spread will keep up to a week in the refrigerator.

NO-CHEESE SPREAD

Makes 2 cups

Are you easing up on dairy foods, but missing cheesy spreads and pizza? This is your answer. No-Cheese Spread tastes great on crackers and is delicious on pizza.

5   **tablespoons olive oil**
1   **small red bell pepper, seeded and coarsely chopped**
1½ **cups raw cashews**
¼   **cup raw sesame seeds**
½   **cup water**
⅓   **cup nutritional yeast flakes**
¼   **cup freshly squeezed lemon juice**
¼   **cup canola or safflower oil**
1   **tablespoon Bragg Liquid Aminos**

Heat 1 tablespoon of the olive oil in a small frying pan over medium-high heat. Add the bell pepper and cook until tender, 5 to 7 minutes. Transfer the pepper to a blender.

Add all the remaining ingredients and blend until smooth. The spread will keep up to a week in the refrigerator.

SPINACH-DILL DIP

Makes 3 cups

1 **ripe medium avocado, peeled, stone removed, and quartered**

1 **ripe medium tomato, quartered**

½ **medium red onion, quartered**

2 **garlic cloves, crushed**

3 **tablespoons chopped fresh dill**

3 **tablespoons freshly squeezed lemon juice**

2 **tablespoons Bragg Liquid Aminos**

¼ **teaspoon grated nutmeg**

¼ **teaspoon freshly ground black pepper**

1¼ **pounds spinach, well washed, stems removed**

In a food processor fitted with the metal blade, pulse all the ingredients except the spinach until puréed. Add the spinach in batches, and process until each batch is puréed before adding the next.

Transfer the dip to a serving dish, cover, and refrigerate for at least 1 hour before serving. The dip keeps, covered and refrigerated, for 1 day.

"When you see the Golden Arches, you are probably on the road to the pearly gates."—William Castelli, M.D., Director, Framingham Heart Study

CHUNKY GUACAMOLE

Makes 2 cups

Everyone loves guacamole. While traditionally served as a dip with corn chips or fresh vegetables, this chunky version can be used as a topping for salads, a spread on toasted bagels, or a condiment for Mexican dishes such as Enchiladas Supremas (page 332).

2 avocados, peeled, stones removed, and chopped

2 green onions, with tops, chopped

1 rib celery, with leaves, chopped

1 tomato, chopped

½ green bell pepper, seeded and chopped

1 fresh hot chile pepper, seeded and minced, or more to taste

1 garlic clove, minced

2 tablespoons freshly squeezed lemon juice

¾ teaspoon fine sea salt

Mix all the ingredients together in a medium bowl.

The guacamole will keep for up to a day in the refrigerator, with a piece of waxed paper pressed directly onto its surface to prevent discoloration.

Amount of nutrient wasted by cycling grain through beef cattle:
Protein: 90 percent
Carbohydrate: 99 percent
Fiber: 100 percent

> *"The fact is that there is enough food in the world for everyone. But tragically, much of the world's food and land resources are tied up in producing beef and other livestock— food for the well-off—while millions of children and adults suffer from malnutrition and starvation."*
> —Dr. Walden Bello, Executive Director, Institute for Food and Development Policy

SALSA

Makes 3 cups

A spicy, uncooked sauce made with tomatoes and other vegetables makes a tasty dip for vegetables or corn chips, or a sauce for many Mexican dishes. Salsa can be mild or hot depending on how many jalapeño peppers you use. The oils from these hot peppers can irritate the eyes, so wash your hands after handling them.

 3 **medium tomatoes, cut into chunks**

 1 **medium green bell pepper, seeded and cut into chunks**

 1 **green onion, with top, cut into large pieces**

 2 **tablespoons chopped fresh cilantro, optional**

 ½ **jalapeño pepper, seeded and minced (include seeds for a hotter salsa)**

 1 **tablespoon freshly squeezed lime juice**

 ½ **teaspoon fine sea salt**

Put all the ingredients into a food processor fitted with the metal blade, and pulse to coarsely chop. The salsa will keep up to a week in the refrigerator.

MEXICAN BLACK BEAN DIP

Makes 3 cups

You can keep a few cans of black beans in your pantry to make this dip when you don't have time to soak and cook the beans. Serve this hearty dip with corn chips and vegetables.

1 cup dried black beans, picked over and rinsed, or
1 16-ounce can black beans, rinsed and drained

1 small Anaheim chile pepper or green bell pepper, seeded and finely chopped

1 fresh hot chile pepper, seeded and minced

1 medium avocado, peeled, stone removed, and finely chopped

2 medium tomatoes, finely chopped

6 green onions, with tops, finely chopped

2 garlic cloves, minced

¼ cup finely chopped fresh cilantro, optional

3 tablespoons Bragg Liquid Aminos

2 tablespoons freshly squeezed lime juice

Pinch of cayenne pepper

If using dried beans, put the beans into a large bowl and add enough cold water to cover by 2 inches. Put the bowl in a cool place and let the beans soak for 8 hours, or overnight. Drain and rinse the beans.

Put the soaked beans into a pot and add enough fresh water to cover the beans by 2 inches. Cover and bring to a boil over high heat, then immediately reduce the heat and simmer, stirring occasionally, until the beans are tender 45 minutes to 1 hour. Thoroughly drain the beans and let them cool.

Put the cooked or canned beans into a large bowl and mash them with a fork. Add the remaining ingredients and stir together. The dip keeps up to 5 days in the refrigerator.

FOURTEEN

Soups

In this chapter, there are recipes for three different kinds of soups: uncooked soups, creamy soups, and broths. Once you learn the easy cooking principles behind each one, you can create unlimited variations. Uncooked soups are an easy way to introduce enzyme-rich raw foods into your diet. They are healthy, delicious, and easy to prepare. Just blend the ingredients in a blender or food processor and serve. Our creamy soups use vegetables, nuts, and seeds to achieve a creamy texture without the cholesterol and saturated fat associated with dairy products. Broths are made by cooking a variety of vegetables, herbs, and spices in water. Cooked beans, grains, and pasta can be added to broths to make a thicker soup.

VEGETABLE STOCK

Makes 2 quarts

Use this stock as an ingredient in other dishes, or enjoy it on its own as a soup. Cool the stock to room temperature, then store in the refrigerator for up to five days, or freeze for up to three months. Vegetable bouillon cubes and bouillon flakes, available at health food stores in both salted and salt-free varieties, can be dissolved in boiling water to substitute for freshly made stock.

2½ **quarts water**
  2 **medium onions, chopped**
  2 **medium ribs celery, with leaves, chopped**
  2 **medium carrots, chopped**
  2 **medium baking potatoes, unpeeled, cut into 2-inch pieces**
  1 **head garlic, unpeeled, cut in half horizontally**
  4 **parsley sprigs**
  ½ **teaspoon fine sea salt**
  ⅛ **teaspoon black peppercorns**

In a large pot, combine all the ingredients and bring to a boil over high heat. Reduce the heat to low and simmer, partially covered, for about 3 hours. (Do not boil, or the potatoes will fall apart and cloud your stock.)

Carefully spoon the stock and the vegetables into a strainer set over a large bowl. Discard the solids remaining in the strainer. Cool the stock completely before storing.

Let us bless the source of life that brings forth bread from the Earth.
Let our lives be a blessing to the Earth that sustains us,
And to all the creatures who, like us, call this planet home.

> *When it comes to food that is healthy, hearty, and wholesome,*
> *there is nothing like homemade soup.*

GAZPACHO

Makes 6 servings

This refreshing soup is made with raw fresh vegetables and is traditionally served chilled. It was popular in Spain and Mexico long before the health advantages of raw foods were discovered in America. Serve gazpacho as a first course to an elegant dinner, or with Spanakopita (page 340) for a light meal.

6 medium tomatoes, quartered

2 unwaxed cucumbers, coarsely chopped

1 green bell pepper, seeded and coarsely chopped

½ cup coarsely chopped fresh basil

¼ cup chopped fresh parsley

2 tablespoons freshly squeezed lemon juice

2 garlic cloves, minced

½ teaspoon ground cumin

½ teaspoon fine sea salt

⅛ teaspoon cayenne pepper

2 cups tomato-vegetable juice

2 green onions, with tops, chopped

Herbed Croutons (page 227)

In a food processor fitted with the metal blade, combine the tomatoes, cucumbers, green pepper, basil, parsley, lemon juice, garlic, cumin, salt and cayenne. Pulse until coarsely chopped. Transfer to a large bowl, stir in the tomato-vegetable juice, and refrigerate for at least 1 hour before serving.

Serve the gazpacho in individual bowls, with the green onions and croutons in separate bowls on the side.

BORSCHT ENERGY SOUP

Makes 6 servings

This soup is a delectable blend of fresh vegetables and sprouts.

- 1 medium beet, scrubbed and cut into chunks
- 1 medium carrot, sliced
- 1 medium Kirby cucumber, cut into chunks
- 1 medium green bell pepper, seeded and coarsely chopped
- 1 lemon, peeled, halved, and seeds removed
- 1 ripe avocado, peeled, stone removed, and quartered
- ½ packed cup spinach leaves
- ½ packed cup alfalfa sprouts
- ½ cup chopped fresh dill
- 2 tablespoons Bragg Liquid Aminos
- ⅛ teaspoon freshly ground black pepper
- 2 cups Vegetable Stock (page 250) or vegetable bouillon

Alfalfa sprouts, for garnish

In a food processor fitted with the metal blade, pulse the beet, carrot, cucumber, bell pepper, and lemon until finely chopped. Add the avocado, spinach, alfalfa sprouts, dill, liquid aminos, and pepper. With the machine running, gradually add the Vegetable Stock and process until smooth. Transfer the borscht to a bowl, cover, and refrigerate until chilled, at least 2 hours.

Serve the soup in individual bowls, garnishing each one with alfalfa sprouts.

Amount of U.S. cropland producing livestock feed:
64 percent
Amount of U.S. cropland producing fruits and vegetables:
2 percent

As the aroma of a soup cooking on the stove steams its way into the atmosphere of our kitchens, our lives are enriched in ways beyond telling. A good soup, gently simmering away, makes the whole house feel welcoming.

CREAMY CARROT SOUP

Makes 6 servings

Uncooked soups like this one are very quick and easy to make. Be sure the vegetables and juice are well chilled.

> 1 ripe avocado, peeled, stone removed, and quartered
> 1 medium red bell pepper, seeded and coarsely chopped
> 1 medium tomato, halved
> ½ small red onion
> 2 tablespoons Bragg Liquid Aminos
> ¾ teaspoon ground cumin
> Pinch of cayenne pepper, optional
> 3½ cups fresh carrot juice, chilled
> 2 medium carrots, grated

In a food processor fitted with the metal blade, combine the avocado, bell pepper, tomato, red onion, liquid aminos, cumin, and cayenne and process until finely chopped. With the machine running, add the carrot juice, and process until blended. Pour the soup into a serving bowl, and stir in the grated carrots. Serve immediately.

Spotted on a child's T-shirt: "If you love me, don't feed me junk food."

CREAMY BUTTERNUT SQUASH SOUP

Makes 6 servings

Butternut squash gives this soup a creamy, smooth texture, a naturally sweet taste, and a lovely autumnal color. Serve at your holiday dinners, or with Sweet and Spicy Couscous Salad (page 284) for a simple meal.

   1 **butternut squash (about 1¾ pounds), skin left on, cut into 2-inch cubes**

4½ **cups Vegetable Stock (page 250) or vegetable bouillon**

  ½ **cup raw almonds**

1½ **teaspoons curry powder**

  ½ **teaspoon fine sea salt**

  ⅛ **teaspoon freshly ground black pepper**

Parsley sprigs, for garnish

   1 **tart apple, such as Granny Smith, peeled, cored, and finely chopped**

Put the squash and 3 cups of the Vegetable Stock in a large pot. Bring to a simmer over medium heat, then reduce the heat, cover and cook until the squash is tender, 15 to 20 minutes. Remove from the heat, and let the squash cool in the cooking water.

Using a slotted spoon, remove the squash from the pot. Peel the squash, and set aside. Set aside the pot of cooking liquid.

Blanch the almonds in boiling water for 30 seconds. Drain, and plunge the almonds into cold water. Drain, and squeeze the almonds between your fingertips to remove the skins. Compost or discard the skins.

Put the blanched almonds and the remaining 1½ cups Vegetable Stock into a blender. Blend until smooth, about 1 minute. Add the cooked squash, curry, salt, and pepper and process until smooth.

Add the squash mixture to the pot of cooking liquid, and bring just to a simmer over medium heat.

Serve hot, garnished with parsley sprigs and the apple.

YELLOW PEPPER SOUP

Makes 6 servings

Sweet yellow peppers and cashews give this soup its creamy texture.

2 **tablespoons olive oil**

3 **large yellow bell peppers, seeded and coarsely chopped**

4 **shallots, finely chopped**

1½ **cups raw cashews**

3½ **cups Vegetable Stock (page 250) or vegetable bouillon**

1 **teaspoon dry mustard**

½ **teaspoon fine sea salt**

⅛ **teaspoon freshly ground black pepper**

Parsley sprigs, for garnish

In a medium skillet, heat the olive oil over medium heat. Add the bell peppers and shallots, cover, and cook, stirring occasionally, until the peppers are very soft, 8 to 10 minutes. Remove from the heat.

Put the cashews and 1½ cups of the Vegetable Stock in a blender. Blend until smooth, about 1 minute. Add the cooked peppers, mustard, salt, and pepper, and purée.

Pour the soup into a medium saucepan, and stir in the remaining 2 cups Vegetable Stock. Bring just to a simmer over medium heat. Serve hot, garnished with parsley sprigs.

"The American fast-food diet and the meat-eating habits of the wealthy around the world support a world food system that diverts food resources from the hungry. A diet higher in whole grains and legumes and lower in beef and other meat is not just healthier for ourselves but also contributes to changing the world system that feeds some people and leaves others hungry."
—Dr. Walden Bello, Executive Director,
Institute for Food and Development Policy

POTATO PARSLEY BISQUE

Makes 6 servings

This creamy soup is similar to the classic French leek and potato soup, but is made with an almond milk instead of dairy cream. It has the fresh taste of leeks and parsley and is thick with lots of potatoes. Any variety of potatoes can be used, but try the sweet, delicate flavor of red-skinned potatoes.

 1 **cup raw almonds or cashews**

 5 **cups Vegetable Stock (page 250) or vegetable bouillon**

 1 **pound red-skinned potatoes, unpeeled, cut into
     ½-inch cubes**

 2 **medium leeks, sliced and thoroughly washed**

 1 **cup finely chopped fresh parsley**

 1 **teaspoon freshly squeezed lemon juice**

 1 **teaspoon fine sea salt**

 ¼ **teaspoon freshly ground black pepper**

Blanch the almonds in boiling water for 30 seconds. Drain, and plunge the almonds into cold water. Drain, and squeeze the almonds between your fingertips to remove the skins. Compost or discard the skins.

Put the blanched almonds and 1 cup of the Vegetable Stock in a blender, and blend until smooth, about 1 minute.

In a large pot, combine the potatoes, leeks, and the remaining 4 cups Vegetable Stock and bring to a simmer over medium heat. Cover and boil until the potatoes are tender, about 10 to 15 minutes.

Stir the blanched almond mixture, parsley, lemon juice, salt, and pepper into the soup. Bring to a simmer and cook, stirring often, until thickened, about 2 minutes. Transfer the soup to a food processor and process, in batches if necessary, until smooth.

Serve immediately.

CREAM OF BROCCOLI SOUP

Makes 6 servings

Cream soups bring out the natural taste of vegetables and do not need a lot of spices. You can vary this basic recipe by substituting asparagus, cauliflower, or peas for the broccoli. For a complete meal, serve with Spicy Corn Bread (page 228) and a green salad with Rose's Sweet and Sour Dressing (page 293).

1 cup raw cashews

5 cups Vegetable Stock (page 250) or vegetable bouillon

2 medium boiling potatoes, unpeeled, cut into ½-inch cubes

1 medium onion, finely chopped

1 bunch broccoli, trimmed and coarsely chopped (about 4½ cups)

1 teaspoon dried basil

1 teaspoon fine sea salt

¼ teaspoon freshly ground black pepper

Put the cashews and 1 cup of the Vegetable Stock into a blender. Blend until smooth, about 1 minute.

Put the remaining 4 cups Vegetable Stock, the potatoes, and onion in a large pot. Bring to a simmer, cover, and cook for 5 minutes. Stir in the broccoli and basil and return to a simmer. Cover and cook until the potatoes are tender, about 10 minutes.

Stir in the reserved cashew mixture, the salt, and pepper and bring just to a simmer. Remove from the heat, transfer about half of the soup to a blender, and purée. Return the purée to the pot and stir well. Serve immediately.

Amount of U.S. land that could be returned to forest for each American who adopts a meat-free diet: **35,000 square feet**

POTATO CORN CHOWDER

Makes 6 servings

Creamy soups can be quickly prepared with soy milk, almond milk, or cashew milk. This soup is like a chowder, thick with potatoes, onions, and corn. Serve with Garlic Herb Bread (page 225) and a green salad with John's Tahini Dressing (page 301).

2½ cups Vegetable Stock (page 250) or vegetable bouillon
½ pound boiling potatoes, unpeeled, cut into ½-inch cubes
1 medium onion, finely chopped
1 medium red bell pepper, seeded and finely chopped
1 medium rib celery, finely chopped
2 ears corn, kernels cut off the cob, or 1½ cups (thawed) frozen corn
2 cups soy milk
1 teaspoon celery seeds
1 teaspoon fine sea salt
¼ teaspoon freshly ground black pepper

Put the vegetable stock, potatoes, onion, red pepper, and celery in a large pot. Bring to a simmer over medium heat, cover, and cook until the potatoes are tender, about 15 minutes.

Stir in the corn, soy milk, celery seeds, salt, and pepper. Return to a simmer, and cook until heated through, about 3 minutes. Serve immediately.

One of the best things about cooked soups is that you can make them in large quantities and keep the extra in the refrigerator or freezer. In fact, soups usually taste even better if the flavors have had a day or so to blend with one another.

CREAMY VEGETABLE TAHINI SOUP

Makes 6 servings

Tahini gives this garden vegetable soup its creamy base. It has a rich but delicate flavor and will make a colorful addition to your table. Serve with Vegetable Rye Bread (page 223) and Mediterranean Salad (page 279).

⅓ cup raw tahini

⅓ cup water

3 tablespoons tamari

1 tablespoon freshly squeezed lemon juice

1 teaspoon ground cumin

Pinch of cayenne pepper

4 cups Vegetable Stock (page 250), vegetable bouillon, or water

2 medium carrots, chopped

2 cups finely chopped broccoli florets and stalks

2 medium leeks, sliced and thoroughly washed

2 medium tomatoes, coarsely chopped

¼ cup finely chopped fresh parsley

Put the tahini, the ⅓ cup water, the tamari, lemon juice, cumin, and cayenne in a small bowl, and stir together.

Put the Vegetable Stock and carrots in a large pot, cover, and bring to a boil over medium-high heat. Immediately reduce the heat, and simmer for 5 minutes. Stir in the broccoli, leeks, tomatoes, and parsley. Cover and return to a boil over medium-high heat, then immediately reduce the heat and simmer until the vegetables are tender, about 5 minutes.

Add the tahini mixture and stir until mixed. Bring just to a simmer, and serve immediately.

MILLET SOUP

Makes 6 servings

Millet, a grain commonly used in Asia and Africa, is available in health food stores. This thick, hearty soup is a delicious introduction to this nutritious grain. Try it with Spicy Corn Bread (page 228).

> 3½ cups Vegetable Stock (page 250) or vegetable bouillon
> ½ cup millet
> ½ small cauliflower, cut into florets
> 1 medium carrot, coarsely chopped
> 1 rib celery, with leaves, sliced
> 2 garlic cloves, minced
> ½ teaspoon dried rosemary
> ½ teaspoon dried thyme
> 1 teaspoon dried basil
> ¼ teaspoon freshly ground black pepper
> 1½ cups sliced mushrooms
> 3 green onions, with tops, finely chopped
> 2 cups soy milk
> 3 tablespoons tamari
> 2 tablespoons nutritional yeast flakes, optional

Put the stock and millet in a large pot. Bring to a simmer over medium heat, cover, and cook for 12 minutes.

Stir in the cauliflower, carrot, celery, garlic, rosemary, thyme, basil, and pepper and return to a simmer. Cover and cook, stirring occasionally, until the vegetables are almost tender, about 8 minutes.

Stir in the mushrooms and green onions, cover, and simmer until the mushrooms are tender, about 5 minutes.

Stir in the soy milk, tamari, and yeast flakes, and bring just to a simmer. Serve immediately.

TOFU NOODLE SOUP

Makes 6 servings

This soup has the taste of traditional chicken noodle soup. The tofu is frozen and then thawed to make it chewy.

½ **pound firm tofu**

2 **cups noodles made without eggs**

5 **cups Vegetable Stock (page 250) or vegetable bouillon**

1 **medium carrot, chopped**

1 **rib celery, with leaves, chopped**

1 **medium onion, chopped**

2 **garlic cloves, minced**

½ **teaspoon dried marjoram**

½ **teaspoon dried thyme**

½ **teaspoon rubbed sage**

1 **bay leaf**

1 **teaspoon fine sea salt**

¼ **teaspoon freshly ground black pepper**

1 **pound fresh peas, shelled, or 1 cup (thawed) frozen peas**

½ **cup finely chopped fresh parsley**

Drain and rinse the tofu. Put the tofu in a plastic bag or container, close it tightly, and freeze until the tofu is frozen hard. Remove the bag or container from the freezer and put it in a bowl of hot water, or let the tofu thaw at room temperature. Gently squeeze the water from the tofu, using your hands, and then squeeze it dry between two towels. Cut the tofu into ½-inch cubes.

In a large pot of lightly salted boiling water, cook the noodles just until tender, about 8 minutes. Drain, rinse well under cold running water, and drain again.

In a large pot, combine the Vegetable Stock, carrot, celery, onion, garlic, marjoram, thyme, sage, bay leaf, salt, and pepper. Bring to a simmer over medium heat and cook for 5 minutes.

Stir in the cubed tofu, peas, and parsley, return to a simmer, and cook for 2 minutes. Stir in the cooked noodles and bring just to a simmer. Remove the bay leaf and serve immediately.

VEGETABLE-BEAN CHILI

Makes 8 to 10 servings

Hearty chili is a classic. Serve it over rice, or with Spicy Corn Bread (page 228) and a green salad with Poppy Seed Dressing (page 292). You can make a big pot of chili as it keeps up to five days in the refrigerator; the flavors intensify as it keeps.

2 cups dried kidney beans, picked over and rinsed

2 tablespoons olive oil

1 medium onion, coarsely chopped

2 medium carrots, finely chopped

2 ribs celery, with leaves, finely chopped

1 medium green bell pepper, seeded and chopped

3 garlic cloves, minced

2 tablespoons chili powder

2 teaspoons ground cumin

2 teaspoons dried oregano

2 bay leaves

1 teaspoon fine sea salt

⅛ teaspoon cayenne pepper, plus more to taste

1 16-ounce can unsweetened tomato sauce

2 medium tomatoes or 1 14-ounce can unsweetened Italian tomatoes, coarsely chopped

1 cup Vegetable Stock (page 250), vegetable bouillon, or water

2 ears corn, kernels cut off the cob, or 1½ cups (thawed) frozen corn

Put the beans in a large bowl and add enough water to cover by 2 inches. Put the bowl in a cool place and let the beans soak for 6 to 12 hours. Drain and rinse the beans; drain again.

Put the beans into a large pot and add enough fresh water to cover the beans by 2 inches. Bring to a boil over high heat. Reduce the heat to low, cover, and simmer, stirring occasionally, until the beans are tender, 1¼ to 2 hours, (depending on the age of the beans). Thoroughly drain the beans and let them cool.

In a large pot, heat the olive oil over medium heat. Add the onion, carrots, celery, bell pepper, and garlic, cover, and cook, stirring occasionally, until softened, about 7 minutes.

Add the chili powder, cumin, oregano, bay leaves, salt, and pepper, and stir for 30 seconds. Stir in the cooked beans, tomato sauce, tomatoes, and Vegetable Stock. Cook, partially covered, until thickened, about 20 minutes.

Stir in the corn and cook for 5 minutes, or until heated through.

Remove the bay leaves and serve immediately.

One of California's leading environmental problems: **Drought**
Water needed in California to produce one edible pound of:

Tomatoes	**23 gallons**
Lettuce	**23 gallons**
Potatoes	**24 gallons**
Wheat	**25 gallons**
Carrots	**33 gallons**
Apples	**49 gallons**
Eggs	**544 gallons**
Chicken	**815 gallons**
Pork	**1630 gallons**
Beef	**5214 gallons**

MINESTRONE

Makes 8 servings

Full of vegetables and noodles, this hearty Italian soup is a meal all by itself. Garlic Herb Bread (page 225) is a must with minestrone.

  4 ounces (2 cups) sesame shell macaroni or other shell macaroni made without eggs
  1 tablespoon olive oil
  1 medium onion, chopped
  1 medium carrot, chopped
  1 medium rib celery, with leaves, chopped
  4 garlic cloves, minced
  8 cups Vegetable Stock (page 250) or vegetable bouillon
  3 medium tomatoes, finely chopped, or 1 14-ounce can unsweetened Italian tomatoes, undrained, chopped
  1 medium potato, unpeeled, cut into ½-inch pieces
  1 teaspoon dried rosemary
  2 teaspoons dried basil
  1 teaspoon dried oregano
  1 bay leaf
  ½ teaspoon fine sea salt
  ¼ teaspoon freshly ground black pepper
  3 cups finely shredded green cabbage (about ½ small head)
  ½ cup finely chopped fresh parsley

In a medium pot of lightly salted boiling water, cook the noodles until just tender, about 6 minutes. Drain, rinse under cold water, and drain again. Set the noodles aside.

In a large pot, heat the olive oil over medium heat. Add the onion, carrot, celery, and garlic, and cook, stirring occasionally, until softened, about 5 minutes.

Stir in the vegetable stock, tomatoes, potato, rosemary, basil, oregano, bay leaf, salt, and pepper. Bring to a simmer and cook, partially covered, until the potatoes are almost tender, about 8 minutes.

Stir in the cabbage and parsley and simmer, partially covered, until the cabbage is tender, about 15 minutes.

Stir in the cooked noodles and simmer until heated through, about 5 minutes. Remove the bay leaf, and serve immediately.

HEARTY PEA SOUP

Makes 6 to 8 servings

This recipe is easy and always comes out well. You can make a big potful to have on hand for an instant meal any time of day.

7   cups water
1½ cups split peas, picked over and rinsed
2   onions, chopped
1   bunch broccoli, trimmed and coarsely chopped
3   carrots, sliced
2   zucchini, sliced
½   cup tahini
¼   cup Bragg Liquid Aminos
2   teaspoons chili powder
1   teaspoon ground cumin

In a large pot, combine 6 cups of the water and the split peas. Add the onions, broccoli, carrots, and zucchini and bring to a boil over medium high heat. Immediately reduce the heat, cover, and simmer, stirring occasionally, until the peas are very soft, about 1½ hours.

Meanwhile, in a food processor or blender, combine the remaining 1 cup water and the remaining ingredients and process until smooth.

Stir the tahini mixture into the soup, and serve immediately.

> "I have no doubt that it is a part of the destiny of the human race in its gradual improvement to leave off eating animals."—Henry David Thoreau

DAL

Makes 8 servings

In India, dals are the ubiquitous accompaniment to rice and Chapatis (page 220). They can be served as a side dish or as a rich, thick soup made with split peas, Indian spices, and lots of vegetables. It is no wonder this is one of India's most popular dishes.

7   cups Vegetable Stock (page 250) or vegetable bouillon

1   pound yellow or green split peas

1   medium onion, chopped

2   medium carrots, sliced into ¼-inch rounds

2   medium boiling potatoes, unpeeled, cut into ½-inch cubes

2   tablespoons canola oil

2   teaspoons cumin seeds

1   teaspoon black mustard seeds

2   teaspoons curry powder

1   teaspoon ground coriander

1   teaspoon ground cumin

1   teaspoon turmeric

1   teaspoon finely grated fresh gingerroot

2   garlic cloves, minced

1   teaspoon fine sea salt

⅛   teaspoon cayenne pepper

Put the vegetable stock and split peas in a large pot. Cover and bring to a boil over medium-high heat, then immediately reduce the heat and simmer until the peas are beginning to get tender, about 25 minutes.

Stir in the onion, carrots, and potatoes, cover, and return to a boil over medium-high heat. Immediately reduce the heat and simmer, stirring occasionally, until the potatoes are almost tender, about 15 minutes.

Meanwhile, in a small frying pan, heat the canola oil over medium heat. Add the cumin seeds, mustard seeds, curry powder, coriander, cumin, turmeric, ginger, garlic, salt, and cayenne. Cook, stirring constantly, until the mustard seeds begin to pop, about 30 seconds. Remove from the heat.

Stir the spice mixture and lemon juice into the split peas. Cover and return to a boil over medium-high heat, then immediately reduce the heat and simmer, stirring occasionally, for 5 minutes. Mash some of the vegetables and split peas until the dal reaches the desired consistency. Serve immediately.

VEGETABLE MISO SOUP

Makes 6 servings

This soup, a harmonious blend of vegetables with the wonderful, warm flavor of miso, is a tasty example of why miso is a staple food in Japanese cuisine. Remember, to maintain its full nutritional value, never boil miso.

- 6 **cups water**
- 6 **tablespoons white miso**
- ¾ **pound fresh peas, shelled, or 3 cups (thawed) frozen peas**
- 3 **green onions, with tops, thinly sliced**
- 1 **jalapeño pepper, seeded and sliced into thin rings**
- 1 **garlic clove, minced**
- 1 **medium piece dulse, finely chopped**
- 2 **teaspoons freshly squeezed lemon juice**
- ¼ **teaspoon hot sesame oil**

Put 1 cup of the water and the miso in a small bowl and stir together. In a large pot, combine the remaining 5 cups water, the peas, green onions, jalapeño pepper, and garlic. Cover and bring to a boil over medium-high heat, then immediately reduce the heat and simmer for 3 minutes. Stir in the miso mixture, dulse, lemon juice, and hot sesame oil. Bring barely to a simmer over medium-high heat. Serve immediately.

VEGETABLE LENTIL SOUP

Makes 8 servings

7 cups Vegetable Stock (page 250) or vegetable bouillon

1 cup lentils, picked over and rinsed

1 small bunch Swiss chard (about 14 ounces), well rinsed

2 medium boiling potatoes, unpeeled, cut into ½-inch cubes

1 rib celery, with leaves, chopped

1 medium onion, chopped

2 garlic cloves, minced

¼ cup unsweetened tomato paste

2 cups sliced shiitake mushrooms or cultivated mushrooms

½ cup finely chopped fresh parsley

1½ teaspoons dried thyme

½ teaspoon ground cumin

1 teaspoon fine sea salt

¼ teaspoon freshly ground black pepper

3 tablespoons freshly squeezed lemon juice

Put the vegetable stock and lentils in a large pot. Cover and bring to a boil over medium-high heat, then immediately reduce the heat and simmer until the lentils are almost tender, 30 to 45 minutes (depending on the age of the lentils).

Meanwhile, slice off the stems from the Swiss chard. Keeping the stems and leaves separate, cut into small pieces.

Stir the Swiss chard stems, potatoes, celery, onion, garlic, and tomato paste into the lentils. Cover and bring to a boil over medium-high heat, then immediately reduce the heat and simmer until the potatoes are almost tender, 6 to 8 minutes.

Stir in the Swiss chard leaves, mushrooms, parsley, thyme, cumin, salt, and pepper. Cover and return to a boil over medium-high heat, then immediately reduce the heat and simmer until all the vegetables are tender, about 5 minutes.

Stir in the lemon juice. If desired, mash some of the vegetables and lentils until the soup reaches the desired consistency. Serve immediately.

FIFTEEN

Vegetable Salads

The word salad *comes from the Latin* salus, *meaning "to bring health." Other words stemming from the same root word include* salubrious *("promoting healing"),* salubrity *("wholesomeness"), and* salutary *("contributing to some beneficial purpose"). And, of course, there is the toast, "Salud!"—"To your health!"*

SPINACH WALNUT SALAD

*Makes 2 to 3 main-course servings or
4 first-course servings*

A lovely spinach salad with the flavors of garlic and walnuts. Serve it as a side salad with Herbed Croutons (page 227) or in warm pita bread with Vegetable Lentil Soup (page 268).

2 tablespoons freshly squeezed lemon juice

⅓ cup olive oil

1 small garlic clove, minced

½ teaspoon Dijon mustard

½ teaspoon fine sea salt

⅛ teaspoon freshly ground black pepper

6 green onions, with tops, thinly sliced

1 pound spinach, well washed, stems removed and leaves torn in pieces

1 cup raw walnuts, toasted and finely chopped

Put the lemon juice, olive oil, garlic, mustard, salt, and pepper in a small jar. Cover with the lid and shake until the ingredients are well mixed.

In a salad bowl, toss together the green onions, spinach, and walnuts. Shake the Lemon Garlic Dressing and pour it over the salad. Toss until well coated.

Historic cause of demise of many great civilizations:
Topsoil depletion
*Amount of U.S. topsoil depletion directly associated with
livestock raising:* **85 percent**

MARINATED TOFU SPINACH SALAD

*Makes 2 to 3 main-course servings or
4 to 6 first-course servings*

Spicy marinated tofu and toasted sesame seeds give this spinach salad a distinctive Oriental flair. Start with Vegetable Miso Soup (page 267). This is great with fresh shiitake mushrooms, but try other varieties.

¼ cup apple cider vinegar

1 tablespoon toasted sesame oil

3 tablespoons canola oil

2 tablespoons soy sauce

1 teaspoon curry powder

⅛ teaspoon freshly ground black pepper

½ pound firm tofu, cut into ½-inch cubes

10 ounces spinach, well washed, stems removed and leaves torn into pieces

1 cup mung bean sprouts

1 cup thinly sliced mushrooms

6 to 8 radishes

6 green onions, with tops, thinly sliced

¼ cup sesame seeds, toasted

Put the vinegar, sesame and canola oils, soy sauce, curry powder, and pepper in a large jar. Cover with the lid and shake until the ingredients are well mixed. Add the tofu, cover with the lid, and turn the jar several times until the tofu is coated. Refrigerate for at least 30 minutes to allow the tofu to absorb the flavors, turning the jar occasionally to keep the tofu coated.

In a salad bowl, toss together the spinach, sprouts, mushrooms, radishes, and green onions. Shake the Marinated Tofu Dressing and pour it over the salad. Toss until well coated. Sprinkle with the sesame seeds.

FRESH HERB SALAD

*Makes 2 to 3 main-course servings or
4 to 6 first-course servings*

A simple lemon dressing and fresh basil and dill give this leafy green salad a refreshing flavor. It is quick to make and goes with everything.

⅓ cup freshly squeezed lemon juice

⅓ cup olive oil

½ teaspoon fine sea salt

⅛ teaspoon freshly ground black pepper

1 head leaf or romaine lettuce, torn into small pieces

2 medium tomatoes, cut into wedges

1 avocado, peeled, stone removed, and chopped

1 cup thinly sliced mushrooms

6 green onions, with tops, thinly sliced

½ cup coarsely chopped fresh basil

¼ cup coarsely chopped fresh dill

½ cup raw almonds, toasted and coarsely chopped

Put the lemon juice, olive oil, salt, and pepper in a small jar. Cover with the lid and shake until the ingredients are well mixed.

In a salad bowl, toss together the lettuce, tomatoes, avocado, mushrooms, green onions, basil, and dill. Shake the Lemon Dressing and pour it over the salad. Toss until well coated. Sprinkle the toasted almonds over the top.

Average bone loss of female meat eaters at age 65:
35 percent
Average bone loss of female vegetarians at age 65:
18 percent

"Until he extends the circle of his compassion to all living things, man will not himself find peace."—Albert Schweitzer

SUNNY SALAD

Makes 2 main-course servings or
4 first-course servings

A salad with no leafy greens, just lots of vegetables and toasted sunflower seeds.

    3 tablespoons freshly squeezed lemon juice
    3 tablespoons olive oil
    1 tablespoon water
    ½ teaspoon fine sea salt
    ⅛ teaspoon freshly ground black pepper

    ¼ cup tamari-toasted raw sunflower seeds (page 274)
    1 avocado, peeled, stone removed, and cut into ½-inch cubes
    1 medium tomato, cut into ½-inch cubes
    1 medium red bell pepper, finely chopped
    1 cup thinly sliced mushrooms
    ¼ small red onion, finely chopped
    ½ cup finely chopped fresh basil
Green leaf lettuce leaves, for serving

Put the lemon juice, olive oil, water, salt, and pepper in a small jar. Cover with the lid and shake until the ingredients are well mixed.

In a large bowl, toss together the toasted sunflower seeds, avocado, tomato, bell pepper, mushrooms, onion, and basil. Shake the Lemon Oil Dressing and pour it over the salad. Toss until well coated.

Arrange several lettuce leaves on each plate, and spoon the salad over. Serve immediately.

TAMARI-TOASTED NUTS

Makes ½ cup

Many of the recipes in this book use tamari-toasted nuts as a garnish to add flavorful crunch. You may find yourself doubling the recipe to eat them as a snack.

½ **cup raw walnuts, cashews, almonds, pecans, or peanuts**

1 **tablespoon tamari**

In a large dry skillet over medium heat, cook the nuts, stirring often, until toasted, 3 to 5 minutes. Remove from the heat and immediately stir in the tamari. Stir to coat the nuts, then immediately transfer the nuts to a plate. Cool completely before serving.

Tamari-Toasted Seeds For ¼ cup sesame or sunflower seeds, toast as above, and stir in 1 teaspoon tamari.

Beautiful God,
Beautiful Earth.
Show us how to help.
Make us strong so that we can bring more love into the world.
Make us strong so that we can bring more peace into the
world.
Thank you for this food
Beautiful God,
Beautiful Earth.

POTATO SALAD

Makes 6 side-dish servings

Delicious made with any potato, but best with small new potatoes. This salad is a traditional favorite for picnics.

1½ **pounds new potatoes or other boiling potatoes, unpeeled**
1 **large carrot, finely chopped**
2 **ribs celery, with leaves, finely chopped**
1 **pound fresh peas, shelled, or 1 cup (thawed) frozen peas**
½ **small red onion, finely chopped**

½ **cup tofu mayonnaise**
1 **tablespoon Dijon mustard**
¼ **cup chopped fresh parsley**
¼ **cup chopped fresh dill**
¾ **tablespoon fine sea salt**
¼ **teaspoon freshly ground black pepper**

Lettuce leaves, for serving
Paprika, for garnish

In a large pot with enough lightly salted boiling water to cover, cook the potatoes until just tender when pierced with the tip of a sharp knife, 10 to 15 minutes depending on their size. Drain, rinse under cold water, and cool completely.

Cut the potatoes into ½-inch cubes, and put them in a salad bowl. Add the carrot, celery, peas, and onion and stir until mixed well.

Put the tofu mayonnaise, mustard, parsley, dill, salt, and pepper into a small bowl and stir to combine. Pour the dressing over the salad and toss to coat. Refrigerate until well chilled.

Serve chilled on a bed of lettuce, with a sprinkle of paprika on top.

VEGETARIAN BURRITOS

Makes 6 servings

Beans, vegetables, and olives are layered on warm tortillas. Offer a choice of mild Avocado Dressing or spicy Salsa Vinaigrette. Serve the ingredients as a buffet and let your guests build their own burritos.

> 6 whole wheat flour tortillas
>
> 2 tablespoons canola or safflower oil
>
> 2 16-ounce cans refried pinto beans (without lard)
>
> 1 small head lettuce, shredded
>
> 1 cup alfalfa sprouts
>
> 1 medium carrot, grated
>
> 1 small unwaxed cucumber, peeled and finely chopped
>
> 1 small red onion, finely chopped
>
> 2 medium tomatoes, finely chopped
>
> 1 cup Mediterranean black olives, pitted and chopped
>
> Avocado Dressing (page 292) or Salsa Vinaigrette
>   (page 294)
>
> ½ cup tamari-toasted sunflower seeds (page 274)

Preheat the oven to 350°F. Stack the tortillas and wrap tightly in aluminum foil. Bake until heated through, about 15 minutes.

Meanwhile, heat the oil in a medium saucepan over medium-low heat. Add the pinto beans and heat until they are hot, stirring often, about 3 minutes.

Put each vegetable, your choice of dressing, and the sunflower seeds in separate bowls.

Serve all the ingredients buffet style and let your guests make their own burritos, or assemble them as follows: Put a warm tortilla on each salad plate. Spread a layer of warmed pinto beans over each tortilla. Layer the vegetables in the order they are listed, ending with the black olives on top. Pour over a little dressing and sprinkle the toasted sunflower seeds over the top. Roll the tortillas up into cylinders and serve immediately.

BEETS AND GREENS WITH LEMON-BASIL DRESSING

Makes 4 side-dish servings

This simple salad is best in the early summer when baby beets are available. Use ¼ cup fresh tarragon or thyme leaves, if you like, instead of the basil, but *fresh* herbs are a must!

12 small or 6 medium beets, with greens

LEMON-BASIL DRESSING
⅓ **cup freshly squeezed lemon juice**
⅓ **cup olive oil, preferably extra virgin**
½ **teaspoon fine sea salt**
⅛ **teaspoon freshly ground black pepper**
½ **cup chopped fresh basil**

Cut the greens from the beets, and separate the stems from the leaves. Scrub the beets well. Wash the stems and leaves separately in several changes of water to remove any grit. Cut the stems into ½-inch pieces. Cut the leaves into 1-inch-wide strips.

Put 1 inch of water in a large saucepan with a steamer basket, cover with the lid, and bring to a boil. Add the beets and steam until almost tender, 8 to 12 minutes. Add the beet stems and steam for 3 minutes. Add the leaves and steam for 2 minutes. Transfer the cooked beets, stems, and greens to a serving bowl.

In a small bowl, whisk together the lemon juice, oil, salt, and pepper. Pour over the warm beets and toss well.

Just before serving, add the chopped basil to the beets and toss well. Serve the salad either warm, chilled, or at room temperature. The salad will keep up to a day in the refrigerator.

"I never eat when I can dine."—Maurice Chevalier

BLACK BEAN AND CORN SALAD

*Makes 4 to 5 main-course servings or
8 to 10 side-dish servings*

This salad is a delightful fiesta of brightly colored vegetables and black beans. Serve with Spicy Corn Bread (page 228). This substantial salad travels well so it is ideal for picnics. Made without the avocado, it will keep in the refrigerator up to a week. Then add the avocado, if desired, just before serving.

2 cups dried black beans, picked over and rinsed, or
  2 15-ounce cans black beans, rinsed and drained
⅓ cup freshly squeezed lime juice
½ cup olive oil
1 garlic clove, minced
1 teaspoon fine sea salt
⅛ teaspoon cayenne pepper

2 ears corn, kernels cut off the cob, or 1½ cups (thawed) frozen corn
1 avocado, peeled, stone removed, and cut into ½-inch pieces
1 small red bell pepper, seeded and cut into ½-inch pieces
2 medium tomatoes, cut into ½-inch pieces
6 green onions, with tops, finely chopped
1 fresh hot chile pepper, seeded and minced
½ cup coarsely chopped fresh cilantro, optional

If using dried beans, place the beans in a large bowl and add enough water to cover by 2 inches. Place the bowl in a cool place and let the beans soak for 6 to 12 hours. Drain and rinse the beans.

Put the beans into a large pot and add enough fresh water to cover the beans by 1 inch. Bring to a simmer over medium high heat, reduce the heat, cover, and simmer until the beans are barely tender, 1½ to 2 hours (depending on the age of the beans). Thoroughly drain the beans and let them cool.

Put the lime juice, olive oil, garlic, salt, and cayenne in a small jar. Cover with the lid and shake until the ingredients are well mixed.

In a salad bowl, combine the cooked or canned beans, corn, avocado, bell pepper, tomatoes, green onions, chile pepper, and cilantro. Shake the Lime Dressing and pour it over the salad. Stir until well coated. (The salad can be prepared a few hours ahead, but don't add the avocado until serving time. Refrigerate, and adjust the seasonings before serving.)

MEDITERRANEAN SALAD

*Makes 2 to 3 main-course servings or
4 to 6 first-course servings*

Freshly squeezed lemon juice really brings out the flavors of this vegetable salad. Serve with pasta dishes.

3 medium tomatoes, cut into ½-inch pieces

2 unwaxed cucumbers, cut into ½-inch cubes

1 large avocado, peeled, stone removed, and cut into ½-inch pieces

½ small red onion, sliced into thin rings

10 Mediterranean green olives, pitted and chopped

¼ cup coarsely chopped fresh basil

⅓ cup olive oil

¼ cup freshly squeezed lemon juice

1 garlic clove, minced

½ teaspoon fine sea salt

⅛ teaspoon freshly ground black pepper

Green leaf lettuce leaves, for serving

In a large bowl, combine the tomatoes, cucumbers, avocado, onion, olives, and basil.

In a small bowl, whisk together the oil, lemon juice, garlic, salt, and pepper. Pour the dressing over the vegetables and toss well.

Place the lettuce leaves on individual plates and spoon the salad on top.

GARDEN VEGGIE ANTIPASTO

Makes 4 to 6 servings

Lightly steamed chunks of vegetables marinated in a tangy vinegar-herb dressing can be served as appetizers or as a dinner salad on lettuce leaves. Keep on hand in the refrigerator for snacks.

1 small cauliflower, cut into florets

½ bunch broccoli, trimmed and cut into florets

3 medium carrots, cut into sticks

⅓ cup red wine vinegar

¼ cup olive oil

1 teaspoon dried basil

1 teaspoon dried oregano

1 teaspoon dried thyme

1 garlic clove, minced

½ teaspoon fine sea salt

¼ teaspoon freshly ground black pepper

Put 1 inch of water in a large saucepan with a steamer basket, cover with the lid, and bring to a boil. Put the cauliflower, broccoli, and carrots in the steamer basket, cover, and steam until the broccoli is bright green in color, about 3 minutes. Remove the steamed vegetables from the steamer basket; they should still have a crunch. Put the vegetables in a salad bowl.

Put the vinegar, olive oil, basil, oregano, thyme, garlic, salt, and pepper in a jar. Cover with the lid and shake until the ingredients are well mixed.

Pour the vinaigrette over the steamed vegetables. Toss until well coated. Refrigerate for at least 30 minutes before serving. Serve chilled.

LOTSA PASTA SALAD

Makes 4 main-course servings or
6 to 8 first-course servings

A substantial pasta salad with crisp, fresh vegetables and a tangy dressing. Serve this salad with Garlic Herb Bread (page 225) for a tasty meal.

- 1 **pound spiral noodles or other noodles made without eggs**
- 4 **ribs celery, with leaves, finely chopped**
- 2 **medium carrots, finely chopped**
- 2 **medium red bell peppers, seeded and finely chopped**
- 1 **small red onion, finely chopped**
- 1 **cup Mediterranean black olives, pitted and chopped**
- 1½ **cups Creamy Italian Dressing (page 297)**

In a large pot of lightly salted boiling water, cook the noodles until barely tender, about 6 minutes. Drain, rinse under cold running water, and let cool.

Put the cooked noodles, celery, carrots, bell peppers, onion, and olives into a salad bowl. Pour the Creamy Italian Dressing over and stir until well coated. Refrigerate for at least 30 minutes before serving.

In a salad, the freshness, flavor, and texture of any vegetable is markedly apparent. A poor thing that has been grown with an array of petrochemicals, sprayed with poisons, waxed, and then shipped thousands of miles won't be a match for one that has been grown in good Earth without adulteration, picked only after it has fully ripened, and taken to your table without delay.

LENTIL SALAD

*Makes 3 to 4 main-course servings or
6 to 8 first-course servings*

This hearty salad is made with vegetables and lentils marinated in oil and vinegar. Lentils are a tasty legume that require no soaking and take only about forty-five minutes to cook. This salad keeps well in the refrigerator up to five days. Serve in warmed pita bread with slices of avocado.

   2 cups lentils, picked over and rinsed
3½ cups water

   ⅓ cup red wine vinegar
   ⅓ cup olive oil
   2 garlic cloves, minced
   2 teaspoons dried basil
   1 teaspoon fine sea salt
   ¼ teaspoon freshly ground black pepper

   2 medium tomatoes, cut into ½-inch pieces
   1 medium red bell pepper, seeded and cut into
       ½-inch pieces
   1 unwaxed cucumber, cut into ½-inch pieces
   1 small red onion, finely chopped
   1 cup coarsely chopped fresh parsley

Put the lentils and water in a large pot. Bring to a simmer over medium heat, cover, and cook until the lentils are just tender, 30 to 45 minutes (depending on the age of the lentils). Thoroughly drain the lentils and let cool.

Put the vinegar, olive oil, garlic, basil, salt, and pepper in a jar. Cover with the lid and shake until the ingredients are well mixed.

Put the cooked lentils and the remaining ingredients into a salad bowl. Shake the Red Wine Vinaigrette and pour it over the salad. Stir until well coated. Refrigerate for at least 1 hour to allow the flavors to blend. Serve chilled. (If the salad is prepared more than a few hours ahead, adjust the seasonings before serving.)

QUINOA TABOULEH

*Makes 3 to 4 main-course servings or
6 to 8 side-dish servings*

Quinoa, pronounced "keen-wa," was known as "the mother grain" by the Incas. This ancient grain continues to be a staple food in much of South America and is fast becoming popular elsewhere because the tiny seeds are quick to prepare, easy to digest, and have a light, delicate flavor.

1 cup quinoa
2 cups water
2 medium tomatoes, cut into ½-inch cubes
6 green onions, with tops, finely chopped
1 medium unwaxed cucumber, cut into ½-inch cubes
1 small green bell pepper, seeded and cut into ½-inch cubes
1 cup finely chopped fresh parsley
½ cup finely chopped fresh mint

⅓ cup freshly squeezed lemon juice
⅓ cup olive oil
1 garlic clove, minced
1 teaspoon fine sea salt
⅛ teaspoon cayenne pepper

Put the quinoa in a wire strainer and thoroughly rinse with hot water to remove any bitter flavor.

In a medium saucepan, bring the water and quinoa to a boil over high heat. Reduce the heat to low, cover, and simmer until the quinoa is tender and the water is absorbed, 10 to 12 minutes. Transfer the quinoa to a bowl and cool completely.

Stir the tomatoes, green onions, cucumber, bell pepper, parsley, and mint into the quinoa.

In a small bowl, whisk together the lemon juice, oil, garlic, salt, and cayenne pepper. Pour over the quinoa and toss well. Cover and refrigerate for at least 30 minutes before serving. (If the salad is prepared longer than 2 hours ahead, adjust the seasonings before serving.)

SWEET AND SPICY COUSCOUS SALAD

*Makes 3 to 4 main-course servings or
6 to 8 side-dish servings*

Couscous, fresh vegetables, and a sweet-spicy currant dressing give this salad a uniquely delicious flavor. Serve it with warm whole wheat flatbread and Tahini Miso Spread (page 241).

½ cup currants
¼ cup freshly squeezed orange juice
¼ cup freshly squeezed lemon juice
⅓ cup canola or safflower oil
¼ teaspoon ground cinnamon
½ teaspoon fine sea salt
⅛ teaspoon cayenne pepper

3 cups water
1 tablespoon canola or safflower oil
1½ cups couscous, preferably whole wheat
1 medium carrot, finely chopped
1 cup sliced green beans or yellow wax beans (cut into ¼-inch pieces)
1 medium red bell pepper, seeded and finely chopped
½ small red onion, finely chopped
¼ cup finely chopped fresh mint or parsley
½ cup tamari-toasted almonds (see page 274), coarsely chopped, optional

Put the currants, orange juice, lemon juice, ⅓ cup oil, cinnamon, salt, and cayenne in a jar. Cover with the lid and shake until the ingredients are well mixed.

In a medium saucepan, bring the water and 1 tablespoon oil to a boil. Stir in the couscous. Immediately remove from the heat, cover, and let stand until the water is absorbed, about 6 minutes. Transfer the couscous to a large bowl, and fluff with a fork. Cool completely.

Put 1 inch of water in a large saucepan with a steamer basket, cover with the lid, and bring to a gentle boil. Put the carrot, green beans, and bell pepper in the steamer basket, cover the steamer, and steam until the vegetables are a bright color, about 3 minutes. Remove the steamed vegetables from the basket; they should still have a crunch. Rinse under cold water, drain, and cool completely.

Stir the steamed vegetables, onion, and mint into the couscous. Shake the Spicy Currant Dressing and pour it over the salad. Stir until well coated. Refrigerate for at least 30 minutes to allow the flavors to blend. Sprinkle the toasted almonds over the top just before serving and serve chilled. (If the salad is prepared more than a few hours ahead, adjust the seasonings before serving.)

What images come to your mind when you think of salads? For much of my life, all I would visualize was a chunk of iceberg lettuce, so identical to millions of others that it might have come from a factory assembly line. It was accompanied by pale greenish-red slabs, reputed to be tomatoes, and immersed in a mixture of oil, vinegar, salt, and sugar that was mistakenly called a dressing. But now I see a wide variety of colors, shapes, and textures so aesthetically pleasing that my hunger for beauty is fed as well as my body. I see all the colors of creativity—purple cabbage, yellow corn, red and green peppers. I see the orange of grated carrots, the reddish-purple of sliced beets, the deep green of chopped parsley, and all the wonderful shades of red, green, purple, and white lettuces.

INDIAN RICE SALAD

*Makes 2 main-course servings or
4 side-dish servings*

This vegetable-rice salad has the spicy Indian flavors of cumin and turmeric with the sweetness of raisins and cinnamon. An attractive way to serve the salad is to press it into a well-oiled mold or tube pan, put a serving dish on top of the mold, and turn both over together. Gently tap the mold or pan and lift it off the rice salad. Serve with Chapatis (page 220).

¼ cup canola or safflower oil
2 teaspoons yellow mustard seeds
2 teaspoons cumin seeds
2 garlic cloves, minced
1 teaspoon finely grated fresh gingerroot
1 teaspoon turmeric
⅛ teaspoon cayenne pepper
2½ cups water
1 bay leaf
1 cinnamon stick
1 cup long-grain brown rice
½ cup raisins
3 tablespoons rice vinegar
2 tablespoons dark Oriental sesame oil
2 tablespoons tamari
1 medium carrot, finely chopped
4 green onions, with tops, thinly sliced
1 pound fresh peas, shelled, or 1 cup (thawed) frozen peas

In a medium saucepan, heat 1 tablespoon of the oil over medium heat. Add the mustard seeds, cumin seeds, garlic, ginger, turmeric, and cayenne pepper and cook, stirring, until the mustard seeds begin to pop, about 30 seconds.

Add the water, bay leaf, and cinnamon, cover, and bring to a boil. Add the rice, cover, reduce the heat to low, and simmer until the water is absorbed, 30 to 40 minutes. Remove the rice from the heat and let stand, covered, for 10 minutes.

Put the rice into a medium bowl, and remove the bay leaf and cinnamon stick. Stir in the raisins.

In a small bowl, whisk the rice vinegar, the remaining 3 tablespoons canola oil, the sesame oil, and tamari until combined. Pour over the rice. Add the carrot, green onions, and peas and stir well. Refrigerate until well chilled. Serve chilled.

CUCUMBER RAITA

Makes 4 side-dish servings

A refreshing cucumber salad, made with a creamy tahini dressing, cooling raita is traditionally made with yogurt and served with spicy Indian curries like Curried Potatoes, Cauliflower, and Peas (page 344) and Chapatis (page 220).

  2 tablespoons raw tahini
  2 tablespoons freshly squeezed lemon juice
  1/2 teaspoon ground cumin
  1/4 teaspoon cumin seeds
  1/4 teaspoon fine sea salt
Pinch of cayenne pepper
  2 large unwaxed cucumbers, thinly sliced

Put the tahini, lemon juice, ground cumin, cumin seeds, salt, and cayenne in a small bowl. Stir together until well mixed.

Place the cucumber slices in a salad bowl. Pour the dressing over the salad and stir until well coated. Refrigerate.

Serve well chilled.

THAI VEGETABLE SALAD

*Makes 3 to 4 main-course servings or
6 to 8 side-dish servings*

Thailand is known for its beautiful salads such as this one, which combines vegetables and sprouts with peanuts and traditional Thai flavors.

- 3 tablespoons freshly squeezed lime juice
- ¼ cup toasted sesame oil
- 3 tablespoons tamari
- ¼ cup finely chopped fresh mint
- 3 tablespoons rice syrup
- 1 teaspoon curry powder

- ½ small head Napa or green cabbage, shredded fine (about 7 cups)
- 1 medium carrot, grated
- 6 ounces daikon, peeled and grated
- 1 medium tomato, cut into ½-inch pieces
- 1 cup mung bean sprouts
- 6 green onions, finely chopped
- ½ cup raw peanuts, toasted and coarsely chopped

Put the lime juice, oil, tamari, mint, rice syrup, and curry in a jar. Cover with the lid and shake until the ingredients are well mixed.

In a salad bowl, combine the cabbage, carrot, daikon, tomato, sprouts, and green onions. Shake the Thai Vinaigrette and pour it over the salad. Toss until well coated. Sprinkle the toasted peanuts over the salad, and refrigerate. Serve chilled.

Good salads speak of exuberance and vitality.

THAI NOODLE SALAD

Makes 6 to 8 main-course servings

The dressing for this vegetable pasta salad is an exotic blend of peanuts and spices. Udon noodles are available at health food or Oriental grocery stores. This hearty salad goes well with Vegetable Miso Soup (page 267), and makes a wonderful picnic lunch.

8 ounces udon noodles

½ cup unsalted crunchy peanut butter

½ cup soy milk

1 teaspoon finely grated fresh gingerroot

1 small garlic clove, minced

3 tablespoons rice vinegar

3 tablespoons soy sauce or Bragg Liquid Aminos

1 tablespoon toasted sesame oil

⅛ teaspoon crushed red pepper flakes

1 medium unwaxed cucumber, cut into matchsticks

2 cups mung bean sprouts

1 medium carrot, grated

6 to 8 green onions, thinly sliced

¼ cup chopped fresh mint

1 cup raw peanuts, toasted and coarsely chopped

Romaine lettuce leaves, for serving

In a large pot of lightly salted water, cook the noodles until just tender, about 5 minutes. Drain, rinse the noodles under cold running water, and let cool.

Put the peanut butter, soy milk, ginger, garlic, vinegar, soy sauce, sesame oil, and red pepper flakes in a small bowl. Whisk until well mixed.

In a salad bowl, combine the cooked noodles, cucumber, sprouts, carrot, green onions, and mint. Whisk the Spicy Peanut Dressing and pour it over the salad. Stir until well coated.

Serve chilled on a bed of lettuce leaves. Sprinkle the roasted peanuts over the salad.

MARINATED TOFU CABBAGE SALAD

*Makes 2 to 3 main-course servings or
4 to 6 side-dish servings*

Red cabbage and other bright vegetables make this a colorful salad. The dressing adds a tangy taste of vinegar with celery seeds.

- ⅓ cup apple cider vinegar
- ⅓ cup olive oil
- 1 tablespoon celery seeds
- 1¼ teaspoons fine sea salt
- ¼ teaspoon freshly ground black pepper
- ½ pound firm tofu, cut into ¼-inch cubes

- 4 cups finely shredded red cabbage (about ½ medium head) or 2 cups *each* shredded green and red cabbage
- 1 medium carrot, grated
- 1 bunch radishes, grated
- 4 green onions, finely chopped
- ½ cup raw sunflower seeds, toasted

In a medium bowl, whisk together the vinegar, olive oil, celery seeds, salt, and pepper. Add the tofu, and stir gently to coat. Cover and refrigerate for at least 30 minutes, stirring occasionally to keep the tofu coated.

In a salad bowl, toss together the cabbage, carrot, radishes, and green onions. Shake the Marinated Tofu Dressing and pour it over the salad. Toss until well coated. Sprinkle with the sunflower seeds before serving. Serve chilled.

S I X T E E N

Dressings and Sauces

Homemade dressings are better than any you can buy, because they are fresh and do not have to be processed for shipping and storing. When preparing dressings, make some extra to have on hand for the next day.

POPPY SEED DRESSING

Makes 1⅓ cups

This dressing has a spicy-sweet flavor, and the poppy seeds add a pleasing texture.

- ¼ small red onion
- ½ cup canola oil
- ¼ cup red wine vinegar
- ¼ cup water
- ¼ cup pure maple syrup
- 1 tablespoon dry mustard
- 1 teaspoon fine sea salt
- 2 tablespoons poppy seeds

Put all the ingredients except the poppy seeds into a blender and blend until smooth. Add the poppy seeds and pulse just to mix. This keeps in the refrigerator for 3 days.

AVOCADO DRESSING

Makes 1⅔ cups

A pleasantly tart dressing with the creamy texture and flavor of avocado. Make it thicker or thinner by varying the amount of water. Use on leafy green salads and Mexican dishes.

- 1 medium avocado, peeled, stone removed, and quartered
- ½ green bell pepper, seeded and coarsely chopped
- ¼ small red onion
- ½ cup water
- ⅓ cup freshly squeezed lemon juice
- 1 small garlic clove, peeled
- 1 teaspoon fine sea salt

Put all the ingredients into a blender and blend until smooth. This keeps no longer than one day in the refrigerator.

ROSE'S SWEET AND SOUR DRESSING

Makes 2¹/₂ cups

This all-purpose dressing was created by Rose Thompson. It is good with everything from salads to main courses.

    1   cup water
    ½   cup canola oil
    ⅓   cup apple cider vinegar or freshly squeezed lemon juice
    2   to 5 tablespoons nutritional yeast flakes (to taste), optional
    3   to 5 pitted dates
    2   tablespoons soy sauce
    2   teaspoons curry powder
    2   teaspoons Dijon mustard
    2   teaspoons umeboshi plum paste
    1   teaspoon finely grated fresh gingerroot
    ⅛   teaspoon freshly ground black pepper

Put all the ingredients into a blender and blend until smooth. The dressing keeps up to 5 days in the refrigerator.

The dairy industry claims: **Whole milk is 3.5 percent fat. *Fact:* The 3.5 percent figure is based on weight, and most of the weight in milk is water. Half the real calories in whole milk are fat.**

May the beauty and variety of the food at this table
Kindle my wonder and appreciation for life.
May the good taste of the food at this table
Kindle the joy in my heart.
May this time of nurture
Kindle my gratitude for all that gives me strength and
*   nourishment.*
May the friendship at this table
Help me to understand my place in the living Earth
*   community.*

SALSA VINAIGRETTE

Makes 2¹/₂ cups

Spicy flavors give this traditional vinaigrette a Mexican twist. If you want a hotter taste, just add a few of the hot chile pepper seeds. Toss this dressing with Romaine lettuce and sliced red onions.

   1 **large tomato, quartered**
  ¼ **small red onion**
  ½ **cup olive oil**
  ¼ **cup red wine vinegar**
  ½ **cup chopped fresh cilantro, optional**
  ¼ **cup freshly squeezed lime juice**
   1 **garlic clove, peeled**
   1 **fresh hot chile pepper, seeded and minced**
  ½ **teaspoon fine sea salt**
  ⅛ **teaspoon freshly ground black pepper**

Put all the ingredients into a blender and blend until smooth. This keeps in the refrigerator for 5 days.

SPICY RASPBERRY DRESSING

Makes 1 1/3 cups

Colorful and zesty, this dressing is delicious on sliced orange and red onion salad.

½ cup pure maple syrup

½ cup canola oil

⅓ cup freshly squeezed lemon juice

⅓ cup fresh or (thawed) frozen raspberries

1 teaspoon dry mustard

¼ teaspoon fine sea salt

¼ teaspoon freshly ground black pepper

2 tablespoons poppy seeds

1 tablespoon minced red onion

Put the maple syrup, oil, lemon juice, raspberries, dry mustard, salt, and pepper in a blender and blend until smooth. Add the poppy seeds and onion, and pulse briefly until mixed.

"Most people are largely unaware of the wide-ranging effects cattle are having on the ecosystems of the planet and the fortunes of civilization. Yet, cattle production and beef consumption now rank among the gravest threats to the future well-being of the earth and its human population."
—Jeremy Rifkin

TOFU DILL DRESSING

Makes 3 cups

Dill has been used as a love potion, appetite inhibitor, digestive aid, and protector against evil for thousands of years. It also gives this tofu dressing a refreshing flavor. Use this salad dressing as a dip for raw vegetables or as a delicious topping for baked potatoes.

½ **pound soft tofu, crumbled**
½ **cup water**
¼ **cup olive oil**
¼ **cup freshly squeezed lemon juice**
¼ **cup soy sauce**
2 **tablespoons chopped fresh dill or 2 teaspoons dried dillweed**
1 **teaspoon pure maple syrup**
⅛ **teaspoon cayenne pepper**

Put all the ingredients into a blender and blend until smooth. This keeps 4 to 5 days in the refrigerator.

"It is easy to take a stand on a remote issue, but [one] reveals his true nature when the issue comes nearer home. To protest about bullfighting in Spain or the slaughter of baby seals in Canada while continuing to eat chickens that have spent their lives crammed into cages, or veal from calves that have been deprived of their mothers, their proper diet, and the freedom to lie down with their legs extended, is like denouncing apartheid in South Africa while asking your [white] neighbors not to sell their houses to blacks."—Peter Singer

CREAMY ITALIAN
DRESSING

Makes 2¹/₄ cups

Tofu makes this dressing creamy, and herbs add a delicious Italian
flavor.

½ **pound soft tofu, crumbled**

½ **cup water**

½ **cup olive oil**

⅓ **cup red wine vinegar**

1 **tablespoon Dijon mustard**

1 **teaspoon dried basil**

1 **teaspoon dried oregano**

½ **small red onion**

1 **garlic clove, peeled**

1 **teaspoon fine sea salt**

Put all the ingredients into a blender and blend until smooth. This
keeps in the refrigerator for 4 to 5 days.

TANGY PESTO DRESSING

Makes 1 1/2 cups

A bright green dressing with a tangy lemon taste. The basil, pine nuts, and garlic add the flavor of classic Italian pesto. Use on rice, pasta, and cooked vegetables.

- 1/2 cup olive oil
- 1/2 cup pine nuts
- 1/2 cup chopped fresh basil
- 1/3 cup freshly squeezed lemon juice
- 1/4 cup water
- 1 garlic clove, peeled
- 1/2 teaspoon fine sea salt
- 1/8 teaspoon freshly ground black pepper

Put all the ingredients into a blender and blend until smooth. This keeps for 3 days in the refrigerator.

PARSLEY-TAMARI-LÉMON DRESSING

Makes 1 1/2 cups

A John Robbins creation, this delightfully lemony dressing uses lots of parsley for a fresh accent.

- 1 cup extra virgin olive oil
- 1/3 cup freshly squeezed lemon juice
- 1/3 cup tamari
- 1 cup loosely packed chopped parsley
- 1 tablespoon minced onion

Combine all the ingredients in a blender and blend until smooth. The dressing keeps in the refrigerator for 2 to 3 days.

SWEET GINGER DRESSING

Makes 1 cup

Ginger and miso give this dressing a spicy Oriental flavor while the rice syrup adds a touch of sweetness. Use it on your favorite leafy greens and top with toasted sesame seeds.

    2   tablespoons sesame seeds, toasted
    2   tablespoons dark Oriental sesame oil
    6   tablespoons canola or safflower oil
    ⅓   cup rice vinegar
    2   tablespoons rice syrup
    1½ tablespoons finely grated fresh gingerroot
    1   tablespoon brown rice miso
    1   small garlic clove, peeled
    ⅛   teaspoon freshly ground black pepper

Put all the ingredients into a blender and blend until smooth. This keeps for 2 weeks in the refrigerator.

*Calories of fossil fuel expended to produce 1 calorie of protein
from beef:* **78**
*Calories of fossil fuel expended to produce 1 calorie of protein
from soybeans:* **2**

SUMMER TOMATO SAUCE

Makes 5 cups

Make this sauce when fresh tomatoes and herbs are in season.

      5 **pounds plum tomatoes**
      2 **tablespoons olive oil**
      1 **large onion, finely chopped**
      3 **garlic cloves, minced**
      1 **cube or 2 tablespoons vegetable bouillon**
      1 **teaspoon fine sea salt**
    ⅛ **teaspoon freshly ground black pepper**
      1 **cup chopped fresh basil or 2 teaspoons dried basil**
    ¼ **cup chopped fresh oregano or 1 teaspoon dried oregano**
      3 **tablespoons chopped fresh rosemary or 1 teaspoon dried rosemary**
    ¼ **cup unsweetened tomato paste, optional**

Blanch the tomatoes in boiling water for 30 seconds. Immediately drain off the water and plunge the tomatoes into cold water. Drain, peel, and compost or discard the skins. Working over a sieve placed in a large bowl, cut the tomatoes in half and gently squeeze to remove the seeds. Discard the seeds in the sieve, and reserve the juice. Coarsely chop the tomato pulp.

Heat the olive oil in a large saucepan over medium heat. Add the onions and garlic and cook until the onions are softened, 5 to 6 minutes.

Add the tomatoes, the reserved tomato juice, the bouillon, salt, and pepper. If using dried herbs, add them now; if using fresh herbs, stir them into the sauce during the last 15 minutes of cooking. If the sauce seems pale, stir in the tomato paste. Cover and bring to a boil over high heat, then reduce the heat to low and simmer, stirring occasionally, until the sauce has reduced to about 5 cups, 1 hour to 1 hour 15 minutes.

JOHN'S TAHINI DRESSING

Makes about 1 1/2 cups

This dressing keeps well in the refrigerator but it never seems to stay around long. Try it on vegetables and grain dishes as well as salads.

¼ cup freshly squeezed lemon juice

½ cup canola or safflower oil

¼ cup tamari

⅓ cup tahini

1 tablespoon finely chopped onion

1 garlic clove, peeled

1 tablespoon pure maple syrup

¼ cup water

Combine all the ingredients in a blender and blend until smooth.

> *"Love all God's creation, the whole of it and every grain of sand. Love every leaf, every ray of God's light! Love the animals, love the plants, love everything. If you love everything, you will perceive the divine mystery in things. And once you have perceived it, you will begin to comprehend it ceaselessly, more and more every day. And you will at last come to love the whole world with an abiding universal love. Love the animals: God has given them the rudiments of thought and untroubled joy. Do not, therefore, trouble them, do not torture them, do not deprive them of their joy, do not go against God's intent."*—Fyodor Mikhail Dostoyevski

> *"I feel that spiritual progress does demand at some stage that we should cease to kill our fellow creatures for the satisfaction of our bodily wants."*—Mahatma Gandhi

WINTER TOMATO SAUCE

Makes 4 cups

When fresh, ripe tomatoes are out of season, this is the sauce to make.

- 2 tablespoons olive oil
- 1 medium onion, finely chopped
- 2 garlic cloves, minced
- 1 14-ounce can unsweetened Italian tomatoes, undrained, coarsely chopped
- 1 cup Vegetable Stock (page 250), vegetable bouillon, or water
- 1 6-ounce can unsweetened tomato paste
- 1 teaspoon dried basil
- ½ teaspoon dried oregano
- ½ teaspoon dried thyme
- 1 bay leaf
- ¼ teaspoon fine sea salt
- ⅛ teaspoon crushed red pepper flakes

Heat the olive oil in a large saucepan over medium heat. Add the onion and garlic and cook until softened, about 6 minutes.

Stir in the tomatoes, Vegetable Stock, tomato paste, basil, oregano, thyme, bay leaf, salt, and red pepper flakes. Cover and bring to a simmer, then reduce the heat to low, and cook, stirring occasionally, for 45 minutes. Remove the lid and cook, stirring often, until thickened, about 10 minutes longer.

MUSHROOM MISO SAUCE

Makes about 3 cups

You can use this sauce on mashed potatoes, steamed vegetables, and nut loaves because it looks like old-fashioned gravy and has a full, rich taste.

¼ cup whole wheat pastry flour

⅓ cup nutritional yeast flakes

¼ cup brown rice miso

½ cup hot water

1 tablespoon olive oil

1 small onion, finely chopped

1 cup thinly sliced mushrooms

2 cups water

Put the flour in a small dry frying pan over medium heat and toast, stirring often, until it has darkened evenly to a light brown. Transfer the flour to a medium bowl.

In a small bowl, stir the nutritional yeast, miso, and hot water together.

In a medium saucepan, heat the olive oil over medium heat. Add the onion and cook, stirring until softened, about 5 minutes. Add the mushrooms and cook, stirring, until lightly browned, about 5 minutes.

Meanwhile, add the 2 cups water to the browned flour and whisk until combined.

Whisk the flour mixture into the mushrooms, and simmer, whisking often, until the mixture is thickened, 1 to 2 minutes. Stir in the nutritional yeast and miso mixture. Bring just to a simmer, and remove from the heat. Serve hot.

Cattle ranching has destroyed more rain forest in Central America than any other activity.

WALNUT SAUCE

Makes 2¼ cups

Developed especially for Zucchini Boats (page 336), this sauce is also good over brown rice and cooked vegetables.

¼ cup whole wheat flour

½ cup raw walnuts

3 tablespoons Bragg Liquid Aminos

1 tablespoon freshly squeezed lemon juice

2 cups Vegetable Stock (page 250) or vegetable bouillon

1 garlic clove, minced

⅛ teaspoon freshly ground black pepper

Put the flour in a small dry frying pan over medium heat and toast, stirring often, until it has darkened evenly to a light brown. Transfer the flour to a blender. Add the walnuts, liquid aminos, lemon juice, garlic, pepper, and ½ cup of the Vegetable Stock to the blender and blend until smooth. Add the remaining 1½ cups stock and blend until smooth.

Scrape the mixture into a medium saucepan. Bring to a simmer over low heat, and simmer, stirring often, until the mixture is thickened, about 2 minutes. Serve hot.

As I sit before my plate full of food,
Relishing the pleasure of eating all that I want,
May my heart not forget the many
Who are hungry but whose plates are never full.
May this food become fuel for a life that is of use to those who
*   are hungry.*

> *"A missionary was walking in Africa when he heard the ominous padding of a lion behind him. 'Oh Lord,' prayed the missionary, 'Grant in Thy goodness that the lion walking behind me is a good Christian lion.' And then, in the silence that followed, the missionary heard the lion praying too: 'Oh Lord,' he prayed, 'We thank Thee for the food which we are about to receive.' "*—Cleveland Amory

TOFU "CHEESE" SAUCE

Makes 1¹/₂ cups

Nutritional yeast mixed with lemon and tahini gives this sauce a rich cheeselike flavor, and the tofu gives it a creamy texture. It is a delicious topping for baked potatoes.

½   pound firm tofu, crumbled
⅓   cup freshly squeezed lemon juice
⅓   cup nutritional yeast flakes
⅓   cup raw tahini
3   tablespoons tamari
3   tablespoons water
1   teaspoon dried basil
⅛   teaspoon turmeric
1   garlic clove, peeled
¼   teaspoon freshly ground black pepper

Put all the ingredients into a blender and blend until smooth. Serve this sauce warm or at room temperature.

"Forget the soggy sterile slices that pop up dourly in three million automatic toasters every morning . . . and instead cut for yourself . . . a slice of bread that you have seen mysteriously rise and redouble and fall and fold under your hands. It will smell better, and taste better, than you remembered anything could possibly taste or smell, and it will make you feel, for a time at least, newborn into a better world than this one often seems."—M.F.K. Fisher

NUTTY BASIL PESTO

Makes 1 1/2 cups

Pesto is traditionally served on pasta, but it is also good on baked potatoes and as a topping for Pesto Pizza (page 361). This pesto is made with fresh basil, pine nuts, and something different, a taste of miso.

    5 cups tightly packed fresh basil leaves, coarsely chopped
    ½ cup pine nuts
    ¾ cup olive oil
    2 tablespoons brown rice miso
    3 tablespoons freshly squeezed lemon juice
    3 garlic cloves, peeled

Put all the ingredients into a food processor fitted with the metal blade, and process until smooth.

SAVORY TOFU SAUCE

Makes 2 cups

A unique sauce that will turn plain rice and vegetables into a memorable meal.

½ **pound firm tofu, crumbled**

¾ **cup Vegetable Stock (page 250), vegetable bouillon, or water**

¼ **cup canola oil**

2 **tablespoons tamari**

2 **tablespoons nutritional yeast flakes**

2 **tablespoons chopped fresh basil or 1 teaspoon dried basil**

2 **tablespoons freshly squeezed lemon juice**

1 **garlic clove, peeled**

1 **teaspoon Dijon mustard**

Put all the ingredients into a blender and blend until smooth. Serve hot or cold.

Most common cause of death in U.S.: **Heart disease**
Risk of death from heart disease for average American man:
50 percent
*Risk of death from heart disease for average American man
who consumes no meat:* **15 percent**
*Risk of death from heart disease for average American man
who consumes no meat, dairy products, or eggs:* **4 percent**

GINGER PEANUT SAUCE

Makes 3 cups

Many Asian and African dishes use peanut sauces like this one. This spicy sauce gives rice, noodle dishes, and cooked vegetables an exotic flavor.

1   tablespoon canola or safflower oil
1   medium onion, finely chopped
1   tablespoon finely grated fresh gingerroot
2   garlic cloves, minced
½   teaspoon curry powder
1   cup hot water
1   cup unsalted crunchy peanut butter
¼   cup tamari
¼   cup freshly squeezed lime juice
1   tablespoon dark Oriental sesame oil
⅛   teaspoon cayenne pepper

Heat the canola oil in a skillet over medium heat. Add the onion, ginger, and garlic and cook, stirring occasionally, until the onion is lightly browned, about 6 minutes. Add the curry powder and stir until fragrant, about 20 seconds. Remove from heat.

In a small bowl, whisk the hot water, peanut butter, tamari, lime juice, sesame oil, and cayenne until smooth.

Stir the peanut butter mixture into the onions. Bring just to a simmer, and remove from the heat. Serve hot or at room temperature.

> *"I know, in my soul, that to eat a creature who is raised to be eaten, and who never has a chance to be a real being, is unhealthy. It's like . . . you're eating misery. You're eating a bitter life."*—Alice Walker

TERIYAKI MARINADE

Makes ¾ cup

This marinade gives bland tofu and tempeh a spicy, delicious flavor. You can marinate cut up vegetables in it for kebabs, or for flavorful Teriyaki-Roasted Vegetables (page 345).

½ cup soy sauce

2 tablespoons freshly squeezed lemon juice

1 tablespoon pure maple syrup

1 tablespoon dark Oriental sesame oil or hot sesame oil

2 teaspoons finely grated fresh gingerroot

1 garlic clove, minced

Put all the ingredients into a large jar, cover with the lid, and shake until mixed.

This marinade is enough to marinate 1 pound of tofu, tempeh, or slightly steamed vegetables. Cut the tofu, tempeh, or vegetables into the desired shape and add to the jar of marinade. Cover and turn the jar until the contents are coated. Marinate in the refrigerator for at least 30 minutes, turning the jar occasionally. Use within 24 hours.

GOMASHIO

Makes 1 cup

Gomashio, made from toasted sesame seeds, has a nutty, salty flavor. Put a small bowl of gomashio on your table and use it in place of salt.

1 cup sesame seeds, toasted

½ teaspoon fine sea salt

Pinch of cayenne pepper

Put all the ingredients into a blender and pulse until the seeds are coarsely chopped (be careful not to process the mixture into sesame seed butter). This keeps for up to 3 weeks in the refrigerator.

PAPAYA SAUCE

Makes 1²/₃ cups

This rich, creamy sauce looks beautiful over fruit when served in a stemmed glass.

½ cup unsweetened papaya juice
1 small ripe papaya, peeled, seeded, and coarsely chopped
1 ripe banana
4 pitted dates

Put all the ingredients into a blender or a food processor fitted with the metal blade, and process until smooth.

MANGO-STRAWBERRY SAUCE

Makes 2¹/₂ cups

The soft pink color, inviting fragrance, and sweet taste of this luscious sauce delight the senses. Enjoy it over a salad of your favorite fresh fruit. You can substitute papaya juice for the mango juice.

½ cup mango juice
2 ripe bananas
1 cup fresh or (thawed) frozen strawberries
4 pitted dates

Put all the ingredients into a blender or a food processor fitted with the metal blade, and process until smooth.

S E V E N T E E N
Main Dishes

Whenever we cook for others, we are making a statement to them. If what we prepare and present to our family and guests is attractive, tasty, and health-supporting, we are saying that we want them to be well and happy, to feel nurtured and strengthened. When we offer cuisine that is made from wholesome and natural ingredients, we are saying that we want them to have all the energy they need in order to make every aspect of their lives richer. We are saying that we honor them.

TAGINE OF MOROCCAN
VEGETABLES WITH COUSCOUS

Makes 4 to 6 servings

When you want to impress your guests, try this impressive, colorful *tagine*, or Moroccan stew, an exotically spiced vegetable stew spooned over a platter of steaming whole wheat couscous. The list of ingredients may seem long, but the cooking procedure is easy.

- 2 tablespoons olive oil
- 2 medium onions, sliced
- 1 red bell pepper, seeded and cut into ¾-inch-wide strips
- 2 garlic cloves, peeled
- 1 teaspoon turmeric
- 1 teaspoon ground ginger
- ½ teaspoon ground cinnamon
- ½ teaspoon fine sea salt
- ¼ teaspoon cayenne pepper
- ¼ teaspoon crushed saffron threads, optional
- 4 medium carrots, cut into 1-inch lengths
- 1 butternut squash (about 2 pounds), pared, seeded, and cut into 2-inch pieces
- 1 15-ounce can unsweetened tomatoes
- 1 cup Vegetable Stock (page 250), vegetable bouillon, or water
- 2 medium zucchini, cut into 1-inch chunks
- 1 cup cooked garbanzo beans (chickpeas)
- ½ cup raisins

- 3 cups water or 2 cups Vegetable Stock (page 250) or vegetable bouillon and 1 cup water
- 2 tablespoons olive oil
- ½ teaspoon fine sea salt
- 1½ cups whole wheat couscous
- ½ cup coarsely chopped almonds, toasted

Make the tagine: In a large saucepan, heat the oil over medium heat. Add the onions and cook, stirring often, until lightly browned, about 6 to 8 minutes. Add the bell pepper, garlic, turmeric, ginger, cinnamon, salt, cayenne, and saffron, and stir for 1 minute.

Stir in the carrots, squash, tomatoes with their juice, and Vegetable Stock, breaking up the tomatoes with the spoon. Bring to a simmer over high heat. Reduce the heat to low, cover, and simmer for 20 to 30 minutes, until the vegetables are just tender.

Stir in the zucchini, garbanzo beans, and raisins. Cover and continue cooking until the squash is tender, about 5 to 10 minutes.

Make the couscous: Meanwhile, in a large saucepan, combine the water, oil, and salt and bring to a boil over high heat. Stir in the couscous. Immediately remove from the heat, cover, and let stand until the couscous has absorbed all the liquid, about 5 minutes.

Place the couscous on a warmed serving platter and make a well in the center. With a slotted spoon, spoon the vegetables into the well. Pour the *tagine* cooking juices over the couscous, sprinkle with the almonds, and serve.

Eternal Spirit of Justice and Love,
At this time of Thanksgiving
We would be aware of our dependence on the Earth
And on the sustaining presence
Of other human beings both living and gone before us.
As we partake of bread and wine, may we remember
That there are many for whom sufficient bread is a luxury,
Or for whom wine, when attainable, is only an escape.
Let our thanksgiving for Life's bounty include a commitment
To changing the world, that those who are now hungry may be
*   filled*
And those without hope may be given courage. Amen.

—Congregation of Abraxas

How beautiful this food.
How beautiful these friends.
We give thanks.

BROWN RICE AND VEGETABLE PAELLA

Makes 4 servings

This paella is another colorful dish that is easy to prepare, yet ideal for guests.

2 tablespoons olive oil

1 medium onion, chopped

1 medium red bell pepper, seeded and chopped

2 garlic cloves, minced

1 cup brown rice

2 cups Vegetable Stock (page 250) or vegetable bouillon

1 cup tomato juice

½ teaspoon crushed saffron threads, optional

¼ teaspoon fine sea salt

Pinch of cayenne pepper

1 12-ounce package frozen artichoke hearts, thawed

1 16-ounce can garbanzo beans (chickpeas), rinsed and drained

1 cup fresh or (thawed) frozen peas

½ cup Mediterranean green olives, pitted and chopped

Lemon wedges, for garnish

Preheat the oven to 350°F.

In a large skillet, heat the oil over medium heat. Add the onion, bell pepper, and garlic, and cook, stirring often, until softened, about 5 minutes. Add the brown rice and cook, stirring, until the rice turns opaque, about 2 minutes.

Stir in the Vegetable Stock, tomato juice, saffron, salt, and cayenne, and bring to a boil. Transfer to a 2-quart baking dish. Stir in the artichoke hearts. Cover tightly and bake until the liquid is absorbed and the rice is tender, about 1 hour.

Stir in the garbanzo beans, peas, and olives. Cover and bake just until heated through, about 5 minutes.

Garnish the paella with the lemon wedges, so each guest can squeeze on lemon juice to taste, and serve immediately.

"I think in the next ten or twenty years, we'll have evidence [showing that a vegetarian diet is superior] that is as strong as the evidence that cigarette smoking causes lung cancer. In my view, it's plenty strong enough now."
—T. Colin Campbell, Ph.D., director of the
China Health Project, the largest
study of diet and health in medical history

315

"People often say that humans have always eaten animals, as if this is a justification for continuing the practice. According to this logic, we should not try to prevent people from murdering other people, since this has also been done since the earliest of times."—Isaac Bashevis Singer

ITALIAN VEGETABLE AND POTATO STEW

Makes 4 to 6 servings

In Italy, this is known as *ciambotta*, and every household has its own version. While it is hearty enough to stand on its own, it can also be spooned over cooked brown rice or pasta.

1 large eggplant, peeled and cut into 1-inch cubes

1½ teaspoons fine sea salt

3 tablespoons olive oil, or more as needed

1 medium onion, chopped

2 ribs celery, with leaves, chopped

1 green bell pepper, seeded and chopped

2 garlic cloves, minced

3 medium boiling potatoes, cut into ½-inch thick slices

1 28-ounce can unsweetened tomatoes in purée

1 cup Vegetable Stock (page 250), vegetable bouillon, or water

⅛ teaspoon crushed red pepper flakes

½ cup chopped fresh basil or 1 teaspoon dried basil

1 cup Mediterranean black olives, pitted and chopped

Place the eggplant in a colander and toss with 1 teaspoon of the salt. Let stand for 1 hour to draw out the bitter juices. Rinse well, drain, and pat dry with kitchen towels.

Heat 2 tablespoons of the oil in a large saucepan over medium heat. Add the eggplant and cook, stirring often, until lightly browned, about 4 minutes. (You may have to add a little more oil if the eggplant sticks.) Transfer to a plate and set aside.

Heat the remaining 1 tablespoon oil in the pan, and add the onion, celery, bell pepper, and garlic. Cook, stirring often, until softened, about 5 minutes. Stir in the reserved eggplant, the potatoes, the tomatoes with their purée, Vegetable Stock, the remaining ½ teaspoon salt, and the red pepper flakes; if using dried basil, add it now. Bring to a simmer, then reduce the heat to low, cover, and simmer, stirring occasionally, until the potatoes are tender, about 45 minutes to 1 hour.

Stir in the olives and, if using, the fresh basil, and continue cooking to blend the flavors, about 5 minutes. Serve the stew hot, warm, or at room temperature.

The food which we are about to eat
Is Earth, Water, and Sun,
Compounded through the alchemy of many plants.
Therefore Earth, Water, and Sun will become part of us.
This food is also the fruit of the labor of many beings and
*   creatures.*
We are grateful for it.
May it give us strength, health, joy.
And may it increase our love.

—Unitarian prayer

ITALIAN BROWN RICE CROQUETTES

*Makes ten 2-inch croquettes or
forty 1-inch croquettes*

A delectable blend of vegetables and herbs in a creamy mixture of rice and tofu makes hearty appetizers or a main course.

2 cups water
1 cup long-grain brown rice

1 tablespoon olive oil
2 ribs celery, with leaves, finely chopped
1 medium onion, finely chopped
2 garlic cloves, minced
½ pound firm tofu, crumbled
1 cup Vegetable Stock (page 250) or vegetable bouillon
¼ cup rolled oats
3 tablespoons soy sauce
1 cup finely chopped fresh parsley
½ cup finely chopped fresh basil or 2 teaspoons dried basil
¼ teaspoon freshly ground black pepper
Pinch of cayenne pepper
1 cup whole wheat bread crumbs
1 cup finely chopped Mediterranean black olives
1 cup Herbed Bread Crumbs (page 225)
Nutty Basil Pesto (page 306)

In a medium saucepan, bring the water to a boil over medium-high heat. Add the rice, cover, and return to the boil. Immediately reduce the heat to low and simmer until the water is absorbed, 30 to 40 minutes.

Meanwhile, in a large skillet, heat the oil over medium heat. Add the celery, onion, and garlic and cook, until softened, about 6 minutes. Transfer to a large bowl.

Put the tofu, Vegetable Stock, oats, and soy sauce in a blender, and blend until smooth. Add the parsley, basil, black pepper, and cayenne and pulse until blended. Add to the onion mixture.

Add the cooked rice to the onion mixture, along with the whole wheat bread crumbs and olives, and mix well.

Preheat the oven to 400°F. Lightly oil a baking sheet.

Shape the rice mixture into 2-inch balls (about ½ cup) for a main dish or 1-inch balls about (⅛ cup) for an appetizer. Roll each ball in the Herbed Bread Crumbs, patting to make the crumbs adhere, and put the croquettes on the baking sheet. Bake until lightly browned, 20 to 30 minutes.

Arrange the croquettes on a serving platter and serve the Nutty Basil Pesto on the side.

Amount you reduce your risk of heart disease by reducing your consumption of meat, dairy products, and eggs by 10 percent: **8 percent**

Amount you reduce your risk of heart disease by reducing your consumption of meat, dairy products, and eggs by 50 percent: **45 percent**

Amount you reduce your risk of heart disease by reducing your consumption of meat, dairy products, and eggs by 100 percent: **90 percent**

"American feed [for livestock] takes so much ener
counting fuel for farm machinery and for mak
and pesticides—that it might as well be a
product."—Alan Durning, Worldwat

VEGETABLE TOFU LOAF

Makes 6 to 8 servings

This fragrant tofu and vegetable loaf is adapted from a dish served at
The Vegan, a restaurant in Maui, Hawaii.

- 4 slices whole wheat bread, cut into ½-inch cubes
- 1 tablespoon canola or safflower oil
- 2 ribs celery, with leaves, finely chopped
- 1 large carrot, finely chopped
- 1 medium onion, finely chopped
- 3 garlic cloves, minced
- 1¼ pounds firm tofu
- 1 cup nutritional yeast flakes
- ½ cup raw tahini
- ½ cup finely chopped fresh basil or 1 teaspoon dried basil
- ¼ cup finely chopped fresh oregano or 1 teaspoon dried oregano
- ½ teaspoon turmeric
- 3 tablespoons tamari
- ¼ teaspoon freshly ground black pepper

Mushroom Miso Sauce (page 303)

Preheat the oven to 350°F. Lightly oil a 9½- by 5½-inch loaf pan.

Put the bread cubes on an ungreased baking sheet and bake for 5 to 7 minutes. Stir the bread and bake until lightly browned, 3 to 5 minutes more.

Heat the oil in a large frying pan over medium heat. Add the celery, carrot, onion, and garlic and cook until almost tender, 4 to 6 minutes. Remove from the heat.

Put the tofu in a large bowl, and mash well. Add the nutritional yeast, tahini, basil, oregano, turmeric, tamari, and pepper, and stir until well mixed. Add the toasted bread cubes and the cooked vegetables and mix well.

Press the mixture firmly into the prepared loaf pan. Bake until browned on top, 50 to 60 minutes.

Let the loaf stand for 5 minutes, then invert onto a serving platter to unmold. Cut into slices and serve the Mushroom Miso Sauce on the side.

> *"Family farmers are victims of public policy that gives preference to feeding animals over feeding people. This has encouraged the cheap grain policy of this nation and has made the beef cartel the biggest hog at the trough."*
> —Howard Lyman, former senior lobbyist
> for the National Farmers Union

VEGETABLE WALNUT PATTIES

*Makes eight 3-inch patties or
about forty 1-inch patties*

These savory little patties are a blend of vegetables, walnuts, millet, and herbs, all baked instead of the traditional deep frying. Millet is a good grain for making patties because it holds together well. Always use freshly cooked millet when making these. Mini-patties make great appetizers.

1½ cups water
½ cup millet
1 tablespoon canola or safflower oil
1 rib celery, with leaves, finely chopped
1 medium onion, finely chopped
4 slices whole wheat bread, torn into large pieces
2 cups walnuts
1 cup chopped fresh parsley
½ cup coarsely chopped fresh basil or 2 teaspoons dried basil
2 tablespoons chopped fresh thyme or 1 teaspoon dried thyme
3 tablespoons tamari
¼ teaspoon freshly ground black pepper
1 medium carrot, grated
1⅓ cups Herbed Bread Crumbs (page 225)
Walnut halves or parsley sprigs, for garnish

In a medium saucepan, bring the water to a boil over medium-high heat. Stir in the millet, cover, reduce the heat, and simmer until the water is absorbed, 20 to 30 minutes. (The millet must be freshly cooked and still warm to form the patties.)

Meanwhile, heat the oil in a large frying pan over medium-high heat. Add the celery and onion and cook, until softened, about 6 minutes.

Transfer to a large bowl.

In a food processor fitted with the metal blade, combine the bread, walnuts, parsley, basil, thyme, and tamari and process until coarsely chopped. Add to the onion/celery mixture.

Add the cooked millet to the onion mixture, along with the grated carrot, and stir to mix.

Preheat the oven to 400°F. Lightly oil a baking sheet.

Shape the warm millet mixture into 2-inch patties (about ½ cup) to serve as a main dish or 1-inch patties (about ⅛ cup) for an appetizer. Roll each patty in the Herbed Bread Crumbs, patting to make the crumbs adhere, and put on the baking sheet. Bake until lightly browned, 20 to 30 minutes.

Arrange the patties on a serving platter and garnish each one with a walnut half or a sprig of parsley.

PEPPERED CABBAGE

Makes 4 servings

This peppery-good cabbage dish takes minutes to prepare and is especially good with steamed new potatoes.

1 medium head green or red cabbage, cored and coarsely shredded

5 tablespoons raw tahini

2 tablespoons brown rice miso

½ teaspoon freshly ground black pepper, or more to taste

Put 1 inch of water in a large saucepan with a steamer basket, cover, and bring to a boil. Put the cabbage in the steamer basket, cover, and steam until the cabbage is tender, about 8 minutes. Drain, reserving the cooking liquid. Put the cabbage in a serving bowl.

In a medium bowl, whisk the tahini, miso, pepper, and ¼ cup of the cooking liquid until smooth, adding another tablespoon of the cooking liquid if necessary. Pour the tahini mixture over the cabbage, toss to combine, and serve immediately.

"I don't understand why asking people to eat a well-balanced vegetarian diet is considered drastic, while it is medically conservative to cut people open or put them on powerful cholesterol-lowering drugs for the rest of their lives."
—Dean Ornish, M.D.

HERBED LENTIL LOAF

Makes 6 to 8 servings

4½   cups water

  2   cups lentils, picked over and rinsed

½   pound firm tofu, crumbled

¼   cup rolled oats

¼   cup soy sauce

¼   teaspoon freshly ground black pepper

  1   cup minced fresh parsley

½   cup finely chopped fresh basil or 2 teaspoons dried basil

  2   tablespoons finely chopped fresh thyme or 1 teaspoon dried thyme

  1   teaspoon rubbed sage

  1   tablespoon olive oil

  3   ribs celery, with leaves, finely chopped

  1   medium onion, finely chopped

  3   garlic cloves, minced

TOPPING

  1   cup raw almonds

  2   tablespoons nutritional yeast flakes

  1   tablespoon soy sauce

Mushroom Miso Sauce (page 303)

Preheat the oven to 350°F. Lightly oil an 8- by 8-inch baking pan.

Put 3½ cups of the water and the lentils in a large saucepan. Cover and bring to a boil over medium-high heat, then immediately reduce the heat and simmer until the water is absorbed, 50 to 60 minutes.

Meanwhile, put the tofu, the remaining 1 cup water, the oats, soy sauce, and pepper in a blender and blend until smooth. Add the parsley, basil, thyme, and sage and pulse just to mix. Transfer to a large bowl.

Heat the olive oil in a large frying pan over medium-high heat. Add the celery, onion, and garlic and cook until softened, about 6 minutes. Add to the tofu mixture.

Add the cooked lentils to the tofu-vegetable mixture, and stir to mix. Press the mixture firmly into the prepared pan, and bake for 15 minutes.

Meanwhile, put the almonds, yeast flakes, and soy sauce in a food processor fitted with the metal blade, and pulse to coarsely chop.

Sprinkle the topping over the top of the lentil loaf and bake for 15 minutes more. Let the loaf cool for 10 minutes before cutting into squares. Serve with the Mushroom Miso Sauce on the side.

Increased risk of breast cancer for women who eat meat daily compared to those who eat it less than once a week:
3.8 times higher
Increased risk of breast cancer for women who eat eggs daily compared to those who eat them once a week:
2.8 times higher
Increased risk of breast cancer for women who eat butter and cheese three times a week compared to those who eat them once a week: **3.2 times higher**

SPINACH TOFU QUICHE

Makes one 9-inch pie

1 recipe Whole Wheat Pie Dough (page 368)

1 pound firm tofu, crumbled

¼ cup brown rice vinegar

1 teaspoon onion powder

1 teaspoon fine sea salt

½ teaspoon dry mustard

1 tablespoon olive oil

1 medium onion, finely chopped

1 garlic clove, minced

2 cups thinly sliced mushrooms

1 tablespoon tamari

1 pound spinach, well washed, stems removed and leaves cut
   small

¼ cup tightly packed fresh basil leaves, finely chopped

1 large tomato, sliced

Preheat the oven to 350°F.

Roll out the pie dough and fit it into a 9-inch pie pan. With a fork, prick holes all over the bottom and sides of the pie shell. Bake until a light golden color, 20 to 25 minutes. Let cool.

Put the tofu, rice vinegar, onion powder, salt, and mustard in a blender and blend until smooth. Transfer to a large bowl.

Heat the oil in a large frying pan over medium heat. Add the onion, garlic, mushrooms, and tamari and cook until the mushrooms are browned, about 6 minutes. Add the spinach, cover, and cook until the spinach is wilted, 2 to 3 minutes. Uncover and cook, stirring often, until the excess moisture has evaporated, about 3 minutes. Add to the tofu mixture, along with the basil, and stir to mix.

Pour into the baked pie crust. Arrange the tomato slices, overlapping in a circle, on top. Bake until the top is lightly browned and the filling seems firm in the center, 40 to 50 minutes. Let cool 15 minutes. Serve warm or at room temperature.

BROCCOLI-MUSHROOM BAKED POTATOES

Makes 4 servings

Baked potatoes have always been treated as side dish, but the delectable broccoli-mushroom sauce elevates these potatoes to main-dish status.

    4 large baking potatoes, scrubbed and pricked with a fork

    2 cups broccoli florets and sliced stalks

¼ cup water

Mushroom Miso Sauce (page 303), heated

¼ cup finely chopped fresh chives

Preheat the oven to 400°F.

Bake the potatoes until tender when poked with a fork, 50 to 60 minutes.

Meanwhile, in a medium saucepan, combine the broccoli and water and bring to a boil over high heat. Cover and cook until the broccoli is crisp-tender, 3 to 4 minutes; drain. Stir the broccoli into the Mushroom Miso Sauce, and keep warm.

Place one potato in each individual bowl. Slice the potatoes open lengthwise, and squeeze the ends together to break up the potato flesh. Pour the warm sauce over the potatoes, sprinkle with the chives, and serve immediately.

Worldwide, one of the primary causes of the destruction of trees is animal agriculture, as forests are leveled to make way for pastures.

CREAMY CORN BAKED POTATOES

Makes 4 servings

Corn and leeks simmered in a creamy almond sauce is a rich-tasting topping for baked potatoes.

4   large baking potatoes, scrubbed and pricked with a fork

1   tablespoon canola or safflower oil

1   medium leek, sliced into ¼-inch rings and thoroughly washed

1   rib celery, finely chopped

1   red bell pepper, seeded and finely chopped

2   cups Almond Milk (page 209), almond beverage, or soy milk

¼   cup whole wheat pastry flour

2   ears corn, kernels cut off the cob, or 1½ cups (thawed) frozen corn

¼   cup finely chopped fresh dill

1   tablespoon freshly squeezed lemon juice

¾   teaspoon fine sea salt

¼   teaspoon freshly ground black pepper

Preheat the oven to 400°F.

Bake the potatoes until tender when poked with a fork, 50 to 60 minutes.

Meanwhile, heat the oil in a large skillet over medium heat. Add the leek, celery, and red pepper and cook until softened, about 5 minutes. In a small bowl, whisk the Almond Milk and flour together until combined, and stir into the leeks. Bring to a simmer, reduce the heat to low, and simmer, whisking often, until thickened, about 2 minutes.

Stir in the corn, dill, lemon juice, salt, and pepper and simmer until heated through, 1 to 2 minutes.

Place one potato in each individual bowl. Slice the potatoes open lengthwise and squeeze the ends together to break up the potato flesh. Pour the warm sauce over the potatoes and serve immediately.

CREAMY VEGETABLE-MILLET CASSEROLE

Makes 4 servings

Broccoli, carrots, and onions, in a creamy tahini sauce served over a bed of millet, will satisfy the biggest of appetites. Cook some extra millet for making Waste-Not Brown Rice-and-Raisin Breakfast Pudding (page 195), and enjoy this hearty grain for breakfast.

3½ cups water
1 cup millet
8 medium carrots, sliced diagonally into ¼-inch-thick slices
2 broccoli stalks, cut into small florets, stalks sliced ½ inch thick
1 medium onion, finely chopped
½ cup raw tahini
½ cup hot water
2¼ tablespoons brown rice miso
3 tablespoons toasted sesame seeds or Gomashio (page 309)

In a medium saucepan, bring 3 cups of the water to a boil over high heat. Add the millet, cover, and return to the boil. Immediately reduce the heat, and simmer until the water is absorbed, 20 to 30 minutes.

Meanwhile, put the carrots, broccoli, onion, and the remaining ½ cup water in a large saucepan. Cover and bring to a boil over high heat, then immediately reduce the heat and simmer until the vegetables are crisp-tender, about 3 minutes. Drain well.

Put the millet into a 1½-quart baking dish. Pour the tahini-vegetable mixture over and sprinkle the sesame seeds over the top. Bake, uncovered, until heated through, about 15 minutes. Serve immediately.

> *"If you have men who will exclude any of God's creatures from the shelter of compassion and pity, you will have men who will deal likewise with their fellow men."*—Francis of Assisi

BOSTON BAKED BEANS

*Makes 3 to 4 main-course servings or
6 to 8 side-dish servings*

A flavorsome old favorite that is surprisingly easy to make. It takes just minutes to put the ingredients together, but you do have to plan ahead since soaking the beans requires six to twelve hours and cooking them an additional hour and a half.

  2 **cups navy beans, picked over and rinsed**
  1 **tablespoon canola or safflower oil**
  1 **medium onion, finely chopped**
  ⅓ **cup fruit-sweetened catsup**
  ¼ **cup unsulphured molasses**
  3 **tablespoons tamari**
  3 **tablespoons pure maple syrup**
  1 **tablespoon dry mustard**
  1 **teaspoon fine sea salt**

Put the beans into a large bowl and add enough water to cover by 2 inches. Put the bowl in a cool place and let the beans soak for 6 to 12 hours. Drain and rinse the beans.

Put the beans in a large pot and add enough fresh water to cover by 2 inches. Cover and bring to a boil over medium-high heat, then immediately reduce the heat and simmer until the beans are tender, 45 minutes to 1½ hours (depending on the age of the beans). Drain the beans, reserving the cooking liquid. Put the beans in a 2-quart baking dish.

Preheat the oven to 300°F.

Heat the oil in a large skillet over medium heat. Add the onion and cook until softened, about 6 minutes.

Stir the onion into the beans, along with all the remaining ingredients. Add enough of the cooking liquid to barely cover the beans.

Bake covered, until all of the liquid is absorbed, 1 to 1½ hours. Serve hot.

HOT TAMALE PIE

Makes one 8-inch square pie

This irresistible tamale pie is made with beans, lots of vegetables and spices, and a crust of cornmeal. It keeps well in the refrigerator for up to five days. Just reheat in the oven for about thirty minutes and serve.

1 tablespoon olive oil

1 medium onion, finely chopped

1 medium yellow, red, or green bell pepper, seeded and finely chopped

2 garlic cloves, minced

1 16-ounce can unsweetened tomato sauce

1 16-ounce can pinto beans, rinsed and drained

1 ear corn, kernels cut off the cob, or ¾ cup (thawed) frozen corn

1 teaspoon chili powder

1 teaspoon ground cumin

½ teaspoon fine sea salt

Pinch of cayenne pepper

3 cups water

1 cup yellow stone-ground cornmeal

1 tablespoon freshly squeezed lemon juice

1 teaspoon Dijon mustard

½ teaspoon fine sea salt

Heat the olive oil in a large frying pan over medium-high heat. Add the onion, bell pepper, and garlic and cook until softened, 6 to 8 minutes. Remove from the heat and stir in the tomato sauce, pinto beans, corn, chili powder, cumin, salt, and cayenne. Pour into an 8- by 8-inch glass baking dish.

Preheat the oven to 350°F.

Boil the water, add the cornmeal, lemon juice, mustard, and salt in a large saucepan, and stir until mixed. Bring to a boil over medium-high heat, then immediately reduce the heat to low and simmer, stirring often, until thickened, 3 to 5 minutes.

Spread the cooked cornmeal over the bean mixture. Bake for 30 minutes. Cool for 10 minutes before serving.

> *"And there are the ideas of the future ... of freeing the slaves, of giving equality to women, [and] of ceasing to use flesh food."*—Leo Tolstoy

ENCHILADAS SUPREMAS

Makes 4 to 6 servings

Enchiladas filled with spicy tofu and vegetables. The tofu is frozen and then thawed to make it chewy.

- 1 **pound firm tofu**
- ¼ **cup tamari**
- 2 **tablespoons unsalted smooth peanut butter**
- 2 **tablespoons unsweetened tomato paste**
- 1 **tablespoon olive oil**
- 2 **medium onions, finely chopped**
- 1 **medium green bell pepper, seeded and finely chopped**
- 1 **fresh hot chile pepper, seeded and minced**
- 2 **garlic cloves, minced**
- 2 **ears corn, kernels cut off the cob, or 1½ cups (thawed) frozen corn**
- 1 **16-ounce can unsweetened tomato sauce**
- 1 **16-ounce can unsweetened tomato purée**
- 1 to 2 **tablespoons chili powder, or to taste**
- 1 **teaspoon dried oregano**
- 1 **teaspoon ground cumin**
- 12 **corn tortillas**

Canola oil, for brushing the tortillas

- ½ **cup Mediterranean black olives, pitted and chopped, for garnish**

Drain and rinse the tofu. Put the tofu in a plastic bag or container, close it tightly, and freeze until the tofu is frozen hard. Remove the bag or container from the freezer and put it in a bowl of hot water, or let the tofu thaw at room temperature. Gently squeeze the water from the tofu with your hands, and then squeeze it between two kitchen towels. Cut the tofu into ¼-inch cubes.

In a large bowl, stir the tamari, peanut butter, and tomato paste until blended.

Heat the olive oil in a large frying pan over medium heat. Add the tofu, onions, bell pepper, chile pepper, and garlic. Cook until softened, about 6 minutes. Stir into the tamari mixture. Stir in the corn.

In a medium bowl, combine the tomato sauce, tomato purée, chili powder, oregano, and cumin.

Preheat the oven to 350°F. Lightly oil a 9- by 13-inch baking dish.

Spread about 1 cup of the tomato sauce over the bottom of the baking dish.

Heat a dry frying pan or griddle over medium heat. Brush each tortilla lightly on both sides with oil. Add the tortillas, one at a time, to the pan or griddle and heat for about 15 seconds on each side so they are warm and flexible. Put ½ cup of the tofu-vegetable mixture in the center of each tortilla. Roll up tightly and place in the baking dish seam side down. Pour the remaining tomato sauce over the enchiladas. Cover with aluminum foil, and bake until bubbling, 30 to 35 minutes.

Scatter the chopped black olives over the enchiladas and serve hot.

Dr. Maria Simonson, Director of the Health, Weight, and Stress Clinic at Johns Hopkins University in Baltimore, observed eighteen groups of thirty people each during mealtime over a five-year period. Diners who listened to relaxing music during their meals ate much more slowly, reported being more satisfied, and even said the food tasted better— compared to diners who ate the same food while listening to rock music, or no music. Those who listened to rock music ate almost twice as fast.

ITALIAN STUFFED PEPPERS

Makes 8 bell pepper cups

Italians love to stuff vegetables. Bell peppers are filled with tomatoes, rice, mushrooms, and zucchini, topped with a cheeselike sauce.

  2 cups water

  1 cup long-grain brown rice

  8 large green bell peppers

TOMATO SAUCE

  1 tablespoon olive oil

  1 small onion, finely chopped

  1 garlic clove, minced

  1 16-ounce can unsweetened tomatoes, undrained, coarsely chopped

  1 6-ounce can unsweetened tomato paste

  1 teaspoon dried basil

  1 teaspoon dried oregano

  ½ teaspoon dried thyme

  1 teaspoon fine sea salt

  ¼ teaspoon freshly ground black pepper

  1   tablespoon olive oil

  1 medium onion, chopped

  1 cup chopped mushrooms

  1 medium zucchini, chopped

  2 garlic cloves, minced

In a medium saucepan, bring the water to a boil over high heat. Add the rice, cover, reduce the heat, and simmer until the water is absorbed, 30 to 40 minutes. Transfer the rice to a large bowl.

Put 1 inch of water into a large saucepan with a steamer basket, cover with the lid, and bring to a boil. Carefully trim the bottoms of the bell peppers so they sit straight. Slice off the tops and carefully remove the seeds and ribs with your fingers. (Save the tops for chopping and using in another recipe.) Put the peppers in the steamer basket, cover, and steam the peppers until they are bright green but still firm, 5 to 8 minutes. Remove from the steamer and set aside.

Preheat the oven to 350°F. Lightly oil a 9- by 13-inch baking dish.

To make the sauce, in a medium saucepan, heat the oil over medium heat. Add the onion and garlic and cook, stirring often, until softened, about 5 minutes. Stir in the tomatoes with their juices, tomato paste, basil, oregano, thyme, salt, and pepper. Bring to a simmer, reduce the heat to low, and cook until slightly thickened, about 20 minutes. Remove from the heat.

Meanwhile, heat the olive oil in a large frying pan over medium heat. Add the onion, mushrooms, zucchini, and garlic and cook until the mushrooms are lightly browned, about 8 minutes. Add to the rice.

Add ½ cup of the tomato sauce to the rice and vegetables and mix well.

Fill the bell pepper cups with the tomato-rice mixture. Put the stuffed peppers into the prepared baking dish. Pour the remaining tomato sauce on and around the peppers. Bake until bubbling, 20 to 30 minutes. Serve immediately.

O, Heavenly father,
We thank thee for food, and remember the hungry.
We thank thee for health, and remember the sick.
We thank thee for friends, and remember the friendless.
We thank thee for freedom, and remember the enslaved.
May these remembrances stir us to service.
That thy gifts to us may be used for others.
Amen.

—Dear Abby (Abigail Van Buren)

> *"The only foods you need to release are those that are harmful to you in some way: foods that you obsess over, that are nutritionally inferior, and that inhibit the clear head and clear heart you need to allow love to enter your life."*
> —Victoria Moran

ZUCCHINI BOATS

Makes 4 servings

Hollowed-out zucchini are filled with bulgur wheat, mushrooms, and herbs and topped with a walnut sauce.

    4 large zucchini, cut in half lengthwise
    2 tablespoons olive oil
    1 medium red bell pepper, seeded and finely chopped
    1 cup chopped mushrooms
    1 medium onion, finely chopped
    2 garlic cloves, minced
 1½ cups water
    2 tablespoons soy sauce
    1 teaspoon dried basil
    ½ teaspoon dried oregano
    ¼ teaspoon freshly ground black pepper
    1 cup bulgur
Walnut Sauce (page 304)

Put 1 inch of water into a saucepan with a steamer basket, cover with the lid, and bring to a gentle boil. Put the zucchini in the steamer basket, cover, and steam until almost tender, 6 to 8 minutes. Remove the zucchini from the steamer and let cool. Scrape out the center of each zucchini using a melon baller or a spoon, reserving the pulp. Set the shells aside.

Preheat the oven to 350°F. Lightly oil a 9- by 13-inch baking dish. Heat the olive oil in a medium saucepan over medium heat. Add the reserved zucchini pulp, the bell pepper, mushrooms, onion, and garlic and cook until softened, about 6 minutes. Add the soy sauce, basil, oregano, and pepper, and bring to a boil. Stir in the bulgur, remove from the heat, cover, and let stand until the liquid is absorbed, about 10 minutes.

Put the zucchini shells in the prepared baking dish. Fill each shell with the bulgur mixture. (Put any extra bulgur mixture into a lightly oiled baking dish.)

Bake the zucchini (and extra stuffing) until heated through, about 20 minutes. Serve with the Walnut Sauce on the side.

Blessed with this food and this life,
We offer thanks.
Thanks to the Earth, to the Sun, to the Moon, to the Stars;
Thanks to the streams of water, to the pools, to the springs, to
the lakes, to the oceans;
Thanks to the mountains, to the forests, to the meadows, to the
valleys;
Thanks to the grasses, to the vegetables, to the fruits, to the
seeds, to the nuts, to the medicinal herbs;
Thanks to the wind, to the clouds, to the rain;
Thanks to the Great One at the source of all things,
Who is the giver of breath and of health and of life.
May this meal be taken in gratitude.
May our lives be lived in gratitude.

Bless this food.
Bless the poor and the hungry.
Bless the wealthy and well fed.
Bless everyone everywhere and always.

DOLMAS

Makes 6 to 8 servings

Dolmas, stuffed grape leaves, are a classic Middle Eastern dish. Here they are stuffed with rice and walnuts and topped with a tangy lemon sauce.

- 2 cups water
- 1 cup long-grain brown rice
- 1 tablespoon olive oil
- 1 medium onion, finely chopped
- 2 garlic cloves, minced
- ½ cup currants
- ½ cup coarsely chopped walnuts
- 1 teaspoon dried mint
- ¼ cup finely chopped fresh parsley
- 1 teaspoon dried oregano
- 1 teaspoon fine sea salt
- ½ teaspoon freshly ground black pepper
- 1 8-ounce jar grape leaves
- 1½ cups Vegetable Stock (page 250), vegetable bouillon, or water
- ¼ cup freshly squeezed lemon juice
- 1 lemon, thinly sliced
- 3 bay leaves

In a medium saucepan, bring the water to a boil over high heat, add the rice, cover, reduce the heat to low, and simmer until the rice is tender and the water is absorbed, 30 to 40 minutes.

Meanwhile, heat the olive oil in a skillet over medium heat. Add the onion and garlic and cook, until softened, about 6 minutes. Transfer to a large bowl.

Add the cooked rice to the onion mixture. Add the currants, walnuts, mint, parsley, oregano, salt, and pepper and stir to mix.

Remove the grape leaves from the jar, being careful not to tear them. Choose 32 of the largest leaves for stuffing. Reserve the smaller or any damaged leaves separately. Put them in a colander, rinse in warm water to remove the salt, and gently separate the leaves. Let the leaves drain and pat them dry with paper towels or dish towels.

Preheat the oven to 350°F. Lightly oil a 9- by 13-inch baking dish.

Line the bottom of the baking dish with some of the rinsed and dried smaller or damaged leaves.

Lay a large leaf flat and put about 1 tablespoon of the rice filling in the middle of the leaf. Fold over the sides and roll up into a cylinder, starting at the bottom. Put the filled leaf seam side down in the prepared baking dish. Repeat until all the filling is used. Cover the dolmas with the remaining smaller leaves.

In a small bowl, combine the Vegetable Stock and lemon juice and stir together. Pour over the dolmas. Arrange the lemon slices and bay leaves on top. Cover with parchment paper or waxed paper and bake until the liquid is absorbed, 30 to 40 minutes.

"The indifference, callousness, and contempt that so many people exhibit toward animals is evil first because it results in great suffering towards animals, and second because it results in an incalculably great impoverishment of human spirit."
—Ashley Montagu

> *"Nothing will benefit human health and increase the chances for survival of life on Earth as much as the evolution to a vegetarian diet."*—Albert Einstein

SPANAKOPITA

Makes 6 servings

Spanakopita is a spinach pie that comes from Greece. The savory spinach filling is layered between sheets of filo dough for a main dish or folded into little triangles for a great appetizer or finger food for picnics and travel. You can find the thin sheets of dough, called filo or phyllo, in the freezer section of your health food store or supermarket. Whole wheat filo dough may be difficult to find, but certain Greek bakeries make it.

2   **tablespoons olive oil**
1   **large onion, finely chopped**
2   **garlic cloves, minced**
2   **pounds spinach, well washed, stems removed and leaves coarsely chopped**
½   **pound soft tofu, crumbled**
2   **teaspoons dried basil**
1   **teaspoon dried thyme**
¼   **cup freshly squeezed lemon juice**
¼   **cup nutritional yeast flakes**
¼   **cup raw tahini**
¼   **cup tamari**
½   **teaspoon grated nutmeg**
¼   **teaspoon freshly ground black pepper**
14   **sheets filo dough, preferably whole wheat, thawed in the refrigerator for 6 to 8 hours**
Olive oil, for brushing the filo

Heat the olive oil in a large skillet over medium heat. Add the onion and garlic and cook until softened, about 5 minutes.

Put the spinach on top of the onions, cover, and cook until the spinach is wilted, 2 to 3 minutes. Remove the lid and cook, stirring often, until the excess liquid is evaporated, about 5 minutes. Stir in the crumbled tofu, basil, thyme, lemon juice, yeast flakes, tahini, tamari, nutmeg, and pepper, and mix well. Remove from the heat and set aside.

Preheat the oven 350°F. Lightly oil an 11- x 7-inch baking dish.

Unroll the filo dough, lay it flat on a dry surface, and cut in half crosswise. Cover the dough with a damp towel to prevent it from drying out as you work. Layer 7 sheets of the dough in the baking dish, lightly brushing each sheet with olive oil.

Spread the tofu-spinach filling evenly over the layered filo dough. Cover the filling with the remaining 7 sheets of dough, brushing each sheet lightly with oil. Brush the top of the last sheet with oil.

Bake until lightly browned on top, 25 to 35 minutes. Use a sharp knife to cut into serving pieces. Serve hot or cold.

The rules of conventional English grammar say not to capitalize the word Earth. *They say to capitalize a person's name,* God, Bible, *the pronoun* I, *and the names of corporations such as* Exxon—*but not the name of our planet. Is this another example of our disconnected attitude toward Nature? I have chosen throughout this book to capitalize the word* Earth.

LEMON RICE AND PEAS

Makes 4 servings

This delicious Indian-flavored rice dish will show you why rice is served as a main course in much of the world. It has the flavors of India and is full of tasty peas and cashews. Serve it rolled in warm chapatis or in a molded shape.

2 cups water

1 cup long-grain brown rice

2 tablespoons olive oil

1 teaspoon cumin seeds

1 teaspoon black mustard seeds

6 green onions, finely chopped

2 cups fresh or (thawed) frozen peas

1 cup raw cashews

3 tablespoons tamari

3 tablespoons freshly squeezed lemon juice

⅓ cup chopped fresh parsley

1 teaspoon turmeric

Pinch of cayenne pepper

8 Chapatis (page 220) or whole wheat tortillas, warmed

In a medium saucepan, bring the water to a boil over high heat. Add the rice, cover, reduce the heat, and simmer until the water is absorbed, 30 to 40 minutes. Remove from the heat.

Heat the olive oil in a large skillet over medium heat. Add the cumin seeds and mustard seeds and cook, stirring, until the mustard seeds begin to pop, about 30 seconds. Add the green onions and cook until softened, about 1 minute. Add the cooked rice, peas, cashews, tamari, lemon juice, parsley, turmeric, and cayenne and cook, stirring often, for 3 minutes. Remove from the heat.

Lay a warm Chapati or tortilla on a work surface, put about ½ cup of the rice mixture in the center, and roll up tightly around the filling. Repeat with the remaining chapatis and rice mixture, serve immediately.

Note: Another attractive way to serve this rice is in a molded shape, with chapatis on the side. Firmly press the rice mixture into a well-oiled 4-cup mold. Put a large serving dish on top of the mold and turn both over together. Gently tap the mold and lift it off the rice.

SPICE ISLANDS CURRIED VEGETABLES AND RICE

Makes 4 servings

2¼ cups water
1 cup long-grain brown rice
2 tablespoons canola or safflower oil
1 medium onion, finely chopped
1 stalk broccoli, cut into small florets, stalk finely chopped
1 medium zucchini, thinly sliced
2 garlic cloves, minced
1 tablespoon finely grated fresh gingerroot
4 medium tomatoes, coarsely chopped
6 ounces snow peas, strings removed, cut in half diagonally
2 teaspoons curry powder
⅛ teaspoon cayenne pepper
3 tablespoons tamari
1 tablespoon rice syrup
½ cup tamari-toasted peanuts (page 274)

In a medium saucepan, bring 2 cups of the water to a boil over high heat. Add the rice, cover, reduce the heat, and simmer until the rice is tender and the water is absorbed, 30 to 40 minutes. Transfer to a serving platter and keep warm.

Meanwhile, in a wok or large frying pan, heat the oil over medium-high heat. Add the onion, broccoli, zucchini, garlic, and ginger and stir-fry until the onions are softened, about 3 minutes. Add the tomatoes, snow peas, curry powder, and cayenne and stir-fry for 2 minutes. Add the remaining ¼ cup water, tamari, and rice syrup, and cook for 1 minute. Stir in the peanuts.

Spoon the vegetables over the cooked rice and serve.

CURRIED POTATOES, CAULIFLOWER, AND PEAS

Makes 4 servings

You can use almost any vegetables to make this tasty dish, served rolled up in flatbread. We call this Curry in a Hurry and sometimes take it on a picnic.

2 tablespoons canola or safflower oil

2 medium baking potatoes, cut into ½-inch cubes

1 large onion, finely chopped

1 large carrot, finely chopped

1 small cauliflower, cut into florets

1 tablespoon curry powder

½ teaspoon ground cumin

½ teaspoon turmeric

Pinch of cayenne pepper

1 cup Vegetable Stock (page 250), vegetable bouillon, or water

1 cup fresh or (thawed) frozen peas

3 tablespoons tamari

Heat the oil in a large skillet over medium heat. Add the potatoes, onion, and carrot, and cook, stirring often, until the potatoes are lightly browned, about 8 minutes.

Add the cauliflower, curry powder, cumin, turmeric, and cayenne and stir for 30 seconds. Add the Vegetable Stock, cover, immediately reduce the heat, and simmer, stirring occasionally, until the potatoes are tender, about 10 minutes.

Stir in the peas and tamari and cook, uncovered, until the liquid has thickened, about 2 minutes. Serve immediately.

TERIYAKI-ROASTED VEGETABLES

Makes 4 servings

Serve these richly flavored vegetables with brown rice or udon noodles.

1 **medium eggplant (about 1 pound), peeled, halved lengthwise and cut into ½-inch-thick slices**

1 **teaspoon fine sea salt**

2 **red bell peppers, seeded and cut into 1-inch-wide strips**

2 **medium zucchini, cut into 1-inch-thick rounds**

Teriyaki Marinade (page 309)

1 **pound mushrooms**

1 **tablespoon dark Oriental sesame oil**

2 **tablespoons raw sesame seeds, toasted**

Place the eggplant slices in a colander and toss with the salt. Let stand at room temperature for 1 hour to draw out the bitter juices. Rinse well under cold water and pat dry with kitchen towels.

In a large bowl, combine the eggplant, bell peppers, and zucchini. Add the Teriyaki Marinade and toss to coat. Cover and refrigerate, tossing occasionally, for at least 3 hours or up to 8 hours. During the last hour of marinating, add the mushrooms. (If added earlier, the mushrooms will soak up too much liquid.)

Preheat the oven to 550°F.

Transfer the vegetables and marinade to a large roasting pan, spreading the vegetables out into a single layer, more or less. Roast until the vegetables are lightly browned and the marinade is reduced to a glaze, 15 to 20 minutes. Serve the vegetables hot, cold, or at room temperature, tossed with the sesame oil, and sprinkled with the sesame seeds.

CHINESE VEGETABLES AND TOFU

Makes 4 to 6 servings

Stir-fried vegetables are served on a bed of crispy noodles.

- 8 ounces spaghetti made without eggs
- ¼ cup canola or safflower oil

SWEET 'N' SOUR SAUCE
- 1 cup unfiltered apple juice
- ¼ cup fruit-sweetened apricot jam
- ¼ cup tamari
- 2 tablespoons arrowroot powder
- 2 tablespoons dark Oriental sesame oil or hot sesame oil
- 2 tablespoons rice vinegar
- 2 teaspoons Dijon mustard
- 2 teaspoons finely grated fresh gingerroot
- 1 garlic clove, minced
- ⅛ teaspoon crushed red pepper flakes

- 1 medium onion, coarsely chopped
- 1 medium green bell pepper, seeded and cut into ¼-inch strips
- 1 cup sliced mushrooms (¼-inch-thick slices)
- 1 stalk broccoli, cut into small florets, stalk finely chopped
- 1 rib celery, with leaves, cut into ½-inch slices
- 1 teaspoon finely grated fresh gingerroot
- 1 garlic clove, minced
- 10 ounces firm tofu, cut into ½-inch cubes
- 4 ounces snow peas, strings removed, cut in half diagonally

In a large pot of boiling salted water, cook the spaghetti about 7 minutes, until just tender. Drain, rinse under cold water, and drain again. Add 1 tablespoon of the canola oil and toss to coat the noodles well.

Preheat the oven to 200°F.

In a large nonstick skillet, heat 1 tablespoon of the remaining canola oil over medium heat, swirling to coat the sides of the pan. Add the noodles and press down with a wooden spoon to form a thick "pancake." Cook until golden brown on the bottom, about 5 minutes. Carefully turn the pancake, and cook until the other side is browned, about 5 minutes longer. Transfer the pancake to a brown paper–lined baking sheet, and keep warm in the oven.

In a medium bowl, whisk together the apple juice, apricot jam, tamari, arrowroot, sesame oil, rice vinegar, mustard, ginger, garlic, and red pepper flakes.

In a wok or large skillet, heat the remaining 2 tablespoons canola oil over medium-high heat. Add the onion, bell pepper, mushrooms, broccoli, celery, ginger, and garlic and stir-fry for 3 minutes. Add the tofu and snow peas, and stir-fry for 2 minutes more. Stir in the sauce and simmer, stirring often, until the mixture is thickened, about 1 minute. Remove from the heat.

Transfer the noodle pancake to a large serving platter, spoon the vegetables and sauce over, and serve immediately.

The meat industry claims: **The USDA protects our health through meat inspection.**
Fact: **Less than one out of every quarter million slaughtered animals is tested for toxic chemical residues.**

SWEET AND SOUR TOFU VEGETABLES

Makes 4 servings

This sweet and sour stir-fried dish is adapted from a recipe from Moosewood Restaurant, the well-known vegetarian restaurant near Ithaca, New York, with a reputation for serving food that is delicious, wholesome, and attractively presented.

- 3 cups water
- 1½ cups long-grain brown rice
- 1 pound firm tofu
- ¼ cup unsweetened pineapple juice
- 2 tablespoons freshly squeezed lemon juice
- 2 tablespoons fruit-sweetened catsup
- 2 tablespoons pure maple syrup
- 2 tablespoons tamari
- 1 tablespoon dark Oriental sesame oil
- 2¼ teaspoons arrowroot powder
- 2½ teaspoons finely grated fresh gingerroot
- 2 tablespoons canola or safflower oil
- 1 large onion, thinly sliced
- 1 medium carrot, sliced diagonally into ¼-inch-thick slices
- 4 ounces green beans, cut into 1-inch pieces
- 1 large red bell pepper, seeded and sliced into ½-inch-wide strips
- 8 ounces mushrooms, thinly sliced
- 1 medium zucchini, sliced into ½-inch-thick rounds
- 1 cup fresh or unsweetened canned cubed pineapple

In a medium saucepan bring 2 cups of the water to a boil over high heat. Add the rice, reduce the heat, and simmer until the rice is tender and the water is absorbed, 30 to 40 minutes. Transfer to a serving platter and keep warm.

Meanwhile, remove excess water from the tofu by squeezing it gently between your hands. Cut the pressed tofu into ½-inch cubes.

In a small bowl, whisk the pineapple juice, lemon juice, catsup, maple syrup, tamari, sesame oil, arrowroot, and ginger together.

In a wok or a large frying pan, heat the canola oil over medium-high heat. Add the onion, carrot, green beans, bell pepper, mushrooms, and zucchini and stir-fry until crisp-tender, 3 to 5 minutes.

Add the pineapple juice mixture, pressed tofu, and pineapple and cook, stirring often, until the sauce is thickened, about 2 minutes.

Spoon the vegetables and sauce over the brown rice and serve immediately.

We honor the farmers of the world in their work,
In stewarding the Earth, in planting the seeds, nourishing
  them,
And bringing them to harvest.
We ask for blessings upon their hands and hearts
As they carry on the ancient work of sustaining cultural
  survival
Through this sacred task.

—Jerilyn Brusseau

STIR-FRIED ORIENTAL VEGETABLES

Makes 4 servings

3 cups water

1½ cups long-grain brown rice

2 tablespoons plus 1 teaspoon arrowroot powder

¼ cup tamari

1 tablespoon canola or safflower oil

1 medium onion, thinly sliced

1 red bell pepper, seeded and cut into strips

2 ribs celery, cut diagonally into ½-inch-thick slices

1 stalk broccoli, cut into small florets, stalks thinly sliced

2 cups shredded Chinese cabbage

1 cup thinly sliced mushrooms

2 tablespoons finely grated fresh gingerroot

2 garlic cloves, minced

4 ounces snow peas, strings removed, cut in half diagonally

1 cup mung bean sprouts

1 cup coarsely chopped raw almonds, toasted

In a medium saucepan, bring 2 cups of water to a boil over high heat. Add the rice, cover, reduce the heat, and simmer until the rice is tender and the water is absorbed, 30 to 40 minutes. Transfer to a serving platter and keep warm.

Meanwhile, in a small bowl, whisk the remaining 1 cup water, the arrowroot, tamari, and thyme until combined.

In a wok or very large frying pan, heat the oil over medium-high heat. Add the onion, bell pepper, celery, broccoli, cabbage, mushrooms, ginger, and garlic and stir-fry for 3 minutes. Add the snow peas and stir-fry for 1 minute more.

Stir in the arrowroot mixture and mung bean sprouts and cook until the mixture is thickened, about 1 minute, stirring often. Spoon over the cooked brown rice and sprinkle with toasted almonds.

EIGHTEEN

Pastas and Pizzas

The myth is that pasta is fattening, but that is not so. It is the rich sauces and toppings made with cream, cheese, butter, and meat that give pasta this undeserved reputation. In fact, plain pasta is so low in fat that a four-ounce serving contains less than seventy-five calories.

FETTUCCINE WITH HERBS

Makes 4 servings

The perfect pasta for summertime, when fresh herbs are available and it's too hot to cook, is simple and quick to make. Serve it with a leafy green salad and Tofu Dill Dressing (page 296).

12 ounces fettuccine made without eggs

2 tablespoons olive oil, preferably extra virgin

1 cup coarsely chopped walnuts

1 cup chopped fresh basil

¼ cup chopped fresh oregano

½ cup finely chopped fresh chives

1 teaspoon fine sea salt

⅛ teaspoon freshly ground black pepper

½ cup Herbed Bread Crumbs (page 225)

In a large saucepan of lightly salted boiling water, cook the noodles until just tender, about 8 minutes. Drain, reserving ½ cup of the cooking water, and transfer to a warmed serving dish.

Add to the fettuccine the olive oil, reserved ½ cup cooking liquid, the walnuts, basil, oregano, chives, salt, and pepper and toss to coat well. Sprinkle with the bread crumbs and serve immediately.

> *Pasta is man at his best—growing and harvesting grain; making it edible by milling it; kneading, shaping, and cooking it.*

FETTUCCINE WITH TOMATO-AVOCADO SAUCE

Makes 4 servings

Avocado adds a surprisingly delicious taste to this quick-to-make pasta dish. Serve with Garlic Herb Bread (page 225) and a green salad topped with Creamy Italian Dressing (page 297).

1 tablespoon olive oil

1 medium onion, finely chopped

2 garlic cloves, minced

1 fresh hot chile pepper, seeded and minced

4 medium tomatoes, cut into ½-inch cubes

¾ teaspoon fine sea salt

⅛ teaspoon freshly ground black pepper

½ cup chopped fresh cilantro, optional

12 ounces fettuccine made without eggs

2 ripe medium avocados, peeled, stone removed, and cut into ¾-inch cubes

3 tablespoons extra virgin olive oil

2 tablespoons freshly squeezed lime juice

Heat the 1 tablespoon olive oil in a large skillet over medium heat. Add the onion, garlic, and chile pepper, and cook until softened, about 5 minutes. Add the tomatoes, salt, and pepper and cook, stirring often, until the sauce has thickened slightly, about 10 minutes.

Remove from the heat, and stir in the cilantro. Keep warm.

Meanwhile, in a large saucepan of lightly salted boiling water, cook the noodles until just tender, about 8 minutes. Drain well and transfer to a warmed serving bowl.

Add the tomato sauce, avocados, extra-virgin olive oil, and lime juice. Toss to mix well, and serve immediately.

RAINBOW PASTA

Makes 4 servings

This colorful pasta dish is made with red bell pepper, corn, red onion, and other bright vegetables. The Spinach Walnut Salad (page 270) is the perfect accompaniment.

 2 tablespoons olive oil

 1 medium red onion, finely chopped

 1 medium zucchini, cut into ½-inch cubes

 2 ears corn, kernels cut off the cob, or 1½ cups (thawed) frozen corn

 1 large red bell pepper, seeded and chopped

 2 garlic cloves, minced

 ½ cup Vegetable Stock (page 250), or vegetable bouillon, or water

 ½ cup chopped fresh dill

 1 teaspoon fine sea salt

 ¼ teaspoon freshly ground black pepper

 12 ounces rainbow fettuccine made without eggs

 2 tablespoons extra virgin olive oil

In a large skillet, heat the 2 tablespoons olive oil over medium heat. Add the red onion, zucchini, corn, bell pepper, and garlic and cook until softened, about 5 minutes. Add the Vegetable Stock and bring to a boil. Remove from the heat and stir in the dill, salt, and pepper. Keep warm.

Meanwhile in a large saucepan of lightly salted boiling water, cook the noodles until just tender, about 8 minutes. Drain well and transfer to a warmed serving bowl.

Add the vegetables and extra-virgin olive oil, toss to mix well, and serve immediately.

*You have every right to be highly pleased with yourself
for making food choices that show wise and
life-affirming judgment.*

"CHEESY" TOMATO PASTA

Makes 4 servings

12 ounces fettuccine or other long noodles made without eggs
1   cup No-Cheese Spread (page 244)
2   cups Summer Tomato Sauce (page 300) or Winter Tomato
    Sauce (page 302), warmed

In a large pot of lightly salted boiling water, cook the noodles until
just tender, about 8 minutes. Drain well, and place in a warmed serving
bowl.

Add the No-Cheese Spread and the tomato sauce of your choice. Toss
well, letting the heat of the hot noodles melt the spread. Serve immediately.

*Japanese soba noodles are made from buckwheat flour, which
gives them a dark brown hue. Sometimes jinenjo flour (made
from a type of wild mountain yam reputed to bring vitality and
health) or dried mugwort (from a plant legendary in Chinese
and Japanese acupuncture for its healing benefits) is used.*

MACARONI AND NO-CHEESE

Makes 4 to 6 servings

Yellow butternut squash is blended with white miso and tahini to create a cheeselike sauce for this baked macaroni dish. Serve with a green salad and Rose's Sweet and Sour Dressing (page 293).

1 **butternut squash (about 2 pounds), unpeeled, cut into 2-inch cubes and seeds removed**

¼ **cup white miso**

¼ **cup hot water**

¼ **cup nutritional yeast flakes**

3 **tablespoons Dijon mustard**

2 **tablespoons raw tahini**

3 **tablespoons tamari**

½ **teaspoon freshly ground black pepper**

1 **pound elbow macaroni made without eggs**

½ **cup Herbed Bread Crumbs (page 225)**

Preheat the oven to 350°F. Lightly oil a round 1½-quart baking dish.

Put 1 inch of water in a large saucepan with a steamer basket, cover with the lid, and bring to a gentle boil. Put the butternut squash in the steamer basket, cover, and steam until the squash is tender, 15 to 20 minutes. Cool, and pare off the squash peel.

Put half the steamed squash, the miso, hot water, yeast flakes, mustard, tahini, tamari, and pepper in a blender, and blend until smooth.

Meanwhile, in a large pot of lightly salted boiling water, cook the macaroni until just tender, about 8 minutes. Drain well. Transfer to a large bowl.

Add the tahini-squash mixture and the cubed squash and mix well. Transfer the macaroni mixture to the baking dish. Sprinkle the top with the bread crumbs.

Bake until heated through, about 20 minutes. Serve immediately.

SPINACH LASAGNA

Makes 4 to 6 servings

12 curly lasagna noodles made without eggs (about 9 ounces)

 2 tablespoons olive oil

1¼ pounds spinach, well washed, stems removed and leaves coarsely chopped

 1 medium onion, finely chopped

 2 broccoli stalks, cut into small florets, stalks finely chopped

 1 pound mushrooms, thinly sliced

 2 garlic cloves, minced

1½ cups Tofu "Cheese" Sauce (page 305)

 2 cups Summer Tomato Sauce (page 300) or Winter Tomato Sauce (page 302)

In a large pot of lightly salted boiling water, cook the lasagna noodles until just tender, about 6 minutes. Drain well. Toss with 1 tablespoon of the oil to keep the noodles from sticking.

Meanwhile, put 1 inch of water into a large saucepan with a steamer basket, cover with the lid, and bring to a gentle boil. Put the spinach in the steamer basket, cover, and steam until the spinach is wilted, 2 to 3 minutes. Drain the spinach and rinse under cold running water. Use your hands to squeeze the excess water from the spinach.

In a large skillet, heat the remaining 1 tablespoon olive oil over medium heat. Add the onion, broccoli, mushrooms, and garlic and cook until the onions are softened, about 5 minutes. Add the spinach and cook, stirring, until all the moisture has evaporated from the spinach, about 2 minutes. Stir in the Tofu "Cheese" Sauce, and remove from the heat.

Preheat the oven to 350°F. Lightly oil a 9- by 13-inch baking dish.

Spread ½ cup of the tomato sauce over the bottom of the baking dish. Place 4 cooked lasagna noodles in the baking dish, overlapping them slightly. Spread with half of the spinach filling. Top with 4 more noodles, and spread with the remaining filling. Top with the remaining noodles, and spread the remaining tomato sauce on top.

Bake until bubbling, 25 to 30 minutes. Let stand 10 minutes before serving.

JAPANESE BUCKWHEAT-GINGER NOODLES

Makes 2 to 4 servings

Made with chewy buckwheat noodles, snow peas, and mushrooms this Japanese noodle dish also has the delightful flavors of freshly grated ginger and toasted sesame oil. For a spicier taste, use hot sesame oil.

1½ cups water
 2 tablespoons arrowroot powder
 3 tablespoons tamari
 1 tablespoon umeboshi plum vinegar
 2 tablespoons canola or safflower oil
1½ cups thinly sliced mushrooms
 6 ounces snow peas, cut diagonally into ½-inch-wide pieces
 2 teaspoons finely grated fresh gingerroot
 2 garlic cloves, minced
 6 green onions, with tops, cut on the diagonal into long slivers
12 ounces soba noodles
 2 tablespoons toasted sesame oil or hot sesame oil
 ¼ cup sesame seeds, toasted

Put the water, arrowroot, tamari, and umeboshi plum vinegar in a small bowl, and whisk until the arrowroot is dissolved.

In a large skillet, heat the canola oil over medium heat. Add the mushrooms, snow peas, ginger, and garlic and cook, stirring often, until the snow peas are crisp-tender, about 3 minutes. Stir in the arrowroot mixture and the green onions. Cook just until the mixture thickens, about 1 minute.

Meanwhile, in a large pot of lightly salted boiling water, cook the soba noodles until just tender, about 5 minutes. Drain well and transfer to a warmed serving bowl. Add the tamari-vegetable mixture and sesame oil, and toss to mix well. Sprinkle with the sesame seeds and serve immediately.

PIZZA DOUGH

Makes one 14-inch pizza crust

This pizza dough has a delicious wholesome texture. It is the base for the pizza recipes in this book, or you can use this dough for your own toppings.

½ cup lukewarm water (100° to 110°F)

2½ teaspoons (1 package) active dry yeast

1 teaspoon pure maple syrup

1 cup water

¼ cup olive oil

2 cups whole wheat flour

1½ cups unbleached white flour

1 teaspoon fine sea salt

In a small bowl, combine the lukewarm water, yeast, and maple syrup; let stand until creamy, about 10 minutes. Stir in the 1 cup water and the olive oil.

In a large bowl, combine the whole wheat flour, white flour, and salt. Add the yeast mixture and stir until well mixed. Turn the dough out onto a floured work surface.

Lightly flour your hands, and shape the dough into a ball. Knead the dough until it is smooth and elastic, 10 to 15 minutes. (To knead, pick up the far edge of the dough, fold it over in half, and press down the center of the dough with the heels of your hands. Turn the dough a quarter turn, and repeat.) Add more flour to the work surface as needed, to keep the dough from sticking.

Shape the dough into a ball, put into a lightly oiled bowl, and turn once to coat it. Cover the bowl with a damp cloth, put it in a warm place, and let the dough rise until it is doubled in size, about 1 hour.

Lightly oil a 14-inch pizza pan and dust it with cornmeal.

Punch the dough down 6 to 8 times by pushing your fist into the center of the dough. Shape the dough into a ball.

Lightly flour a rolling pin. On a floured work surface, roll out the dough to a 16-inch circle. Transfer the dough to the pizza pan. Fold the excess dough over, and pinch to form a thick rim of dough.

MEDITERRANEAN PIZZA

Makes one 14-inch pizza

2 small Japanese eggplants (about 8 ounces), cut into ¼-inch-thick rounds

1¼ teaspoons fine sea salt

2 tablespoons olive oil

1 medium onion, sliced into thin rings

1 medium red bell pepper, seeded and sliced into thin rings

1 medium zucchini, cut into ¼-inch-thick rounds

2 garlic cloves, minced

¼ teaspoon freshly ground black pepper

1 15-ounce can unsweetened tomato purée

1 teaspoon dried basil

1 teaspoon dried oregano

1 recipe Pizza Dough (page 359)

1 cup No-Cheese Spread (page 244)

In a colander, toss the eggplant with 1 teaspoon of the salt. Let stand 1 hour to draw out the bitter juices. Rinse under cold water, drain, and pat dry with kitchen towels.

Preheat the oven to 450°F.

In a large skillet, heat the olive oil over medium heat. Add the onion, bell pepper, eggplant, zucchini, and garlic, and cook, stirring often, until the vegetables are crisp-tender, about 3 minutes. Stir in the remaining ¼ teaspoon salt and the pepper, and remove from the heat.

In a small bowl, stir the tomato purée, basil, and oregano to mix.

Roll out the Pizza Dough and place it on a lightly oiled 14-inch pizza pan (see page 359). Spread the tomato sauce over the dough and arrange the cooked vegetables on top. Drop the No-Cheese Spread by teaspoonfuls over the vegetables.

Bake on the lowest rack of the oven until the bottom of the crust is brown and crisp, 15 to 20 minutes.

How wonderful to slow down and be peaceful.
How wonderful to eat with friends.
How wonderful to share this time of peace and gratitude.

PESTO PIZZA

Makes one 14-inch pizza

1   recipe Pizza Dough (page 359)
1½ cups Tofu "Cheese" Sauce (page 305)
½   cup Nutty Basil Pesto (page 306)

Preheat the oven to 450°F.

Roll out the Pizza Dough and place it on a lightly oiled 14-inch pizza pan (see page 359).

Spread the Tofu "Cheese" Sauce over the dough. Drop the Nutty Basil Pesto by tablespoonfuls over the sauce.

Bake on the lowest rack of the oven until the bottom of the crust is brown and crisp, 15 to 20 minutes.

Pastas are substantial, hearty, and filling. In their capacity to
bring us satisfaction, they speak of the fullness of life.

GARDEN CALZONES

Makes four 10-inch calzones

These little pastry pockets are filled with a tantalizing blend of fresh garden vegetables and basil. Make them ahead of time and warm just before serving, or serve at room temperature.

2   tablespoons olive oil

1   medium onion, finely chopped

1   bunch broccoli, trimmed and finely chopped

2   cups coarsely chopped mushrooms

1   medium red bell pepper, seeded and chopped

2   garlic cloves, minced

10 ounces spinach, well washed, stems removed and leaves coarsely chopped

½   cup chopped fresh basil

1   recipe Pizza Dough (page 359)

1   cup Tofu "Cheese" Sauce (page 305)

In a large skillet, heat the olive oil over medium heat. Add the onion, broccoli, mushrooms, red pepper, and garlic and cook until the onion is softened, about 5 minutes. Add the spinach, cover, and cook until the spinach is wilted, about 2 minutes. Remove the lid and cook until the excess liquid has evaporated, about 3 minutes. Stir in the basil and Tofu "Cheese" Sauce.

Preheat the oven to 350°F. Lightly oil a baking sheet and dust with cornmeal.

Flour your hands and a rolling pin. Turn the Pizza Dough out onto a floured work surface, and punch down (see page 359). Divide the dough into four pieces and shape each one into a ball. Roll each ball into a 10-inch circle, about ⅛ inch thick.

Divide the vegetable filling evenly among the dough circles, placing it in the center of each dough circle. Fold the dough circles in half over the filling. Roll up the edges to form a 1-inch-thick border on each calzone, and flute. Carefully transfer the calzones to the baking sheet.

Bake until lightly browned, 20 to 30 minutes. Serve hot or at room temperature.

NINETEEN

Desserts

> Preparing a wholesome dessert is a way of expressing a special kind of care to your guests. You are telling them that they deserve pleasure, and to be nurtured by the sweet experiences that life has to offer.

SPICY BAKED APPLES

Makes 4 servings

Apples are filled with raisins and nuts and baked in a mixture of apple juice, ginger, and cinnamon. Serve them hot or cold. They keep four to five days in the refrigerator.

> 4 **large Rome or other baking apples**
>
> 1 **cup pecans**
>
> 6 **tablespoons plus ⅓ cup pure maple syrup**
>
> 1 **teaspoon ground cinnamon**
>
> ½ **cup raisins**
>
> 1 **cup unfiltered apple juice**
>
> 2 **teaspoons freshly squeezed lemon juice**
>
> ½ **teaspoon finely grated fresh gingerroot**
>
> 1 **cinnamon stick**

Preheat the oven to 350°F.

Peel the top thirds of the apples. Use the point of the vegetable peeler to core the apples from their tops, making the holes about ¾ inches wide. Compost or discard the seeds and stems.

Put the pecans, 6 tablespoons of the maple syrup, and the ground cinnamon in a food processor fitted with the metal blade, and process until coarsely chopped. Transfer to a bowl and stir in the raisins.

Fill each apple with the chopped nut mixture, mounding it a little on top. Put the apples in a small baking dish just big enough for the apples to stand up in.

In a small bowl, stir the apple juice, the remaining ⅓ cup maple syrup, the lemon juice, ginger, and cinnamon stick together. Pour over the apples, and cover.

Bake until the apples are just tender when pricked with the tip of a sharp knife, 40 to 50 minutes. (Overbaking the apples will cause them to split and lose their good flavor.)

Pour the cooking juices into a medium saucepan. Boil over high heat until thickened and reduced to about ½ cup. Pour over the apples in the baking dish.

Put the baked apples into individual bowls, and serve warm.

FRUIT JELL

Makes 8 servings

This is an exquisite dessert of bright berries in a translucent jell of apple juice topped with a sweet almond sauce. While this gels at room temperature, it keeps well, refrigerated, for up to three days.

- 2 **ripe bananas, thinly sliced**
- 1 **cup berries in season, such as raspberries, blueberries, or sliced strawberries**
- 2 **cups unfiltered apple juice, white grape juice, or cherry juice**
- 1 **tablespoon agar-agar flakes**
- **Almond Cream (page 382), optional**

Arrange the sliced bananas in the bottom of a 10-inch deep-dish glass pie pan. Spread the berries over the bananas.

In a medium saucepan, cook the apple juice and agar-agar over low heat, stirring constantly, until the agar-agar is dissolved, about 5 minutes. Carefully pour the juice mixture over the berries. Let cool. Refrigerate if desired, to chill.

Slice the jell into wedges and top with a dab of Almond Cream.

This we ask:
Help us to learn how to love more fully, more wisely, more calmly.
This we ask:
Help us to bring peace to our lives and this world.

VANILLA TAPIOCA WITH STRAWBERRIES

Makes 4 servings

Tapioca is quick, easy, and light. Serve warm or cold, plain or topped with fresh strawberries.

¼ **cup plus 2 tablespoons maple syrup**

½ **cup granulated tapioca**

3 **cups vanilla soy milk, rice beverage, or almond beverage**

2 **teaspoons pure vanilla extract**

¼ **teaspoon fine sea salt**

1 **pint fresh strawberries, hulled and sliced**

In a medium saucepan, combine the ¼ cup maple syrup, the tapioca, soy milk, vanilla, and salt, and bring to a boil over medium-high heat, stirring constantly. Reduce the heat to low and simmer, stirring, until thickened. Transfer to a large serving bowl, cover, and refrigerate until chilled, at least 2 hours.

Meanwhile in a small bowl, combine the strawberries and the remaining 2 tablespoons maple syrup. Cover and refrigerate for at least 2 hours.

To serve, spoon the pudding into individual bowls, and top with the strawberries and their juices.

Increased risk of fatal ovarian cancer for women who eat eggs three or more days a week compared to those who eat them less than once a week: **3 times higher**
Increased risk of fatal prostate cancer for men who consume meats, dairy products, and eggs daily as compared to those who consume them sparingly: **3.6 times higher**

POACHED PEARS 'N' RASPBERRY SAUCE

Makes 4 servings

These pears are simmered in spiced apple juice and then smothered in a naturally sweetened raspberry sauce.

4	**Bosc pears, peeled**
2½	**cups pear juice**
1	**teaspoon whole cloves**
¼	**teaspoon grated nutmeg**
1	**tablespoon grated fresh gingerroot**
1	**cinnamon stick**
1	**tablespoon arrowroot powder**
2	**cups fresh or frozen (thawed) raspberries**
2	**tablespoons pure maple syrup**

Cut a thin slice from the bottom of each pear to make them stand upright.

Put the pears in a medium saucepan, and add 2 cups of the pear juice, the cloves, nutmeg, ginger, and cinnamon stick. Cover and bring to a boil over medium-high heat, then immediately reduce the heat and simmer until the pears are tender, 20 to 30 minutes; turn the pears once for even cooking.

Carefully remove the pears from the pan and arrange them in a deep serving dish.

Strain out the whole spices from the cooking liquid, and return the liquid to the pan.

Put the remaining ½ cup pear juice and the arrowroot into a small bowl and stir together until the arrowroot is dissolved. Stir into the cooking liquid in the saucepan, and bring to a boil over medium heat. Immediately reduce the heat to low and simmer, stirring constantly, until just thickened, about 1 minute. Transfer to a blender.

Add the raspberries and maple syrup, and blend until smooth. Strain the sauce through a fine wire strainer to remove the raspberry seeds.

Pour the sauce over the pears and serve warm, chilled, or at room temperature.

PEACHES 'N' CREAM

Makes 6 servings

Slices of peaches and bright berries are layered and topped with a sweet almond sauce.

6 ripe peaches, stones removed and sliced into thin wedges
2 cups raspberries, blueberries, strawberries, or other berries in season
Almond Cream (page 382)
¼ cup raw almonds, toasted and slivered or chopped

In individual glass goblets, layer the peaches and berries. Pour the Almond Cream over the tops and sprinkle with the toasted almonds. Chill until ready to serve, up to 3 hours.

WHOLE WHEAT PIE DOUGH

*Makes one 9-inch or
10-inch pie shell*

This simple, wholesome pie crust can be used with any sweet or savory filling.

1½ cups whole wheat pastry flour
½ teaspoon fine sea salt
½ cup plus 1 tablespoon canola or safflower oil
3 tablespoons plus 1½ teaspoons ice water

Put the flour and salt in a bowl and stir together. Add the oil and water and stir until it forms a crumbly meal. Gather up the dough into a ball. (The dough will be moist.)

Press the dough evenly and firmly into the bottom and up the sides of a 9-inch or 10-inch pie plate so it rises about ½ inch above the edge of the pie plate. Flute the edges of the crust, if desired.

> *"The beef industry has contributed to more American deaths
> than all the wars of this century, all natural disasters, and all
> automobile accidents combined."*—Neal Barnard, M.D.,
> President, Physicians Committee for Responsible Medicine

PECAN PIE

Makes one 10-inch pie

    1   recipe Whole Wheat Pie Dough (page 368)
    ½   cup pure maple syrup
    ¼   cup barley malt syrup
    ½   teaspoon ground cinnamon
    1   tablespoon arrowroot powder
    2   tablespoons raw tahini
  2½   cups pecan halves

Preheat the oven to 350°F.

Line a 10-inch pie pan with the pie dough (see page 368). With a
fork, prick holes all over the bottom and sides of the pie shell. Bake
until a light golden color, 10 to 15 minutes. Let cool.

Put the maple syrup, barley malt syrup, cinnamon, arrowroot, and
tahini in a food processor and process until smooth. Add the pecans
and pulse several times to coarsely chop the nuts. Pour the filling into
the baked pie shell. Bake until the filling is bubbly and the top is evenly
browned, 25 to 30 minutes. Cool completely before serving.

WINTER SQUASH PIE

Makes one 9-inch pie

The smooth texture of pumpkin makes it a favorite filling for pies, but most any winter squash, such as butternut, acorn, and delicata, can be substituted. If using pumpkin, do not throw away the pumpkin seeds; they make a delightful snack when roasted and sprinkled with soy sauce.

1   recipe Whole Wheat Pie Dough (page 368)

2   pounds butternut squash or sugar pumpkin, skin left on, cut into 2-inch cubes and seeds removed

1   cup vanilla soy milk

¾   cup pure maple syrup

3   tablespoons arrowroot powder

1   teaspoon agar-agar powder

1   teaspoon finely grated fresh gingerroot

1   teaspoon ground cinnamon

¼   teaspoon ground cloves

¼   teaspoon grated nutmeg

¼   teaspoon fine sea salt

Preheat the oven to 350°F.

Line a 9-inch pie pan with the pie dough (see page 368). With a fork, prick holes all over the bottom and sides of the pie shell. Bake until a light golden color, 10 to 15 minutes. Let cool.

Put 1 inch of water into large saucepan with a steamer basket, cover with the lid, and bring to a gentle boil. Put the squash into the steamer basket, cover, and steam until the squash is tender, 15 to 20 minutes. Cool the squash, then pare off the skin.

Put the peeled squash cubes, soy milk, maple syrup, arrowroot, agar-agar, ginger, cinnamon, cloves, nutmeg, and salt into a blender and blend until smooth. Pour into the baked pie shell. Bake until the center of the filling seems set, 40 to 45 minutes. (The filling will firm up as it cools.) Cool the pie completely before serving.

APPLE-CRANBERRY BREAD PUDDING

Makes 4 to 6 servings

Snappy green apples and tart cranberries combined with a cinnamon-walnut topping make this bread pudding a sure favorite. It's moist, wholesome, and quick, and the end result is an extraordinary dessert.

2   medium-size tart apples, such as Granny Smiths, peeled, cored, and grated

4   cups cubed whole-grain bread (¼-inch cubes)

2½ cups soy milk

½   cup cranberries

½   cup raisins

¼   cup plus 3 tablespoons pure maple syrup

1   tablespoon arrowroot powder

1½ teaspoons ground cinnamon

½   teaspoon fine sea salt

1   cup raw walnuts, coarsely chopped

Pure maple syrup, for serving, optional

Preheat the oven to 350°F.

In a large bowl, combine the apples, bread cubes, soy milk, cranberries, raisins, ¼ cup of the maple syrup, the arrowroot, and 1 teaspoon of the cinnamon. Stir until well mixed, and transfer to a 2-quart round baking dish.

Put the walnuts, the remaining 3 tablespoons maple syrup, and the remaining ½ teaspoon cinnamon in a food processor fitted with the metal blade, and pulse until coarsely chopped. Sprinkle over the top of the apple-bread mixture.

Bake for 45 minutes. Let cool 20 minutes before serving on individual plates. Serve with maple syrup on the side to pour over the pudding, if desired.

PLUM COBBLER

Makes 6 servings

Tender sweet plums with a crunchy nut topping. You can use most any fruit for the filling—apples, apricots, cherries, nectarines, peaches.

2¼ **pounds plums, stones removed and thinly sliced**

1 **cup pure maple syrup**

1 **tablespoon arrowroot powder**

2 **tablespoons freshly squeezed lemon juice**

1 **teaspoon ground cinnamon**

¼ **cup canola or safflower oil**

¾ **cup rolled oats**

½ **cup whole wheat pastry flour**

½ **cup raw walnuts**

¼ **teaspoon fine sea salt**

Preheat the oven to 350°F.

In a large bowl, combine the plums, ½ cup of the maple syrup, the arrowroot, lemon juice, and cinnamon, and stir to mix. Pour into an 11- by 7-inch baking dish.

Put the remaining ½ cup maple syrup and the oil into a small bowl and stir together.

In a large bowl, stir the rolled oats, flour, walnuts, and salt together. Add the maple syrup/oil mixture and stir until the dry ingredients are well coated; the mixture will be crumbly. Sprinkle over the plums.

Bake until the top is lightly browned and the plums are tender, 30 to 40 minutes. Let cool 10 minutes before serving.

> *A good dessert is not one that is so rich or sweet that it does us harm. A good dessert is one that lifts our spirits and helps us savor the experiences of life.*

APPLE-APRICOT COBBLER

Makes 6 servings

This cobbler has a flavorful apple-apricot filling and a sweet crumbly crust.

8 **tart apples, such as Granny Smiths, peeled, cored, and thinly sliced**

½ **cup unsulphured dried apricots, finely chopped**

1 **cup pure maple syrup**

1 **cup apricot juice**

2 **tablespoons freshly squeezed lemon juice**

¾ **cup plus 3 tablespoons whole wheat pastry flour**

1 **teaspoon ground cinnamon**

1 **teaspoon finely grated fresh gingerroot**

¼ **teaspoon ground cardamom**

½ **cup rolled oats**

¼ **cup canola or safflower oil**

½ **cup raw pecans**

Preheat the oven to 350°F.

In a large bowl, combine the apples, apricots, ½ cup of the maple syrup, the apricot and lemon juices, 3 tablespoons of the flour, the cinnamon, ginger, and cardamom and stir together. Pour into an 9- by 13-inch baking dish.

Put the remaining ¾ cup flour, the rolled oats, the remaining ½ cup maple syrup, and the oil in a food processor fitted with the metal blade, and process until well mixed. Add the pecans and pulse several times to coarsely chop the nuts. Sprinkle over the apple mixture.

Bake until bubbling and lightly browned, 30 to 40 minutes. Cool 10 minutes before serving.

CARAMEL APPLE CRUNCH

Makes 4 to 6 servings

FruitSource® is an all-natural sweetener without refined sugar. Made from grape juice concentrate and rice syrup, it is available as a liquid and granules.

  1 **cup rolled oats**

  ¾ **cup granular FruitSource®**

  ½ **cup whole wheat pastry flour**

  1 **teaspoon ground cinnamon**

  ¼ **teaspoon fine sea salt**

  ½ **cup canola or safflower oil**

  3 **tart apples, such as Granny Smiths, peeled, cored, and coarsely chopped**

  ⅓ **cup raisins**

  ¼ **cup coarsely chopped pecans or walnuts**

Preheat the oven to 350°F.

In a medium bowl, combine the oats, FruitSource®, flour, cinnamon, and salt. Stir in the oil and mix just until the dry ingredients are moistened. Put the apples, raisins, and pecans into a 9-inch square baking pan, and stir to mix. Sprinkle with the oat mixture.

Bake until the apples are tender, 30 to 35 minutes. Serve warm or at room temperature.

World populations with high meat intakes that do not have correspondingly high rates of colon cancer: **None**
World populations with low meat intakes that do not have correspondingly low rates of colon cancer: **None**

CARROT-CURRANT COOKIES

Makes about 3 dozen cookies

Oatmeal, fresh ginger, and grated carrots give these cookies an unusual flavor. This is the most popular cookie at the Honey Rose Baking Company in Encinitas, California.

1¼ cups pure maple syrup
½ cup canola or safflower oil
1 teaspoon pure vanilla extract
2 cups whole wheat pastry flour
2 teaspoons nonaluminum baking powder
1 teaspoon baking soda
1 teaspoon fine sea salt
2 cups rolled oats
1 cup grated carrots (about 2 medium carrots)
1 tablespoon finely grated fresh gingerroot
1 cup currants

Preheat the oven to 350°F. Lightly oil 2 baking sheets.

Put the maple syrup, oil, and vanilla in a blender, and blend until smooth.

In a large bowl, whisk the flour, baking powder, baking soda, and salt until combined. Stir in the rolled oats. Add the maple syrup mixture, carrots, and ginger and combine, using as few strokes as possible so you do not overmix the dough. Stir in the currants.

Drop rounded tablespoonfuls of the dough 1 inch apart on the prepared baking sheets. Bake until the edges of the cookies are slightly browned, 14 to 18 minutes. Do not overbake.

Let the cookies cool 2 minutes on the baking sheets, then transfer to a wire rack to cool completely.

GINGER SNAPS

Makes 2¹/₂ dozen cookies

Molasses and maple syrup give these cookies a rich sweet flavor, and the fresh ginger gives them an unforgettable snap.

¾　cup pure maple syrup

¼　cup unsulphured molasses

½　cup canola or safflower oil

3　tablespoons finely grated fresh gingerroot

2½　cups whole wheat pastry flour

1　teaspoon nonaluminum baking powder

1　teaspoon baking soda

½　teaspoon fine sea salt

Preheat the oven to 350°F. Lightly oil 2 baking sheets.

Put the maple syrup, molasses, and oil in a blender and blend until smooth. Add the ginger and pulse until mixed.

In a large bowl, whisk the flour, baking powder, baking soda, and salt until thoroughly mixed. Add the maple syrup mixture and combine, using as few strokes as possible so you do not overmix the dough.

Drop level tablespoonfuls of the dough 1 inch apart on the prepared baking sheets. Bake until the edges of the cookies are firm, 12 to 15 minutes. Do not overbake.

Let the cookies cool 2 minutes on the baking sheets, then transfer to a wire rack to cool completely.

Bless our work and our play.
Bless the elephants and the hummingbirds, the pigs, mice, and
　　ants.
Show us how to live so that
All creatures can live long and happy lives.

A typical four-ounce hamburger made from rain-forest beef represents the destruction of fifty-five square feet of tropical forest, an area the size of a small kitchen.

CAROB WALNUT COOKIES

Makes 2¹/₂ dozen cookies

These scrumptious treats are made with a carob-flavored dough and walnuts.

    1 cup maple syrup
    ½ cup canola or safflower oil
    1 teaspoon pure vanilla extract
    2 cups whole wheat pastry flour
    ½ cup carob powder
    1 teaspoon nonaluminum baking powder
    1 teaspoon baking soda
    ½ teaspoon fine sea salt
    ½ cup raw walnuts, coarsely chopped

Preheat the oven to 350°F. Lightly oil 2 baking sheets.

Put the maple syrup, oil, and vanilla into a blender and blend until smooth.

In a large bowl, whisk the flour, carob powder, baking powder, baking soda, and salt until thoroughly combined. Add the maple syrup mixture and combine, using as few strokes as possible so you do not overmix the dough. Fold in the walnuts.

Drop rounded tablespoonfuls of the dough 1 inch apart on the prepared baking sheets. Bake until the edges of the cookies are slightly browned, 14 to 18 minutes. Do not overbake.

Let the cookies cool 2 minutes on the baking sheets, then transfer to a wire rack to cool completely.

*How liberating it is to enjoy food when you are hungry,
and to find other ways to nourish yourself when you are
not. How freeing it is to learn the difference between feeling
satisfied and feeling stuffed.*

CAROB FUDGE BALLS

Makes about 4 dozen balls

Carob and almond butter give a rich flavor to these little dessert balls,
and rice syrup and dates add the sweetness. They are quick and easy
to make. A great snack for a hike in the countryside, they will keep two
weeks in the refrigerator and one month in the freezer.

 1 **16-ounce jar roasted almond butter**
 ½ **cup currants**
 ½ **cup sunflower seeds**
 ¼ **cup carob powder**
 5 **tablespoons rice syrup**
 6 **pitted dates**
 ½ **teaspoon ground cinnamon**
 ½ **cup finely chopped raw almonds**

In a food processor fitted with the metal blade, combine all the ingredients except the chopped almonds, and process until the mixture is
finely chopped and forms a sticky mass. Roll the dough into 1-inch
balls, then roll each ball in the chopped almonds to coat.

Store the balls in an airtight container in the refrigerator.

CAROB CUPCAKES

Makes 18 cupcakes

1½ cups pure maple syrup

¾ cup canola or safflower oil

4½ ounces firm tofu, crumbled

2 tablespoons pure vanilla extract

½ cup water

3 cups whole wheat pastry flour

¾ cup carob powder

2 teaspoons nonaluminum baking powder

1 teaspoon baking soda

1 teaspoon fine sea salt

Preheat the oven to 350°F. Lightly oil 18 muffin cups. Dust with flour and tap out the excess.

Put the maple syrup, oil, tofu, vanilla, and water into a blender and blend until smooth.

In a large bowl, whisk the flour, carob powder, baking powder, baking soda, and salt together until combined. Add the maple syrup mixture and combine, using as few strokes as possible so you do not overmix the batter.

Spoon the batter into the prepared muffin cups. Bake until a toothpick inserted in the center of a cupcake comes out clean, 15 to 20 minutes.

Let the cupcakes cool for 5 minutes before removing from the muffin tins.

"The vegetarian manner of living, by its purely physical effects on the human temperament, would most beneficially influence the lot of mankind."—Albert Einstein

GINGER CARROT CAKE WITH ORANGE GLAZE

*Makes one 8-inch square cake or
one 9-inch round cake*

This delightful carrot cake is full of spicy goodness and nutty flavors; it travels well and keeps up to a week in the refrigerator.

- ¾ cup unfiltered apple juice
- ½ cup canola or safflower oil
- 1½ cups raisins
- ½ cup pure maple syrup
- Grated zest of 1 orange
- 1½ cups grated carrots (about 3 medium carrots)
- 2 teaspoons finely grated fresh gingerroot
- 2 cups whole wheat pastry flour
- 1 teaspoon nonaluminum baking powder
- 1 teaspoon baking soda
- 1 teaspoon ground cinnamon
- ½ teaspoon grated nutmeg
- ½ teaspoon fine sea salt

- 1 cup coarsely chopped raw walnuts

ORANGE GLAZE
- 3 tablespoons maple syrup
- 2 tablespoons freshly squeezed orange juice

Preheat the oven to 350°F. Lightly oil an 8- by 8-inch cake pan or a 9-inch round pan and dust with flour, shaking out the excess.

Put the apple juice, oil, ½ cup of the raisins, the maple syrup, and orange zest in a blender and blend until smooth. Add the carrots and ginger and pulse just to mix.

In a large bowl, whisk the flour, baking powder, baking soda, cinnamon, nutmeg, and salt together. Add the apple juice mixture and combine, using as few strokes as possible so you do not overmix the batter. Fold in the remaining 1 cup raisins and the walnuts.

Pour the batter into the prepared pan. Use a spatula to spread the batter evenly. Bake until a toothpick inserted near the center of the cake comes out clean, 35 to 45 minutes.

Meanwhile, make the orange glaze: In a small bowl, combine the maple syrup and orange juice and stir together until thoroughly blended.

When the cake is done, remove from the oven and let cool for 10 minutes in the pan. Transfer to a wire rack, and while the cake is still warm, brush on the orange glaze with a pastry brush.

MOCHA CREAM FROSTING

Makes 1³/₄ cups

Use this coffeelike tofu frosting on carob cupcakes or banana cake.

1 **pound firm tofu, crumbled**
½ **cup pure maple syrup**
¼ **cup safflower or canola oil, or more as needed**
2 **teaspoons pure vanilla extract**
Pinch of fine sea salt
2 **tablespoons roasted grain beverage powder**

Using your hands, squeeze the excess water from the tofu.

In a food processor fitted with the metal blade or a blender, combine all the ingredients and process until creamy. (Since tofu varies in consistency, you may need to add a tablespoon or two of additional oil for a smooth frosting.) Transfer to a bowl, cover, and chill until thickened, about 2 hours.

We give thanks for this food.
We give thanks for each other.
We give thanks for our lives.

LEMONY CREAM ICING

Makes about 2 cups

Use this tart, creamy icing on carrot, lemon, or ginger cakes.

- 1 **pound firm tofu, crumbled**
- ½ **cup pure maple syrup**
- 4 **tablespoons freshly squeezed lemon juice**
- 2 **teaspoons pure vanilla extract**
- **Pinch of fine sea salt**
- **Grated zest of 1 lemon**

Use your hands to squeeze the excess moisture from the tofu.

In a food processor fitted with the metal blade or a blender, combine all the ingredients and process until creamy. (Since tofu varies in consistency, you may need to add a tablespoon or two of additional oil for a smooth icing.) Transfer to a bowl, cover, and chill until thickened, about 2 hours.

ALMOND CREAM

Makes 1½ cups

Almond Cream has a smooth texture and a sweet creamy taste. Add to hot roasted grain beverages or pour over fresh fruit.

- 1 **cup raw almonds**
- ¾ **cup Almond Milk (page 209) or almond beverage**
- ¼ **cup pure maple syrup**
- 1 **teaspoon pure vanilla extract**

Blanch the almonds in boiling water for 30 seconds. Drain and plunge the almonds into cold water. Drain, and squeeze the almonds between your fingertips to remove the skins. Compost or discard the skins.

Put the almonds and the remaining ingredients in a blender and blend until smooth, about 2 minutes.

ORANGE ALMOND CREAM

Makes 1½ cups

Orange juice and zest add a refreshing taste to this extravagant delight.
Enjoy it on your favorite desserts, in hot beverages, and over fresh fruit.

1   **cup raw almonds**
¾   **cup freshly squeezed orange juice**
¼   **cup pure maple syrup**
1   **teaspoon pure vanilla extract**
½   **teaspoon finely grated orange zest**

Blanch the almonds in boiling water for 30 seconds. Drain and plunge
the almonds into cold water. Drain, and squeeze the almonds between
your fingertips to remove the skins. Compost or discard the skins.

Put the almonds, orange juice, maple syrup, and vanilla in a blender
and blend until smooth, about 2 minutes. Add the orange zest and pulse
just to mix.

Praise to the chain of life giving.
Praise to the plants
Whose roots, stems, leaves, seeds, and fruits we eat.
Praise to the Earth
Whose elements and myriad life forms nurture the plants.
Praise to the plants and animals
Whose bodies have decomposed and become the Earth.
Praise to the sun, to the rain, to the air.
Praise to the rhythms and cycles of the life spirit.
Praise to the chain of life giving.

CARAMEL POPCORN BALLS

Makes 12 balls

FruitSource® is a new sweetener that is a healthier alternative to refined sugars. These caramel popcorn balls are wonderful made with Fruit-Source.®

½ cup popcorn kernels

1 cup FruitSource®

⅓ cup water

1 teaspoon pure vanilla extract

Pop the popcorn in a hot air popper. Discard any unpopped corn kernels and pour the popcorn into a large bowl.

Preheat the oven to 250°F. Lightly oil a baking sheet.

In a small saucepan, combine the FruitSource® and water and bring to a simmer over low heat, stirring constantly to dissolve the Fruit-Source®. Then cook, stirring often, until a candy thermometer inserted in the syrup reads 265°F, about 8 minutes. Remove from the heat and stir in the vanilla.

Slowly pour the FruitSource® mixture over the popcorn, stirring to coat the popcorn evenly. Spread the caramel popcorn mixture on the prepared baking sheet. Bake for exactly 4 minutes. Allow to cool slightly.

While the popcorn is still warm, shape it into 12 balls, about 3 inches in diameter. Cool completely.

"You have just dined, and however scrupulously the slaughterhouse is concealed in the graceful distance of miles, there is complicity."—Ralph Waldo Emerson

Percentage of Calories from Protein, Fat, and Carbohydrates

VEGETABLES

	Protein	Fat	Carbohydrate
Artichokes	22	3	75
Asparagus	32	6	62
Bamboo shoots	31	8	61
Beet greens	30	9	61
Beets	14	2	84
Broccoli	36	6	58
Brussels sprouts	36	6	58
Cabbage	18	7	75
Carrots	10	4	86
Cauliflower	34	6	60
Celery	17	6	77
Chinese cabbage	28	6	66
Chives	34	0	66
Collards	34	12	54
Corn, sweet	11	7	82
Cucumbers	20	7	73
Dandelion greens	20	13	67
Eggplant	18	9	73
Endive	29	5	66
Garlic	20	0	80
Kale	40	11	49
Lettuce	29	12	59
Mustard greens	31	13	56

Calories from Protein, Fat, and Carbohydrates

	Protein	Fat	Carbohydrate
New Zealand spinach	37	12	51
Okra	22	8	70
Onions	15	3	82
Parsley	30	12	58
Parsnips	9	6	85
Peas, green	30	4	66
Peppers, green bell	20	8	72
Peppers, hot chile	14	4	86
Potatoes	11	1	88
Pumpkin	12	8	80
Radishes	10	1	89
Shallots	16	0	84
Spinach	40	9	51
Squash, summer	20	5	75
Sweet potatoes	6	3	91
Tomatoes	17	8	75
Turnip greens	35	8	57
Turnips	13	7	75
Watercress	40	11	49
Yams	8	2	90
Zucchini	26	6	78

Calories from Protein, Fat, and Carbohydrates

GRAINS

	Protein	Fat	Carbohydrate
Barley	9	3	88
Buckwheat, dark	13	7	80
Corn flour	9	6	85
Oatmeal	15	16	69
Rice, brown	8	5	87
Rice, polished	7	1	92
Rye flour, dark	18	7	75
Rye flour, light	11	2	87
Spaghetti, white	14	3	83
Wheat flour, white	12	3	85
Wheat flour, whole	16	5	79
Wheat germ	29	25	46
Wild rice	16	2	82

LEGUMES

	Protein	Fat	Carbohydrate
Broadbeans	31	3	66
Cowpeas	28	6	66
Garbanzo beans	23	12	65
Kidney beans	26	4	70
Lentils	29	3	68
Lima beans	25	4	71
Mung beans	28	3	69
Mung bean sprouts	34	5	61
Snap beans, green	21	6	73
Soybean curd (tofu)	40	48	12
Soybean flour (full fat)	33	40	27
Soybeans	32	37	31
Soybean sprouts	43	20	37
Soy sauce	31	17	52
Split peas	28	3	69
White beans	26	4	70

NUTS AND SEEDS

	Protein	Fat	Carbohydrate
Almonds	11	77	12
Cashew nuts	12	68	20
Chestnuts	6	7	87
Coconut	4	85	11
Filberts (hazelnuts)	8	81	11
Lychees	6	5	89
Peanuts	18	68	14
Pine nuts	8	80	12
Pistachios	13	74	13
Pumpkin seeds	20	70	10
Sesame seeds	13	75	12
Sunflower seeds	17	69	14
Walnuts, black	13	79	8

FRUITS

	Protein	Fat	Carbohydrate
Apples	1	8	91
Apricots	7	4	89
Avocados	5	81	14
Bananas	5	3	92
Blackberries	7	13	80
Blueberries	5	7	88
Cantaloupes	8	3	89
Cherimoyas	5	4	91
Cherries	8	4	88
Cranberries	3	13	84
Custard-apples	7	5	88
Dates	3	0	97
Figs	6	5	89
Gooseberries	8	5	87
Grapefruit	5	2	93

Calories from Protein, Fat, and Carbohydrates

	Protein	Fat	Carbohydrate
Grapes	8	13	79
Honeydew melons	10	8	82
Lemons	13	7	80
Loganberries	6	8	86
Mangos	4	5	91
Nectarines	4	0	96
Olives	5	91	4
Oranges	8	4	88
Papayas	6	2	92
Peaches	6	2	92
Pears	5	6	89
Persimmons	3	3	94
Pineapples	3	3	94
Plums	3	0	97
Pomegranates	3	5	92
Prunes	4	1	95
Raisins	3	0	97
Raspberries	8	16	76
Strawberries	8	12	80
Tangerines	7	4	89
Watermelons	8	7	85

Calories from Protein, Fat, and Carbohydrates

DAIRY PRODUCTS AND EGGS

	Protein	Fat	Carbohydrate
Butter	0	100	0
Buttermilk	40	3	57
Cheeses			
American	25	73	2
Blue	23	75	2
Brick	24	74	2
Camembert	23	75	2
Cheddar	25	73	2
Cottage	52	37	11
Cottage, nonfat	79	3	13
Cream	8	90	2
Limburger	24	73	3
Parmesan	37	60	3
Swiss	30	68	2
Eggs, chicken	33	65	2
(whites only)	85	7	8
(yolks only)	19	80	1
Eggs, duck	28	71	1
Eggs, goose	30	67	3
Eggs, turkey	31	65	4
Margarine	0	100	0
Milk, cow	21	49	30
(low-fat—2%)	28	31	41
(skim)	41	2	57
Milk, goat	19	54	27
Milk, human	5	46	49
Yogurt, low-fat	27	31	42
Yogurt, whole milk	21	49	30

Calories from Protein, Fat, and Carbohydrates

MEATS AND FISH

	Protein	Fat	Carbohydrate
Bacon	5	95	0
Bass, black sea	26	56	18
Beef, chuck, lean	32	68	0
Beef, corned	25	75	0
Beef, ground	34	66	0
Beef, T-bone, broiled	16	84	0
Caviar, sturgeon	41	54	5
Chicken, without skin, roasted			
dark meat	67	33	0
light meat	81	19	0
Clams	68	21	6
Crab	79	19	2
Lamb			
chops	22	78	0
leg, lean	32	68	0
Lobster	84	15	1
Mackerel	38	62	0
Perch	33	55	12
Pork			
chops	23	77	0
ham	21	79	0
spareribs	16	84	0
Shrimp	91	9	0
Sturgeon	67	33	0
Tuna, canned, in oil	35	65	0
Tuna, canned, in water	60	40	0
Turkey, roasted	41	59	0
Veal, rib roast	36	64	0

Data derived from *Nutritive Value of American Foods in Common Units*, Agriculture Handbook No. 456.

Notes

Part One
Chapter One. The Grace of Eating

1. Aivanhov, O., *The Yoga of Nutrition*, Prosveta, Los Angeles, CA, 1982, p. 21.
2. Siegel, B., quoted in Stanchich, L., *Power Eating Program*, Healthy Products, Coconut Grove, FL, 1989, p. 33.
3. Loehr, J., and Migdow, J., *Take a Deep Breath*, cited in Stanchich, L., as per note 2.
4. Cited in Stanchich, L., as per note 2.
5. Ibid.
6. Hanh, Thich Nhat, *Present Moment, Wonderful Moment*, Parallax Press, Berkeley, CA, 1990, pp. 45–46.
7. Robbins, J., and Mortifee, A., *In Search of Balance*, H. J. Kramer, Tiburon, CA, 1991, pp. 96–97.

Chapter Two. A Bite Felt 'Round the World

1. Robbins, J., *Diet for a New America*, Stillpoint, Walpole, NH, 1987, p. 350.
2. Lappé, F., *Diet for a Small Planet*, Ballantine, NY, 1982, p. 69.
3. Ibid.; Altschul, A., *Proteins: Their Chemistry and Politics*, Basic Books, 1965, p. 264; and Doyring, F., "Soybeans," *Scientific American*, February 1974.
4. Aldridge, T., and Schlubach, H., "Water Requirements for Food Production," *Soil and Water*, Fall 1978, No. 38, University of California Cooperative Extension.
5. Bralove, M., "The Food Crisis," *Wall Street Journal*, October 3, 1974, p. 20.
6. Maidenburg, H. J., "The Livestock Population Explosion," *New York Times*, July 1, 1973, p. 1, Finance section.
   Brody, J., "The Quest for Protein," *Give Us This Day*, Arno Press, New York, 1975, p. 222.
7. *Acres, USA*, Kansas City, MO, Vol. 15, No. 6, June 1985, p. 2.
8. Resenburger, B., "Curb on US Waste Urged to Help World's Hungry," *New York Times*, October 25, 1974.
9. Brown, L., et al., *State of the World 1991*, Worldwatch Institute, W.W. Norton, NY, 1991, p. 15.
10. As per note 8.
11. Rifkin, J., *Beyond Beef*, Dutton, NY, 1992, p. 153.
12. Ibid., pp. 168–169.
13. Ibid., p. 169.
14. Ibid., p. 152.
15. Durning, A., and Brough, H., *Taking Stock: Animal Farming and the Environment*, Worldwatch Paper No. 103, Worldwatch Institute, Washington, DC, 1991, p. 29.
16. Ibid.
17. Ibid.
18. Ibid., pp. 29–30.
19. Ibid., p. 30.
20. Ibid., pp. 30, 33.
21. Ibid., p. 31.
22. DeWalt, B., "Mexico's Second Green Revolution," *Mexican Studies*, Vol. 1, No. 1, Winter 1985, p. 30.
23. Barkin, D., and DeWalt, B., "*Sorghum, the Internationalization of Capital, and the Mexican Food Crisis,*" Paper presented at the American Anthropological Association Meeting, Denver, CO, November 16, 1984, p. 16.
24. Ibid.

25. Ibid.
26. Lappé, F., and Collins, J., *World Hunger—Twelve Myths*, Grove Press, NY, 1986, p. 5.
27. Ibid., p. 40.
28. DeWalt, B., "The Cattle Are Eating the Forest," *Bulletin of the Atomic Scientist*, Vol. 39, No. 1, January 1983, p. 22; and Shane, D., *Hoofprints on the Forest: Cattle Ranching and the Destruction of Latin America's Tropical Forests*, Institute for the Study of Human Issues, Philadelphia, 1986, p. 78.
29. DeWalt, B., as per note 28.
30. Policy Alternatives for the Caribbean and Central America, *Changing Course: Blueprint for Peace in Central America and the Caribbean*, Institute for Policy Studies, Washington, DC, 1984.
31. Lappé, F., and Collins, J., as per note 26, p. 39.
32. Ibid.
33. DeWalt, B., as per note 28.
34. "Latin America Commodities Report," CR–81–15, July 31, 1981, cited in Lappé, F., and Collins, J., as per note 26, p. 86.
35. Lappé, F., and Collins, J., as per note 26, p. 86.

Chapter Three. To Grow Up Big and Strong

1. Hausman, P., *Jack Sprat's Legacy*, Richard Marek Publishers, NY, 1981, pp. 16–17, 25–39.
2. Scrimshaw, N., "An Analysis of Past and Present Recommended Dietary Allowances for Protein in Health and Disease," *New England Journal of Medicine*, January 22, 1976, p. 200; Irwin, M., "A Conspectus of Research on Protein Requirements of Man," *Journal of Nutrition*, 101:385; 1975; and Hegsted, M., "Minimum Protein Requirements of Adults," *American Journal of Clinical Nutrition*, 21:3520; 1968.
3. Reuben, D., *Everything You Always Wanted to Know About Nutrition*, Avon Books, NY, 1978, pp. 154–155.
4. Kofranyi, E., et al., "The Minimum Protein Requirements of Humans . . . ," cited in Akers, K., *A Vegetarian Sourcebook*, G. P. Putnam's Sons, NY, 1983, p. 205; and Rose, W., "The Amino Acid Requirements of Adult Man," *Nutrition Abstracts and Reviews*, 27:631–637, 1957.
5. Markakis, P., "The Nutritive Value of Potato Protein," in *Protein Nutritional Quality of Foods and Feeds*, Pt. 2, ed. M. Friedman, 1975; and Kon, S., "The Value of Potatoes in Human Nutrition," *Journal of Biological Chemistry*, 22:258; 1928.
6. Lappé, F. M., *Diet for a Small Planet*, Ballantine Books, NY, 1971.

7. Lappé, F. M., *Diet for a Small Planet*, Ballantine Books, NY, 1982.
8. Ibid. pp. 162, 172.
9. Ibid. p. 162.
10. Food and Nutrition Board, "Vegetarian Diets," National Academy of Sciences, Washington, DC, 1974, p. 2; see also: Hardinge, M., et al., "Nutritional Studies of Vegetarians, Part V, Proteins...," *Journal of the American Dietetic Association*, Vol. 48, No. 1, January 1966, p. 27, and Hardinge, M., et al., "Nutritional Studies of Vegetarians: Part I...," *Journal of Clinical Nutrition*, Vol. 2, No. 2, March–April 1984, p. 81.
11. Editorial, *Lancet*, London, 2:956; 1959.
12. Hardinge, M., et al., as per note 10.
13. Pritikin, N., quoted in *Vegetarian Times*, No. 43, p. 21.
14. Hardinge, M., as per note 10; and McLaren, D., "The Great Protein Fiasco," *Lancet*, 2:93; 1974.
15. Hegsted, M., cited in Register, U. D., et al., "The Vegetarian Diet," *Journal of the American Dietetic Association*, 62:255; 1973.
16. Schwarzenegger, A., *Arnold's Body-Building for Men*, Simon and Schuster, NY, 1981.
17. National Academy of Sciences, *Recommended Dietary Allowances*, 8th ed., Washington, DC, 1974, p. 43.
18. Barzel, V., *Osteoporosis*, Grune and Stratton, NY, 1970.
19. Ibid.
20. Heaney, R., "Calcium Nutrition and Bone Health in the Elderly," *American Journal of Clinical Nutrition*, 36:986; 1982; Paterson, C., "Calcium Requirements in Man: A Critical Review," *Postgraduate Medical Journal*, 54:244; 1978; Walker, A., "The Human Requirement of Calcium: Should Intakes Be Supplemented?" *American Journal of Clinical Nutrition*, 25:518; 1972; and Symposium of Human Calcium Requirements: Council on Foods and Nutrition, *Journal of the American Medical Association*, 185:588; 1963.
21. Johnson, N., et al., "Effect of Level of Protein Intake on Urinary and Fecal Calcium and Calcium Retention...," *Journal of Nutrition*, 100:1425; 1970; and Allen, L., et al., "Protein-Induced Hypercalcuria: A Longer-Term Study," *American Journal of Clinical Nutrition*, 32:741; 1979.
22. Solomon, L., "Osteoporosis and Fracture of the Femoral Neck in the South African Bantu," *Journal of Bone and Joint Surgery*, 50B:2; 1968; McDougall, J., *McDougall's Medicine*, New Century, Piscataway, NJ, 1985, pp. 61–96; Anand, C., "Effect of Protein Intake on Calcium Balance...," *Journal of Nutrition*, 104:695; 1974; Hegsted, M., "Urinary Calcium and Calcium Balance in Young Men as Affected by Level of Protein and Phosphorous Intake," *Journal of Nutrition*, 111:53; 1981; Walker, R., "Calcium Retention in the Adult Human Male as Affected by Protein Intake," *Journal of Nutrition*, 102:1297; 1972; Johnson, N., et al., as per

note 21; and Linkswiler, H., "Calcium Retention . . . as Affected by Level of Protein and of Calcium Intake," *Transcripts of the New York Academy of Science*, 36:333; 1974.

23. Allen, L., et al., as per note 21; Altchuler, S., "Dietary Protein and Calcium Loss: A Review," *Nutritional Research* 2:193; 1982; and McDougall, J., *The McDougall Plan*, New Century, Piscataway, NJ, 1983, p. 101.

24. As per note 23.

25. McDougall, J., as per note 22, p. 75.

26. Chalmers, J., "Geographic Variations of Senile Osteoporosis," *Journal of Bone and Joint Surgery*, 52B:667; 1970.

27. Walker, A., as per note 20; and McDougall, J., as per note 22, p. 67.

28. Pritikin, N., as per note 13.

29. Walker, A., "Osteoporosis and Calcium Deficiency," *American Journal of Clinical Nutrition*, 16:327; 1965.

30. Smith, R., "Epidemiological Studies of Osteoporosis in Women . . . ," *Clinical Orthopaedics*, 45:32; 1966.

31. Solomon, L., as per note 22; Walker, A., as per note 20; Walker, A., "The Influence of Numerous Pregnancies and Lactations on Bone Dimensions in South African Bantu and Caucasian Mothers," *Clinical Science*, 42:189; 1972; and Walker, A., as per note 29.

32. Mazess, R., "Bone Mineral Content of North Alaskan Eskimos," *Journal of Clinical Nutrition*, 27:916; 1974.

33. Ibid.

34. Ibid.

35. Hegsted, M., "Calcium and Osteoporosis," *Journal of Nutrition*, 116:2316–2319; 1986; McDougall, J., as per note 22, p. 68; Hegsted, M., "Relationships Between Nutrition in Early Life and Late Outcomes, Including Osteoporosis," in *Nutrition and Aging*, Alan Liss, 1990, pp. 73–87; and Ellis, F., et al., "Incidence of Osteoporosis in Vegetarians and Omnivores," *American Journal of Clinical Nutrition*, 25:555; 1972.

36. Kanis, J., "Calcium Supplementation of the Diet," *British Medical Journal*, 298:137–149, 205–208; 1989.

37. Wachman, A., et al., "Diet and Osteoporosis," *Lancet*, May 4, 1968, p. 958.

38. Spencer, H., "Do Protein and Phosphorus Cause Calcium Loss?" *Journal of Nutrition*, 118:657–660; 1988; Spencer, H., "Further Studies of the Effect of a High-Protein Diet as Meat on Calcium Metabolism," *American Journal of Clinical Nutrition*, 37:924–929; 1983; and Spencer H., "Effect of a High-Protein (Meat) Intake on Calcium Metabolism in Man," *American Journal of Clinical Nutrition*, 31:2167–2180; 1978.

39. Marcus, R., "The Relationship of Dietary Calcium to the Maintenance of Skeletal Integrity in Man," *Metabolism*, 31:93–96; 1982; and Kerstetter,

J., Letter, *Journal of Nutrition*, 121:152; 1991.

40. Ellis, F., et al., as per note 35; and Wachman, A., et al., as per note 37.
41. *American Journal of Clinical Nutrition*, March 1983.
42. *Vegetarian Times*, April 1984, p. 32.
43. Recker, R., "The Effect of Milk Supplements on Calcium Metabolism, Bone Metabolism, and Calcium Balance," *American Journal of Clinical Nutrition*, 41:254; 1985.
44. Sorenson, M., *Mega-Health*, 191–240; 1991.
45. Nilas, L., "Calcium Supplementation and Postmenopausal Bone Loss," *British Medical Journal*, 289:1103; 1984.
46. McDougall, J., as per note 22, p. 66.
47. Reichenberg-Ullman, J., "Menopause Naturally," *Natural Health*, March–April 1992, p. 76.
48. Ziel, H., "Increased Risk of Endometrial Carcinoma Among Users of Conjugated Estrogens," *New England Journal of Medicine*, 293:1167–1170; 1975.
49. Ibid.
50. Steinberg, K., "A Meta-Analysis of the Effect of Estrogen-Replacement Therapy on the Risk of Breast Cancer," *Journal of the American Medical Association*, 265:1985–1990; 1991; and Bergkvist, L., "The Risk of Breast Cancer After Estrogen and Estrogen-Progestin Replacement," *New England Journal of Medicine*, 321:293–297; 1989.
51. Ibid.
52. McDougall, J., as per note 22, p. 81.
53. Reichenberg-Ullman, J., as per note 47, p. 80.
54. Horsman, A., "Effect on Bone of Withdrawal of Estrogen Therapy," *Lancet*, ii:33; 1979; Riggs, B., "Short and Long Term Effects of Estrogen and Synthetic Anabolic Hormone in Postmenopausal Osteoporosis," *Journal of Clinical Investigation*, 51:1659–1663; 1972; and Lindsay, R., "Bone Response to Termination of Estrogen Treatment," *Lancet*, 1:1325–1327; 1978.
55. Robertson, W., "Should Recurrent Calcium Oxalate Stone Formers Become Vegetarians?" *British Journal of Urology*, 51:427; 1979; Coe, F., "Eating Too Much Meat Called Major Cause of Renal Stones," *Internal Medicine News*, 12:1; 1979; "Urinary Calcium and Dietary Protein," *Nutritional Review*, 38:9; 1980; "Diet and Urinary Calculi," *Nutritional Review*, 38:74; 1980; and Shah, P., "Dietary Calcium and Idiopathic Hypercalcuria," *Lancet*, 1:786; 1981.
56. Winick, M., quoted in Goodman, D., "Breaking the Protein Myth," *Whole Life Times*, July/August 1984, p. 26.
57. Campbell, T. C., quoted in Lang, S., "Diet and Disease," *Food Monitor*, May–June 1983, p. 24.

58. Chen, J., Campbell, T. C.; et al., *Diet, Lifestyle, and Mortality in China: A Study of the Characteristics of 65 Countries*, Oxford University Press, Cornell University Press, and the China People's Medical Publishing House, 1990.

Chapter Four. Who Decides What You Eat?

1. Imperato, P., and Mitchell, G., *Acceptable Risks*, Viking, NY, 1985.
2. "Dietary Fitness—A Meat Lover's Guide," Oscar Mayer, Inc.
3. Ibid.
4. "Hubbards Awarded for Worst Ads of the Year," Associated Press, *Santa Cruz Sentinel*, June 14, 1985, p. A–6.
5. Liebman, B., Center for Science in the Public Interest, in *Nutrition Action*, cited in *Vegetarian Times*, July 1985.
6. Liebman, B., "Pulling a Fast One," *Nutrition Action*, July–August 1991, p. 8.
7. Oski, F., *Don't Drink Your Milk*, Wyden Books, 1977, p. 6.
8. Bloyd-Peshkin, S., "What's Nutrition Got to Do with It?" *Vegetarian Times*, September 1990, p. 52.
9. Ibid.
10. Ibid.
11. Loggie, J., "Hypertension in the Pediatric Patient," *Journal of Pediatrics*, 94:685; 1979.
12. Ibid.
13. Bucco, G., "Who Decides What You Eat?" *Delicious*, October 1991, p. 10.
14. Kupfer, A., "Where's the Beef? Check This Out," *Fortune*, July 24, 1991, p. 164.
15. Bucco, G., as per note 13.
16. Upton, A., Director, National Cancer Institute, *Status of the Diet, Nutrition and Cancer Program*, Senate Subcommittee on Nutrition, Washington, DC, October 2, 1972; Committee on Diet, Nutrition, and Cancer: Assembly of Life Sciences, National Research Council, *Diet, Nutrition, and Cancer*, National Academy Press, Washington, DC, 1982; "Nutrition and Cancer: Cause and Prevention," American Cancer Society Special Report, *Cancer*, 34:121, 1984; and U.S. Senate Report, *Dietary Goals for the United States*, Washington, DC, 1977.
17. Kolata, G., "Animal Fat Is Tied to Colon Cancer," *New York Times*, December 13, 1990, p. A–1.
18. "Position of the American Dietetic Association: Vegetarian Diets," *Journal of the American Dietetic Association*, 88:351–355; 1988.

19. Morrison, A., "Some International Differences in Treatment and Survival in Breast Cancer," *International Journal of Cancer*, 18:269; 1976; Wynder, E., "A Comparison of Survival Rates Between American and Japanese Patients with Breast Cancer," *Surgery, Gynecology, and Obstetrics*, 117:196; 1963; Nemoto, T., "Differences in Breast Cancer Between Japan and the United States," *Journal of the National Cancer Institute*, 58:193; 1977; Armstrong, B., "Environmental Factors and Cancer Incidence and Mortality in Different Countries, with Special Reference to Dietary Practices," *International Journal of Cancer*, 15:617; 1975; Carroll, K., "Experimental Evidence of Dietary Factors and Hormone-Dependent Cancers," *Cancer Research*, 35:3374; 1975; and Lea, A., "Dietary Factors Associated with Death Rates from Certain Neoplasms in Man," *Lancet*, 2:332; 1966.

20. Wynder, E., "The Dietary Environment and Cancer," *Journal of the American Dietetic Association*, 71:385; 1977; Wynder, E., "Contribution of the Environment to Cancer Incidence: An Epidemiologic Exercise," *Journal of the National Cancer Institute*, 58:825; 1977; Wynder, E., "Epidemiology of Adenocarcinoma of the Kidney," *Journal of the National Cancer Institute*, 53:1619; 1974; Weisburger, J., "Nutrition and Cancer—On the Mechanisms Bearing on Causes of Cancer of the Colon, Breast, Prostate, and Stomach," *Bulletin of the New York Academy of Medicine*, 56:673; 1980; Hill, P., "Environmental Factors and Breast and Prostate Cancer," *Cancer Research*, 41:3817; 1981; and Cunningham, A., "Lymphomas and Animal Protein Consumption," *Lancet*, 2:1184; 1976.

21. Freis, E., "Salt, Volume, and the Prevention of Hypertension," *Circulation*, 53:589; 1976; Sever, P., "Blood Pressure and Its Correlates in Urban and Tribal Africa," *Lancet*, 2:60; 1980; and Finn, R., "Blood Pressure and Salt Intake: An Intra-Population Study," *Lancet*, 1:1097; 1981.

22. As per note 21.

23. Ibid.; Burr, M., "Plasma Cholesterol and Blood Pressure in Vegetarians," *Journal of Human Nutrition*, 35:437; 1981; Sacks, F., "Blood Pressure in Vegetarians," *American Journal of Epidemiology*, 100:390; 1974; Armstrong, B., "Urinary Sodium and Blood Pressure in Vegetarians," *American Journal of Clinical Nutrition*, 32:2472; 1979; and Ophir, O., "Low Blood Pressure in Vegetarians," *American Journal of Clinical Nutrition*, 37:755; 1983.

24. Sacks, F., "Effect of Ingestion of Meat on Plasma Cholesterol of Vegetarians," *Journal of the American Medical Association*, 246:640; 1981; Burstyn, P., "Effect of Meat on Blood Pressure," *Journal of the American Medical Association*, 248:29; 1982; Hartroft, W., "The Incidence of Coronary Artery Disease in Patients Treated with the Sippy Diet," *American Journal of Clinical Nutrition*, 15:205; 1964; and Oski, F., "Is Bovine Milk a Health Hazard?" *Pediatrics*, 75:182; 1985.

25. Virag, R., et al., "Is Impotence an Arterial Disorder?" *Lancet*, 1:181;

1985; and Stamler, J., "Lifestyles, Major Risk Factors, Proof, and Public Policy," *Circulation*, 58:3; 1978.

26. Kuo, P., "Lipemia in Patients with Coronary Heart Disease—Treatment with Low-Fat Diet," *Journal of the American Dietetic Association*, 33:22; 1957; Kuo, P., "Angenia Pectoris Induced by Fat Ingestion in Patients with Coronary Artery Disease," *Journal of the American Medical Association*, 158:1008; 1955; and Kuo, P., "The Effect of Lipemia upon Coronary and Peripheral Arterial Circulation," *American Journal of Medicine*, 26:68; 1959.

27. West, K., *Epidemiology of Diabetes and Its Vascular Lesions*, Elsevier, NY, pp. 353–402, 1978; Kawate, R., "Diabetes Mellitus and Its Vascular Complications," *Diabetes Care*, 2:161:1979; Kiehm, T., "Beneficial Effects of a High-Carbohydrate High-Fiber Diet on Hyperglycemic Diabetic Men," *American Journal of Clinical Nutrition*, 29:895; 1976; Simpson, H., "A High-Carbohydrate Leguminous Fiber Diet Improves All Aspects of Diabetic Control," *Lancet*, 1:1; 1981; Anderson, J., "High-Carbohydrate, High-Fiber Diets for Insulin-Treated Men with Diabetes Mellitus," *American Journal of Clinical Nutrition*, 32:2312; 1979; Simpson, R., "Improved Glucose Control in Maturity-Onset Diabetes Treated with High-Carbohydrate Modified-Fat Diet," *British Medical Journal*, 1:1753; 1979; Singh, I., "Low-Fat Diet and Therapeutic Doses of Insulin in Diabetes Mellitus," *Lancet*, 1:422; 1955; and Barnard, R., "Response of Non-Insulin-Dependent Diabetic Patients to an Intensive Program of Diet and Exercise," *Diabetes Care*, 5:370; 1982.

28. Singh, I., as per note 27; and Barnard, R., as per note 27.

29. Kiehm, T., as per note 27; and Barnard, R., as per note 27.

30. Pixley, F.; Wilson, D.; et al., "Effect of Vegetarianism on Development of Gall Stones in Women," *British Medical Journal*, 291; 1985.

31. Robertson, W.G., et al., "Should Recurrent Calcium Oxalate Stone Formers Become Vegetarians?" *British Journal of Urology*, 51:427; 1979.

32. Lindahl, O., et al., "Vegan Regime with Reduced Medication in the Treatment of Bronchial Asthma," *Journal of Asthma*, 22:45; 1985.

33. Kjeldsen-Kragh, J., "Controlled Trial of Fasting and One-Year Vegetarian Diet in Rheumatoid Arthritis," *Lancet*, October 12, 1991, p. 899.

34. Castelli, W., quoted in Barnard, N., *The Power of Your Plate*, Book Publishing Co., Summertown, TN, 1990, pp. 25–26.

35. Barnard, N., as per note 34, p. 26.

36. In correspondence with the author, experts at the TMJ Clinic at the University of Southern California School of Dentistry estimate that the average American has food in his or her mouth for a total of only twenty minutes a day. They further estimate that the average meat eater has meat in his or her mouth for half that time.

37. Chen, J.; Campbell, T. C.; et al., *Diet, Lifestyle, and Mortality in China:*

A Study of the Characteristics of 65 Countries, Oxford University Press, Cornell University Press, and the China People's Medical Publishing House, 1990.

38. Mead, N., "The Champion Diet," *East-West,* September 1990, p. 46.
39. As per note 37.
40. Campbell, T. C., quoted in Mead, N., as per note 38.
41. Ornish, D., *Dean Ornish's Program for Reversing Heart Disease,* Random House, NY, 1990.
42. Ornish, D., personal communication with author, January 7, 1992.
43. Campbell, T. C., quoted in Attwood, C., "Summit in the Desert," unpublished.
44. Kellock, B., *The Fiber Man—The Life Story of Denis Burkitt,* Lions Publishing, Belleville, MI, 1985.
45. Burkitt, D., "An Approach to the Reduction of the Most Common Western Cancers," *Archives of Surgery,* 126:345; 1991.
46. Barnard, N., "The Need for New Food Recommendations," *PCRM Update,* May–June 1991, p. 3; see also *PCRM Guide to Healthy Eating,* July–August 1991, p. 8.
47. Klaper, M., *Vegan Nutrition,* Gentle World, Maui, HI, p. 8.
48. Ibid.

Chapter Five. What About Chicken, Fish, Milk, and Eggs?

1. O'Brien, B., "Human Plasma Lipid Responses to Red Meat, Poultry, Fish, and Eggs," *American Journal of Clinical Nutrition,* 33:2573; 1980; Flynn, M., "Dietary Meats and Serum Lipids," *American Journal of Clinical Nutrition,* 35:935; 1982; and McDougall, J., *The McDougall Plan,* New Win Publishing, 1983, p. 42.
2. Robbins, J., *Diet for a New America,* Stillpoint, Walpole, NH, 1987, pp. 232–235; Hausman, P., *Jack Sprat's Legacy—The Science and Politics of Fat and Cholesterol,* Richard Marek Publishers, NY, 1981, pp. 40–49.
3. Poulos, J., "A Surprise in Every Package—Nutritional Doubletalk," *Seeing Beyond,* Vol. 2, No. 3, Fall 1991.
4. Toufexis, A., "Playing Politics with Our Food," *Time,* July 15, 1991, p. 58.
5. Ibid.
6. Burros, M., "Eating Well," *New York Times,* July 3, 1991, p. B4.
7. Robbins, J., as per note 2, pp. 48–147.
8. Siess, W., "Platelet-Membrane Fatty Acids, Platelet Aggregation, and Thromboxane Formation During a Mackerel Diet," *Lancet,* 1:441; 1980; and Dyerberg, J., "Haemostatic Function and Platelet Polyunsaturated Fatty Acids in Eskimos," *Lancet,* 2:433; 1979.

9. McDougall, J., *McDougall's Medicine*, New Century, Piscataway, NJ, 1985, p. 111.

10. Kelley, D. S., et al., "Dietary Alpha-Linoleic Acid and Immunocompetence in Humans," *American Journal of Clinical Nutrition*, 53:40; 1991; and Endres, S., et al., "The Effect of Dietary Supplementation with n–3 Polyunsaturated Fatty Acids on the Synthesis of Interleukin–1 and Tumor Necrosis Factor by Mononuclear Cells," *New England Journal of Medicine*, 320:265; 1989.

11. Mazess, R., "Bone Mineral Content of North Alaskan Eskimos," *American Journal of Clinical Nutrition*, 27:916; 1974.

12. "The Truth About Seafood," *Garbage*, September–October 1989, p. 27.

13. "Risk Assessment for 2378-TCDD and 2378-TCDF Contaminated Receiving Waters from US Chlorine-Bleaching Pulp and Paper Mills," EPA, Office of Water Regulations and Standards, August 1990.

14. Jacobson, M., et al., *Safe Food*, Living Planet Press, Venice, CA, 1991, p. 122.

15. Ibid., p. 121.

16. Ibid., p. 122.

17. *Environmental Health Perspectives*, 45:171, 1982.

18. Jacobson, M., et al., as per note 14, pp. 128–130.

19. Viikari, J., "Multicenter Study of Atherosclerosis Precursors . . . ," *Annals of Clinical Research*, 14:103; 1982; Hartcroft, W., "The Incidence of Coronary Artery Disease in Patients Treated with the Sippy Diet," *American Journal of Clinical Nutrition*, 15:205; 1964; and Oski, F., "Is Bovine Milk a Health Hazard?" *Pediatrics*, 75:182; 1985.

20. Truswell, A., "ABC of Nutrition—Reducing the Risk of Coronary Heart Disease," *British Medical Journal*, 291:34, 1985; and *Food Balance Sheets; 1979–1981 Average*, FAO, 1984.

21. Ibid.

22. Duggan, R., "Dietary Intake of Pesticide Chemicals in the US," *Pesticides Monitoring Journal*, 2:140; 1969; Harris, S., "Organochlorine Contamination of Breast Milk," Environmental Defense Fund, Washington, DC, November 7, 1979; and Balbien, J., et al., "Diet as a Factor Affecting Organochlorine Contamination of Breast Milk," Environmental Defense Fund, Washington, DC.

23. Bahna, S., *Allergies to Milk*, Grune and Stratton, NY, 1980.

24. Ibid.

25. Quoted in Liebman, B., "Lactose: Truth or Intolerances," *Nutrition Action*, April 1991, p. 8.

26. Bahna, S., as per note 23; Buisseret, P., "Common Manifestations of Cow's Milk Allergy in Children," *Lancet*, 1:304; 1978; Bahna, S., "Cow's Milk Allergy: Pathogenesis, Manifestations, Diagnosis, and Management," *Ad-*

vances in Pediatrics, 25:1; 1978; Eastham, E., "Adverse Effects of Milk Formula Ingestion on the Gastrointestinal Tract—An Update," *Gastroenterology*, 76:365; 1979; and Gerrard, J., "Milk Allergy: Clinical Picture and Familial Incidence," *Journal of the Canadian Medical Association*, 97:780; 1967.

27. Taube, L., *Food Allergy and the Allergic Patient*, 2nd ed., Charles C. Thomas, Springfield, IL, 1978, p. 22; Boat, T., "Hyperreactivity to Cow's Milk in Young Children . . . ," *Journal of Pediatrics*, 87:23; 1975; Truelove, S., "Ulcerative Colitis Provoked by Milk," *British Medical Journal*, 1:154; 1961; Wright, R., "A Controlled Therapeutic Trial of Various Diets in Ulcerative Colitis," *British Medical Journal*, 2:138, 1965; and Sacca, J., "Acute Ischemic Colitis Due to Milk Allergy," *Annals of Allergy*, 29:268; 1971.

28. "Nutritive Values of Foods," Consumer Food Economics Institute, USDA, US Government Printing Office, Washington, DC.

29. Narins, D., in Bezkorovainy, A., *Biochemistry of Nonheme Iron*, Plenum, NY, 1980, pp. 47–126.

30. Jakobsson, I., "Cow's Milk as a Cause of Infantile Colic in Breast-Fed Infants," *Lancet*, 2:437; 1978; Harris, M., "Cow's Milk Allergy as a Cause of Infantile Colic," *Australian Pediatric Journal*, 13:276; 1977; Lake, A., "Dietary Protein-Induced Colitis in Breast-Fed Infants," *Journal of Pediatrics*, 101:906; 1982; and Gerrard, J., "Allergy in Breast-Fed Babies to Ingredients in Breast Milk," *Annals of Allergy*, 42:69; 1979.

31. McDougall, J., as per note 1, p. 51.

32. McDougall, J., as per note 9, p. 70.

33. McDougall, J., as per note 1, p. 52.

34. Bayless, J., "Lactose and Milk Intolerance: Clinical Implications," *New England Journal of Medicine*, 292:1156; 1975.

35. "Should Humans Drink Milk?" in Physicians Committee for Responsible Medicine, *Guide to Healthy Eating*, November–December 1990, p. 10.

36. Liebman, B., as per note 25.

37. Hurley, J., and Schmidt, S., "Frozen Yogurt: Go Topless," *Nutrition Action*, July–August 1991, p. 10; and Robins-Browne, R., "The Fate of Ingested Lactobacilli in the Proximal Small Intestine," *American Journal of Clinical Nutrition*, 34:514; 1981.

38. Hilton, E., et al., "Ingestion of Yogurt Containing Lactobacillus Acidophillus as Prophylaxis for Candidal Vaginitis," *Annals of Internal Medicine*, 116:353–7, March 1, 1992.

39. Hurley, J., and Schmidt, S., as per note 37.

40. Ibid.

41. Ryan, C., et al., "Massive Outbreak of Antimicrobial-Resistant Salmonellosis Traced to Pasteurized Milk," *Journal of the American Medical Association*, 258:3269; 1987.

42. Ibid.

43. "Update—Listeriosis and Pasteurized Milk," *Journal of the American Medical Association*, 261:1119; 1989.

44. Tham, W., "Listeria Monocytogenes Isolated from Soft Cheese," *Veterinary Record*, 122:539.

45. Schiemann, D., "Yersinia Enterocolitica in Milk and Dairy Products," *Journal of Dairy Science*, 70:383; 1987.

46. Robbins, J., as per note 2, pp. 110–112.

47. "FDA Surveys Not Adequate to Demonstrate Safety of Milk Supply," GAO: 3, 1990.

48. Jacobson, M., et al., as per note 14, pp. 77–88.

49. *Human Food Safety and the Regulation of Animal Drugs Report*, 99th Congress, 1st Session (HR):99–461, 1985; testimony of Michael Jacobson.

50. Jacobson, M., et al., as per note 14, p. 81.

51. "Dairy Dilemma," *Wall Street Journal*, p. A–1, December 29, 1989.

52. As per note 47.

53. Quoted in Moll, L., "FDA Milk Testing Is Not Enough," *Vegetarian Times*, April 1991, p. 16.

54. Ibid.

55. Cited in Giehl, D., *Vegetarianism*, Harper and Row, NY, 1977, p. 3.

56. Mayer, J., "Egg vs. Cholesterol Battle," *New York Daily News*, October 9, 1974, p. 48.

57. Hausman, P., as per note 2, p. 218.

58. Ibid.

59. Ibid., p. 219.

60. "Orders a Stop on Egg Claims," *New York Daily News*, December 12, 1975, p. 62.

61. Ibid.

62. Flynn, M., "Effect of Dietary Egg on Human Serum Cholesterol and Triglycerides," *American Journal of Clinical Nutrition*, 32:1051; 1979; Slater, G., "Plasma Cholesterol and Triglycerides in Men with Added Eggs in the Diet," *Nutrition Report*, 14:249; 1976; Dawber, T., "Eggs, Serum Cholesterol, and Coronary Heart Disease," *American Journal of Clinical Nutrition*, 36:617; 1982; Porter, M., "Effect of Dietary Egg on Serum Cholesterol and Triglyceride of Human Males," *American Journal of Clinical Nutrition*, 34:1103; 1981; and Flaim, E., "Plasma Lipid . . . ," *American Journal of Clinical Nutrition*, 34:1103; 1981.

63. McDougall, J., as per note 1, p. 56.

64. O'Brien, B., as per note 1; Roberts, S., "Does Egg Feeding (i.e., Dietary Cholesterol) Affect Plasma Cholesterol Levels in Humans? The Results of a Double Blind Study," *American Journal of Clinical Nutrition*, 34:2092; 1981; McMurry, M., "Dietary Cholesterol and the Plasma Lipids . . . ," *American Journal of Clinical Nutrition*, 37:741; 1982; and Mattson, F.,

"Effect of Dietary Cholesterol on Serum Cholesterol in Man," *American Journal of Clinical Nutrition*, 25:589; 1972.

65. Hausman, P., as per note 2, p. 214.
66. Glueck, C., quoted in Walles, C., "Hold the Eggs and Butter—Cholesterol Is Proved Deadly and Our Diet May Never Be the Same," *Time*, March 26, 1984, p. 62.
67. Hausman, P., as per note 2, p. 214.
68. Sacks, F., "Ingestion of Egg Raises Plasma Low Density Lipoproteins in Free-Living Subjects," *Lancet*, 1:647; 1984.
69. Glueck, C., as per note 66.
70. U.S. Senate Select Committee on Nutrition and Human Needs Hearing: "Diet Related to Killer Diseases, Vol. 6, Response Regarding Eggs," July 26, 1977.
71. Hausman, P., as per note 2, p. 221.
72. *Time*, "The Worst of 1991 Advertising," January 6, 1992, p. 69.

Chapter Six. Into the Mouths of Babes

1. Supplement 35, *American Journal of Clinical Nutrition*, 1978.
2. Jones, T.W., et al., "Oral Glucose Provokes Excessive Adrenomedullary and Symptomatic Responses in Small Children," *Pediatric Research*, Vol. 27, No. 4, April 1990, Pt. 2, p. 190A, Abstract 1126.
3. Prinoka, E., and Grunewald, K., "Aspartame or Sugar-Sweetened Beverages: Effects on Mood in Young Women," *Journal of the American Dietetic Association*, February 1990, p. 250.
4. "Tale of the Tape," *Nutrition Action*, September 1991, p. 3.
5. Ibid.
6. "Ban Urged on Food Ads Aimed at Children," Associated Press, *San Francisco Chronicle*, p. A3.
7. Ibid.
8. "Cereal Killers?" *Vegetarian Times*, December 1991, pp. 18–19.
9. Quoted in Liebman, B., "Baby Formulas: Missing Key Fats?" *Nutrition Action*, October 1990, p. 9.
10. Welsh, J., "Anti-Infective Properties of Breast Milk," *Journal of Pediatrics*, 94:1; 1979; Addy, D., "Infant Feeding: A Current View," *British Medical Journal*, 1:1268; 1976; Cunningham, A., "Morbidity in Breast-Fed and Artificially Fed Infants, *Journal of Pediatrics*, 90:726; 1977; Goldman, A., et al., "Host Resistance Factors in Human Milk," *Journal of Pediatrics*, 82:1082; 1973; Report of the Task Force on the Assessment of the Scientific Evidence Relating to Infant-Feeding Practices and Infant Health, *Pediatrics*, 74:579; 1984; Victora, C., et al., "Evidence for Protection by

Breastfeeding Against Infant Deaths from Infectious Diseases in Brazil," *Lancet*, 2:319; 1987; Victora, C., et al., "Risk Factors for Deaths Due to Respiratory Infections Among Brazilian Infants," *International Journal of Epidemiology*, 18:918; 1989; Pullan, C., et al., "Breastfeeding and Respiratory Synctial Virus Infection," *British Medical Journal*, 281:1034; 1980; Howie, P., et al., "Protective Effect of Breastfeeding Against Infection," *British Medical Journal*, 300:11; 1990; Chen, Y., et al., "Artificial Feeding and Hospitalization in the First 18 Months of Life," *Pediatrics*, 81:58; 1988; Lepage, P., et al., "Breastfeeding and Hospital Mortality in Children in Rwanda," *Lancet*, 2:409; 1981; Fallot, M., et al., "Breastfeeding Reduces Incidence of Hospital Admissions for Infection in Infants," *Pediatrics*, 65:1121; 1980; Cunningham, A., et al., "Breastfeeding and Health in the 1980s—A Global Epidemiologic Review," *Journal of Pediatrics*, 118:659; 1991; Gross, S., "Growth and Biochemical Response of Preterm Infants Fed Human Milk or Modified Infant Formula," *New England Journal of Medicine*, 308:237; 1983; Frank, A., et al., "Breastfeeding and Respiratory Virus Infection," *Pediatrics*, 70:239; 1982; and Ferguson, D., et al., "Breastfeeding, Gastrointestinal and Lower Respiratory Illness in the First Two Years," *Australian Pediatric Journal*, 17:191; 1981.

11. Reuben, D., *Everything You Always Wanted to Know About Nutrition*, Avon Books, NY, 1978, pp. 196–197.

12. Addy, D., as per note 10.

13. Wiley, C., "Breast-Feeding: Well Worth It," *Vegetarian Times*, August 1991, pp. 22–24.

14. Ironside, A., "A Survey of Infantile Gastroenteritis," *British Medical Journal*, 3:20; 1970.

15. McDougall, J., *The McDougall Plan*, New Win Publishing, 1983, p. 166.

16. Addy, D., as per note 10.

17. Protestos, C., "Obstetric and Perinatal Histories of Children Who Died Unexpectedly (Cot Death)," *Archives of Diseases of Childhood*, 48:835; 1973; Steele, R., "The Relationship of Antenatal and Postnatal Factors to Sudden Unexpected Death in Infancy," *Journal of the Canadian Medical Association*, 94:1165; 1966; Mason, J., "Cot Deaths in Edinburgh: Infant Feeding and Socioeconomic Factors," *Journal of Epidemiology and Community Health*, 34:35; 1980; and Coombs, R., et al., "Allergy and Cot Death: With Special Focus on Allergic Sensitivity to Cow's Milk and Anaphylaxis," *Clinical and Experimental Allergy*, 20:359; 1990.

18. Marano, H., "Breast-Feeding: New Evidence It's Far More Than Nutrition," *Medical World News*, Vol. 20, No. 3, February 5, 1979.

19. Reuben, D., as per note 11, p. 198.

20. Ibid.

21. Brown, R., "Breast-Feeding in Modern Times," *American Journal of Clinical Nutrition,* 26:556; 1973.
22. Reuben, D., as per note 11, pp. 197–198.
23. Marano, H., "Biology Is One Key to the Bonding of Mothers and Babies," *Smithsonian,* Vol. 11, No. 11, February 1981.
24. Ibid.
25. "La Leche League—Because You Care," Publication No. 440, La Leche League, Franklin Park, IL.
26. Quoted in Gotsch, G., "Can Breast-Feeding Become the Cultural Norm?" Publication No. 61, La Leche League, Franklin Park, IL.
27. "Action Update," Action for Corporate Accountability, Fall 1991, p. 1.
28. "The Formula Pushers—Infant Foods Multinationals Breaking the Rules," Action for Corporate Accountability, 1990, p. 3.
29. Quoted in "The Formula Pushers . . . ," as per note 28, p. 6.
30. Chetley, A., "Marketing Breast Milk Substitutes," *Lancet,* 2:258; 1980.
31. Ibid.
32. Editorial, "The Infant Formula Controversy: An International Health Policy Paradigm," *Annals of Internal Medicine,* 95:383; 1981.
33. Quoted in "The Formula Pushers . . . ," as per note 28, p. 7.
34. Ibid., pp. 10–11.
35. Letter from Carol Emerling, Corporate Secretary for American Home Products, to Todd Putnam, Managing Editor, *National Boycott News,* Institute for Consumer Responsibility, September 23, 1991.
36. Quoted in "The Formula Pushers . . . ," as per note 28, p. 14.
37. Ibid.
38. Ibid., p. 13.
39. Ibid.
40. Ibid.
41. Ibid., p. 14.
42. Ibid., p. 9.
43. Quoted in "What You Can Do to Fight This Injustice," in "The Formula Pushers . . . ," as per note 28, p. 15.
44. Cited in Hilts, P., "Study Finds a Decline in Breastfeeding," *New York Times,* October 3, 1991.
45. Quoted in Hilts, P., as per note 44.

Index of Recipes

EarthSave

For memberships and/or to purchase education materials, call 1-800-362-3648.

To receive information about EarthSave, call (408)423-4069, or clip and mail the form below to EarthSave, P.O. Box 68, Santa Cruz, CA 95063-0068

Please send me more information about:

❏ **EarthSave**

❏ **Obtaining copies of *May All Be Fed, Diet for a New America* (the book), *"Diet for a New America"* (the PBS special, on video-cassette), and other related resources**

Name _____

Address _____

State _____ Zip _____ Phone _____